To Nerissa

on your 16th birthday

from Janet & Roger

A History of
CHOBHAM

The Chobham area from the 1816 Ordnance Survey map which was revised to allow for the insertion of railways and other local features. It shows almost all the old farms listed in the Index to this book.

A History of
CHOBHAM

Robert Schueller

Phillimore

1989

Published by
PHILLIMORE & CO. LTD.
Shopwyke Hall, Chichester, Sussex

ISBN 0 85033 671 6

Printed and bound in Great Britain by
Richard Clay Ltd.,
Bungay, Suffolk.

To the Memory
of my old friend the late Jock Crane
from the Westend, Chobham,
who introduced me to Chobham 35 years ago and
taught me how to treat, love and enjoy
Rhododendrons

Contents

List of Illustrations

Frontispiece: The Chobham area from the 1816 Ordnance Survey map

Illustration Acknowledgements

The author wishes to thank the following for permission to reproduce illustrations: Mr. L. G. Bowerman of Send, Ripley, no. 2; British Library, nos. 13, 22, 24, 43 and 44; The Chobham Society, nos. 7, 8, 9, 10, 27 and 28; Mrs. E. M. Dunlop of Chobham, nos. 14, 15, 16 and 36; Mr. Arthur Martin of Bisley, nos. 31, 32, 33, 46, 47 and 51; Mr. J. R. More-Molyneux of Loseley Park, nos. 3, 4, 6 and 39; The Revd. Anthony Salmon, Vicar of Chobham, nos. 18, 19, 20, 29, 30, 34, 35, 37 and 45; Surrey County Archivist (County Record Office), nos. 26, 40, 41, 42, 50 and the endpiece on p. 154, (Guildford Muniment Room), nos. 5, 21, 23, and the endpiece on p. 30; Mr. R. Turner of Auckland, New Zealand, no. 48.

Introduction and Acknowledgements

I moved in 1953 from London to Woking, where I lived for ten years until my house became involved in a local development scheme. To avoid this, I decided to move from the immediate area. It was a fortunate chance that brought me to Chobham in 1963. I retired in 1973, having worked for 21 years in the General Register Office (now the Office of Population Censuses and Surveys), mainly in medical and population statistics and the Census Division. For the last few years I was departmental training officer, in which capacity I had to lecture on the history of registration. My knowledge of British history was rather superficial, owing to the fact that I had taken the equivalent of A-levels in Vienna, where continental history is considered more relevant to Austrian history. In order to make up this shortcoming I joined an evening class on A-level British history and I also spent quite a lot of time in the departmental library, where, in line with my statistical experience, I read Dr. Farr's annual reports to the Registrar General, used the early Census reports of John Rickman and purchased for myself a copy of Wrigley's *Population and History*, with its suggestions for the study of local demography. I was also lucky to find a copy of Graunt's book on London demographic data, as well as some volumes by old German and French authors.

Soon after my retirement and the necessary adjustment to the need of setting myself targets, I followed Wrigley's ideas and, using my now plentiful free time, proceeded to the Census Office in Portugal Street. I was lucky to arrive there before the great increase in demand for its facilities by family historians. I was, in fact, shown the original enumeration books and copied, as my master Wrigley instructs, the details of each household in 1851 on to a separate card, then added (in red) to this data the relating details for 1841. Thus I established a foundation for further work, which led me to the Muniment Room of Guildford Museum. There, to my delight, I found an apparently complete set of Chobham parish registers, beginning in 1654. From these registers, I extracted initially every marriage, hoping that the population of such an isolated village as Chobham would prove rather sedentary before 1800. On each family card (again according to my master Wrigley), I entered the baptisms of each married couple's children, adding their burial and marriage data as it was found. On to those family cards I then transferred the details copied from the 1841 and 1851 Censuses, hoping that I had thus created a sound basis for detailed demographic studies. In a list of documents surrendered by the vicar and parish council of Chobham to the County Record Office in Kingston, I was delighted to find a note that the details of the early Censuses of 1801, 1811 and 1831 had been transferred to Kingston. Again, I copied this data on to my family cards, and thus started the landslide of ever-increasing details which asked for evaluation and comparision with other data. As far as my original aim was concerned, I should have been warned by the absence of the brides' maiden names on nearly all old records.

Adding to the run of basic population data I took note of poor rate records, both of contributions and expenditure, from the early 18th century onwards, the Land Tax records since 1780, Hearth Tax list of 1664 and distribution lists of church collections since 1806.

I must add that, had it not been for the most freely offered help and interest of Miss Beck and her successor, Mrs. Corke at Guildford, and the patience of Dr. Robinson's staff at Kingston, I would have missed all sorts of information and wasted much time on fruitless side issues. Also I must mention the help given me so generously by Miss Cockburn at the L.C.C. Record Office, where she presented me with a complete list of all available records relating to Chobham which included the visitation records of the Surrey Archdiocese and probate records of the Archdeaconry and Commissary Courts of Surrey, from which Mr. Cliff Webb, F.S.G., prepared for me lists of all Chobham people. Mr. Webb's work in issuing lists of tax assessments of West Surrey parishes was most welcome, as was his help when he uncovered any record relating to Chobham people in his work at the Public Record Office. Other persons in the West Surrey Family History Society should also be mentioned, as well as Mr. Marjoribank who brought to my attention the Rev. Jerram's notes in the London Library. Mr. Eric Hall, who had lived in Chobham some time ago when the parish documents were still in the church chest, lent me his notes which enabled me to use them at my leisure at home. I wonder what I would have done without the continuous help and support of Mrs. J. Mason (the authoress of *Cebba's ham*), the guidance of Mr. R. Wilson, Mr. W. Haxworth, the president of the Chobham Society here in Chobham, Mrs. Ann Lee of Chobham and Mr. B. F. J. Pardoe, M.A., of the Chertsey History Research Group, in Ottershaw? Also, I must not forget to thank Mr. Ray Turner from New Zealand, who discovered and edited John Blackman's autobiography. Last, but not least, I must say a very great thank-you to Peter Cleaver for his patience and understanding and to his wife Rosemary who copied my typewritten work on to a word processor – without which I do not think I could have faced my publishers.

Preface

This study enables us to claim that Chobham presents a fascinating, if not unique, example of the growth and development of a village society. A coincidence of favourable circumstances which influenced such growth and preserved the records of such development.

1. The isolated position of a purely agricultural community excluded the village from all influences of the transport and industrial revolutions, thus enabling the preservation well into the 19th century of old established customs and traditions.

2. The absence of a resident Lord of the Manor prevented engrossing by one over-powerful landowner and permitted the early establishment of some farmers who owned their land as freeholders rather than being tenants.

3. With the absence of a resident Lord, the vicar became the main power in the village. Until 1595 the vicars came from the same background as their parishioners, but it was especially the aim of two vicars between then and 1730, who during their long residences assisted the parish officials, to establish a tradition of self-government. The effectiveness of this tradition was put to the test during the very difficult seventy years (from 1730 to 1800) when the vicars, too, became non-resident.

4. In that time the leading farmers, elected to parish office and controlled by the vestry (which often consisted of past and future officials) applied the methods and tradition agreed and established for caring for every member of their community.

5. At the same time the rising price of agricultural produce enabled the richer farmers and tradesmen to increase the comfort of their homes and their general standard of living.

6. It was at this juncture that the arrival of three vicars with completely new views of their place within the community encouraged the newly developed 'class' structure in the village without, however, destroying the caring attitude of the officials elected by the vestry.

7. We shall show that the great variety of documents preserved in the parish chest and from other sources present an illuminating picture of a village community at work.

Chapter One

Chobham under the Abbey of Chertsey

There is no proof of early settlement in the area of Chobham, but:

> Neolithic material has been recorded from a site just outside the area; evidence for activity in this period is therefore possible. The Bronze Age has produced the most important archeological evidence so far. Burial mounds (barrows or tumuli) of the earlier part of the period are known (seven in all, one scheduled as an Ancient Monument). On the Common itself there is a supposed barrow somewhere south of Longcross House and a definite example is scheduled as an Ancient Monument, just on the Common north-west of Pipers Green Stud. In the later Bronze Age this activity continued, as shown by a known urn cemetery just north-west of the Common, and two other possible cemeteries near Chobham Park farm and Chobham Place.[1]

No trace of Roman settlement has been found in the parish but

> the Herestreet or *Via Militaris* of the Chertsey Charters ran through Chobham parish. In 1772 silver coins of Gratian and Valentinian, and copper coins of Theodosius, Honorius and Valentinian, a spear-head and a gold ring, were found near Chobham Park.[2]

The name of our parish has gone through a number of changes: in the Domesday Book it is 'Cebeham' and this name has been traced to a Saxon Lord Cebba. In time Cebeham became 'Chabeham', 'Chabham' and finally our present-day 'Chobham'. We must wait, however, until the 7th century to find the first written reference to the village:

> In the name of the Lord Saviour Jesus Christ.
> I, Frithuwold, concede this donation of my right for the liberty of every single thing.
> How often so ever we devote any thing to the members of Christ as an act of piety, we trust to benefit our soul, because we render to him his own property, and do not bestow ours.
> Wherefore I, Frithuwold, of the province of the men of Surrey, sub-king of Wulfhere, king of the Mercians, of my own free will, being in sound mind and perfect understanding, from this present day grant, concede, transfer and assign from my rightful possession into yours, land for increasing the monastery which was first constructed under King Egbert, 200 hides for strengthening the same monastery, which is called Chertsey, and five hides in the place which is called Thorpe. I not only give the land, but confirm and deliver myself and my only son in obedience to Abbot Eorcenwold. And the land is, taken together, 300 hides, and moreover by the river which is called the Thames, the whole along the bank of the river as far as the boundary which is called the ancient ditch, that is Fullingadic; again, in another part of the bank of the same river as far as the boundary of the next province, which is called Sonning. Of the same land, however, a separate part, of 10 hides, is by the port of London, where ships come to land, on the same river on the southern side by the public way. There are, however, diverse names for the above-mentioned land, namely Chertsey, Thorpe, Egham, Chobham, Gettinges, Molesey, Woodham and Hunewaldesham as far as the above-mentioned boundary . . .[3]

Over two hundred and fifty years ago our knowledge of the Anglo-Saxon Kings was rather scanty so that Nicholas Salmon, writing in 1736, could say with regard to Frithwald's charter:

> Here is the very Scite of the Convent given by one Man whereas another had built it before in a King's reign whom Nobody knows, except he lived above a hundred years after the foundation.[4]

It seemed important to point out this error because Salmon's statement was copied verbatim by other writers such as Thomas Alton in 1829 in his *History of the Counties of Surrey and Sussex* and also G. A. Cooke (in 1802) in his *Topographical & Statistical Description of the County of Surrey*. William Camden, however, in 1607 wrote in his *Britannia*:

To go down the Thames; this river after leaving Berks washes Chertsey, . . . in which, as in a spot unfrequented by men, Frithwald, who styles himself in his charter of foundation, 'petty prince of the province of the Surreians under Wulpher king of the Mercians', and Erchenwald bishop of London, in the early ages of the English church, founded a small monastery, which was some considerable time the burying place of the devout king Henry VI . . . and interred here without any honour.[5]

And the Venerable Bede, a near-contemporary of the Abbey's foundation wrote:

Not long afterwards [A.D. 673] Archbishop Theodore also made Earconwald bishop of the East Saxons . . . Before he became bishop, Earconwald had built two well-known monasteries, one for himself . . . His own monastery stood by the River Thames at Cerotasei [Chertsey] – meaning Cerot's island – in the district of Surrey.[6]

To clarify this complicated history a further extract seems not out of place:

Eorcenberht died in a pestilence which visited England in 664, and Egbert, his eldest son, reigned after him until 673. During at least a part of his reign Egbert must have been recognized as king in Surrey as well as in Kent, for there is almost contemporary evidence that he was the original founder of Chertsey abbey.[7]

To sum up, we have heard that Egbert, King of Kent (664-673) had founded the Abbey of Chertsey in 666, whereas Frithwald, with the approval and confirmation of Wulfhere, King of Mercia, had made the generous gift of land to the Abbey in 673. It would have been useful, if this old spelling could have been preserved. As it was, the *Index Villaris* of 1690 spelled both Chobham and Cobham the same, as 'Cobham', an error which still persists today.

This seems to be right moment to quote F. M. Stenton's *Anglo-Saxon England*:

Like the Saxons of Middlesex, the Saxons of Surrey have no independent history. Their country was in dispute between the kings of Wessex and Kent as early as the year 568, when Ceawlin, king of Wessex, defeated Aethelberht, king of Kent, and drove him into his own land. At different periods in the seventh century Surrey appears as a province of Kent, Wessex and Mercia, and the only one of its early rulers who is known by name – a certain Frithwald, who gave a great estate to Chertsey abbey with the consent of Wulfhere, king of Mercia – looks like an under-king appointed by a superior lord rather than the representative of a local dynasty. The only certainty in the early history of Surrey is the fact that its settlement had begun before the appearance of organized kingdoms in the Thames valley. . . . and the place-names . . . Getingas, the ancient name of Cobham; . . . show that the Wey valley was a region of primary Saxon settlement.[8]

Having thus established how far the charter can be accepted as genuine we ought to add the voice of Dr. Dorothy Whitelock who in the first volume of *English Historical Documents* states:

This is one of the earliest of authentic charters. Though it is preserved only in a late Chertsey cartulary its formulae agree with those of early documents, and there seems no reason to reject it. In the cartulary it is followed by lengthy boundaries in the vernacular, certainly of much later date, which I have not included. It is of historical interest in showing the relationship of Surrey to Mercia in early times.[9]

We must now return to see what happened to our village in these olden times:

In the Danish Wars, traditionally in 871, the abbot and monks were killed, the Abbey burnt and its lands laid waste. It was refounded in the 10th century, traditionally about 933, and reformed under king Edgar (957-75) in the monastic revival inspired by SS. Dunstan and Ethelwold.[10]

The Anglo-Saxon Chronicle for the year 964 states:

In this year King Edgar drove the priests in the city [of Winchester] from the Old Minster and from the New Minster; and from Chertsey and from Milton [Abbas]; and replaced them with monks. And he appointed Abbot Aethelgar as abbot of the New Minster, and Ordberht for Chertsey, and Cyneweard for Milton.[11]

A further quotation, dated 1631, serves to illustrate these words:

'*Nulla Monasteria nisi Benedictina erat apud Angles ab estate Edgari usque ad regnum Guilielmi primi*'. There was no Monasteries, saith an old Writer, amongst the English from the time of King Edgar till the raigne of William The Conqueror, but Benedictine. This order, saith the same Authorer, came first into England with Austin the Monk, Bishop of Canterbury. He, the said Saint Benet, died about the yeare of our Lord five hundred and eitheene, and was buried in his own Oratorie consecrated to Saint John; Where as before was wont to be the Altar of Apollo, He lived 63 yeares.[12]

The Anglo-Saxon Chronicle for the year 508 reads: 'In this year St Benedict the abbot, father of all monks went to heaven'.[13]

We have now reached the year 1066:

William adopted a deliberate and ruthless policy of terrorization, . . . by the mutilation of hostages and the devastation of large areas of arable land. There is, for example, a fearsome connexion between his movements after Hastings and the lands returned as 'waste' to the Domesday commissioners twenty years later: his journey to Dover and thence towards London and his circuit round the north of London can be traced to-day by simply plotting the entries of 'waste lands' in Domesday Book.[14]

Ipſa abbatia ten̄ CEBEHA.T.RE.⁊ m̄ ſe defd ͘p.x.hid.Tra.ē
xii.car̄.In dn̄io.ē una.⁊ xxix.uitti ⁊ vi.bord cū xi.car̄.Ibi.iii.ſerui.
⁊ x.ac̄ p̄ti.Silua de.cxxx.porc̄.
De hac tra ten̄ Odm̄ de abbe.iiii.hid.Corbelin.ii.hid.de tra uitto⁊.
In dn̄io.i.car̄.⁊ vii.uitti ⁊ iiii.bord cū.iii.car̄.Ibi æccta ⁊ alia capella.
Totū m̄ T.R.E.ualb.xvi.lib.Modo pars monacho⁊.xii.lib.
⁊ x.ſolid.Hōum û.ˊlx.ſolid.

The Abbey holds C:IOBHAM itself. Before 1066 and now it answered for 10 hides. Land for 12 ploughs. In lordship 1;
  29 villagers and 6 smallholders with 11 ploughs. 3 slaves.
  Meadow, 10 acres; woodland at 130 pigs.
Odin* holds 4 hides of this land from the Abbot, and Corbelin 2 hides of villagers' land. In lordship 1 plough;
  7 villagers and 4 smallholders with 3 ploughs.
  A church and another chapel.
Value of the whole manor before 1066 £16; now, the monks' part £12 10s; but the men's 60s.

1. The Domesday Book entry relating to Chobham.

So again, the Chertsey Abbey became the victim of an intruder but, as it seems, the monastery and its possessions were soon repaired as is shown by the fact that the church (read chapel) of St Lawrence was rebuilt in the Norman style and its oldest parts are dated to 1080, making it fit to be mentioned in the Survey of 1086:

> The same Abbey holds CEBEHAM [Chobham]. In the time of King Edward, and now, it (was and)
> is assessed for ten hides. There is land for twelve ploughs. In demesne there is one; and (there are)
> twenty-nine villanes and six bordars with eleven ploughs. There are three serfs; and ten acres of
> meadow. Wood for a hundred and thirty hogs. Of this land Odmus holds of the Abbot four hides.
> Corbelin (holds) two hides of the land of the villanes. In demesne there is one plough; and (there
> are) seven villanes and four bordars with three ploughs. There is a church, and another chapel.[15]

The following entry might clear up any doubts:

> The abbots of Chertsey had held the hundred of Godley since the mid-11th century. Within it lay
> the 'four manors' of Chertsey, Chobham, Egham and Thorpe.[16]

There has been quite an amount of argument as to the meaning of the term '*et alia capella*'.
There is good reason to agree with the statement in *Victoria History of Surrey*:

> The Abbot caused the chapel to be repaired in 1318, but after this there is no further mention of a
> chapel. As, however, it seems to have been dedicated in honour of St. Lawrence, it may probably be
> identified with the present church of St. Lawrence, in which case the church was presumably Bisley
> Church.[17]

The details given in the Domesday Book need some explanation:

> In the demesne manors some land was demesne land, that is it was held in the abbot's own hand.
> Some land was freehold, being held of the abbot by tenants in free socage owing rent and perhaps
> some services, including suit of court. . . . Some land was villein or bond land, known later as
> customary or copyhold land, held originally by villeins owing labour services and other obligations,
> . . . Some of the freeholdings in the demesne manors were so extensive that they were subordinate
> manors with their own courts and economic organization. It is uncertain how many of these
> subordinate manors came into existence in the 12th and 13th centuries either by direct grant or by
> a process of accumulation through inheritance, marriage and purchase or by a combination of grant
> and accumulation, and how many may have been in existence earlier: but Domesday Book suggests
> the existence of only a few such subordinate estates in Abbey manors in the 11th century.[18]

The last explanation relates to the abbey's temporalities i.e. the possessions of non-
religious value, in contrast to spiritualities i.e. links with the manor's churches and chapels:

> In the late 12th century the Abbey possessed the patronage of the chapels of Chertsey, Chobham,
> Egham and Thorpe and the churches in all the other parishes in its lands. The first four of these
> were different in character from the rest, since in origin they were merely chapelries of the Abbey
> church on its homeland 'four manors'. . . . the story is instead that of the gradual achievement by
> these chapelries of the status of churches with endowed vicars instead of chaplains but with certain
> rights reserved to the Abbey. . . . Chobham had established the status of a vicarage before the end
> of Abbot Martin's prelacy (1206) for during the vacancy after his death, on 23 March 1207, we find
> Silvester, a royal clerk, getting the King's letters of presentation to the 'perpetual Vicarage of
> Chabbeham'.[19]

A document in the Loseley Papers (dated 1611-32?) states:

> The Hundred of Godley consists of eight parishes, all in the Forrest. Three partes of the ground,
> taken up by heath, parkes and the Kings woods. Among the six market tounes in the Division (West
> division of Surrey). Chertsey, within the Forrest, not standing upon any trade, and full of poore
> people and pestered with cottagers.

John Speed on his famous map of 1610 confirms that his information is 'Described by the
travills of John Norden, Augmented and performed by John Speede'. He further states:

> And for service to the Crown or Common wealths imployments, this Counties division is into
> thirteene Hundreds, wherein are seated eight market Townes, and one Hundred and forty Parish-
> Churches, as in the Table following is inserted.

In this table we find, within the Hundred of Chertsey, these parishes:

> Adleston, S. Annes Hill, Bisley, Buckham Lane, Byflet, Chertsey, Cobham [i.e. Chobham], Egham,

Frimley, Hamhawe, Horstell, Newlodge, Pirford, Potnol, Stroud, Thorpe, Trotworth, Winsham, Wisley, Wodham, Wodham Lane.

All these 21 parishes are also shown on the map proper, if at times in a slightly different spelling.

According to a list of vicars of the parish displayed in the Church of St Lawrence the first vicar was apparently appointed on 31 May 1324 and his patron is shown as the Bishop of Winchester. The Abbot of Chertsey appears as patron for the next vicar in 1343. From that date onwards the abbots are mentioned as patrons until the vicar appointed on 28 May 1557, when the reigning monarch takes over.

The intensity with which the Abbots used to supervise and improve their territories is shown by the extract from Abbot Rutherwyk's cartulary:

In 1307 the Abbot made running water, to run round the manor of Chobham.
In the same year he planted and caused to be enclosed there a certain grove called Suthegrove.
In the same year he caused to be raised a turfhouse in the heath there.
In 1308 he constructed a new mill called Hurstmyll there.
In the same year he stopped up and caused to be made a certain pond called Crachettespond.
In 1310 he caused to be made a new Sheep house in Chabeworthe at Chobham.
In 1311 he purchased a certain moor in Suthemore at Chobham from William Falledle.
And, finally, in 1312 he enclosed a certain pasture called Langeshote.[20]

But their attention also covered the way in which the various tenants in their lands used their land:

When his holdings were confiscated by the Abbot because he was farming it badly in 1332, William de Brok of Chobham owned four oxen, seven steers, two cows, 2½ quarters of winter wheat and 5 quarters of oats – just enough perhaps to feed a family on good white bread and to earn a little money in the market place. As his Holding could not support all his livestock, William de Brok would have run his animals on the common and also cut fern for litter, later to be applied as manure to his meadows. He would also have prepared his pork by smoke strongly impregnated with the pungent aroma of burning peat, also produced by the Forest.[21]

Before we close this chapter, we ought to mention:

The battle of the landless labourers against the farmers backed by the Parliamentary Justices went on, from the time of the Black Death to the rising of 1381 and after. Strikes, riots and the formation of local unions were met by prosecution and imprisonment. The peasantry were divided among themselves as employers and employed, and an early phase of their strife is seen in the famous 'Statutes of Labourers'.[22]

Although there is no documentary evidence of the ravages of the Black Death in the Godley Hundred, the area did not escape from the consequences:

Bondmen and bond-tenants of the Abbot of Chertsey who have long rebelliously withdrawn the customary services due to him for their tenures, and in divers assemblies have mutually confederated and bound themselves, by oath, to resist him and his ministers – at Chobham, Thorpe and Egham.[23]

In the year 1378 the 'Confederation of serfs at Chobham, Thorpe and Egham' was formed, which preceded the large insurrection of 1381. Two disastrous fires at the Abbey must also be mentioned, in 1235 and in 1382. It is, of course, possible that records of the victims of the epidemic were lost in the last-mentioned fire.

At the end of this chapter we feel we ought to mention an event preceding, and relating to, Frithwald's charter of 673. Here is an entry in the Anglo-Saxon Chronicle:

568 – In this year Ceawlin and Cutha fought against Ethelbert and drove him in flight into Kent, and killed two ealdormen, Oslaf and Cnebba, at Wibbandun.[24] [see p. 6]

Among the notes on the Norden and Speed map (of 1610) we find:

Memorable places for Battles fought before the Conquest, WEMBLEBON, where (when the fulnesse of prosperitie burst foorth into CIVILL DISSENSIONS among the SAXONS) a bloudy battle was fought betwixt CHEAULIN the WEST-SAXON and young ETHELBERT OF KENT, wherein he was discomfited, and two of his principall Leaders slaine about the yeere of Christ 560, and three hundred thirty three yeeres after, King ELFRED with a small power overcame the DANES with a great slaughter at FFARNHAM in this County, which somewhat quelled the courage of his savage enemie.

Some say this victorie was obtained at FERNHAM in Kent.

We notice that, in 1610, placenames of historic interest were only vaguely known so it is not surprising that 'WIBBANDUM' was wrongly read as 'WEMBLEDON', again an error often copied in later records. But here is the right place to quote a 'modern' reconstruction of thse events because its originator has shown a very sound appreciation and knowledge of local history.

The charter gives as one point of the border of the donated area a place called Wipandun. Now again we quote:

> Following the boundary marks in a Westerly direction we presently arrive at the 'Hore thorn' (Old thorn). This, I believe, was situated on the hill on the Common immediately South of Long Cross House, where, as I suggested, a game warden may have had his cottage. At one time it was called Thorn Bush Hill, and later Lodge Bush Hill or Old Lodge Hill. Thence, still moving westwards we arrive at the 'Eccan Triewe' mentioned above as having been replaced by the Long Cross. From this point we turn South East, and following the Landmarks we come to the 'Three Burghen', which being interpreted as the three Barrows, otherwise Barrow Hills. And then we come to the 'Shigtren'; here I let my imagination have play, for 'Shigtren' may conceivably mean 'Tree of Victory'. If so, it may have stood where the West Saxons gained their victory over the men of Kent in 568. This was the first internecine battle between the Saxon tribes, and it was fought to decide which tribe should have possession of Surrey. The Anglo-Saxon Chronicle records that it took place at Wipandune. This name occurs amongst the Chertsey Abbey boundary marks, and the spot was somewhere on Chobham Heath, and so it is not unreasonable to imagine that the West Saxons drove their enemy before them and that the men of Kent made their final stand on a mound where a great tree stood and that the victors named this tree 'Shigtren'. In this battle the men of Kent lost two of their leaders and other notable men. I like to think that the three great earth mounds at Barrow Hills cover those mighty dead.
>
> The year 568 may seem to be a late date for Barrow burials, but at a later time than this, when the Anglo-Saxons had been converted to Christianity, they were still clinging to their traditional method of burial, as is proved by the fact that the Church issued an edict ordering them to bury in the Christian Manner.
>
> Nevertheless, in spite of what I have suggested, these barrows may be of a much earlier date. They may conceivably be the work of the Neolithic people.[25]

But apart from the barrows (*see* p. 1 and above) there are two sites on the 1872 Ordnance Map which have in the past attracted the attention of historians and archaeologists. They are called 'BEE GARDEN', a term which requires some explanation:

1. One site lies NE of the old Gracious Pond close to the Parish boundary. It is a large rectangular enclosure carefully constructed which knowledgeable experts have judged not to have been a 'bee garden' but suggest it to have been a PIG-ENCLOSURE which appears to underline the sentence in the Domesday Book 'SILVA DE CXXX PORC'. Perhaps we are correct in taking the word 'SILVA' not to refer solely to oaks which were the main food for pigs but rather to the enclosure's siting 'in the woods'. The site's closeness to the Abbey's pond and the enclosure's sound method of construction point to the monks as responsible for its creation.

2. The second site lies in the ALBURY BOTTOM and has been accepted as correctly named. Its use for keeping bees is reinforced by the early agreed payment of ten pounds of wax by Chobham to the Abbey (*see* p. 7).

Chapter Two

Chobham Park, the House of the Lords of the Manor

Chobham, among the four demesne manors of the Abbey, was the largest in area and the furthest away from the mother house: 'Chobham's development was no doubt due chiefly to its remoteness from the abbey'.[1] So it is not surprising that, although not shown in any written document, a site had been developed where the Abbot could rest on his rounds 'staff in hand' over the abbey's possessions. We find a statement which lets us suggest that the site had been developed by the end of the 13th century:

> John de Rutherwyk, who was abbot from 1307 to 1346 and who was noted for the many improvements which he carried out in his domain, surrounded the manorhouse of Chobham with running water in the first year of his rule as abbot.[2]

John Aubrey, writing at the end of the 17th century, has this to add:

> In the Heath in this Parish [Chobham] is a great Pond call'd Gracious Pond (Where are excellent Carps) above a Mile in Compass, which was made by John Rutherwyke, Abbot of Chertsey, tempore Edward III.[3]

This remark is made in the description of Chobham; from his notes on Egham Church, the following refers, again, to Chobham:

> The Chancel (of the fair old Church in Stone), was built by John Rutherwyke, Abbot of Chertsey in the time of King Edward III, as appears by an Inscription erected in the Chancel, who was also a singular Benefactor to the Publick in the Country, in setting the Poor to work . . . He erected a Mill at Chobham; and in the same year also made the Pond called Gracious Pond. . . . he planted a Coppice called Southmore at Chobham.[4]

It is from this pond that the Abbot obtained the water to increase the security of the moat around the house.

Manning and Bray in 1814 gave full details of the abbot's efforts:

> . . . in 1307 Abbot John surrounded the Manor of Chabeham [the Manor-house] with running water. He planted and inclosed a wood there called Southgrove. . . . In 1308 he built a new mill in Chabeham. . . . He repaired the Chapel of Chabeham in 1312(?). . . . In 1402 a Commission found that the Abbot had the following pensions, viz. from the vicarage of Chabeham 10s. and 6lbs. of wax.[5]

Our attention is now drawn to a completely new development:

> The chief messuage of the manor of Chobham, called Chobham Park, was granted to the King [Henry VIII] by John Cordrey, Abbot of Chertsey, in 1535, two years before the surrender of the entire manor of Chobham.[6]

John Weever, writing in 1631, has this to say about this transaction:

> Services done by the said Cromwell unto King Henry the eight, within a few yeares after his first coming into the favour and service of the said king, copied out of the Original written with his own hand, and now remaining in the Treasury of the Exchequer.
> Imprimis, the King purchased Hampton Court. . . .
> Item, his Highnesse hath purchased the Mannor, and certain other lands in Chombham, whereof a Park is made, of the Abbot of Chensey. . .
> Besides these he did many other services for the King his master, but I will insist only upon two, by which he greatly enriched his Coffers . . .
> The other was his paines and policie in the suppressing of Religious Foundations.

7

This great man gave great reliefe to the poore; two hundred poore people were served at his gates twice every day with bread, meat and drinks sufficient.[7]

Although the following is not strictly related to Chobham, it is rather interesting to hear what John Aubrey has to say about Thomas Cromwell:

Over against Fulham, on the Bank of the River Thames, is situated a small village, and famous for little, but giving birth to that remarkable Instance of the Inconstancy of Fortune, Thomas Cromwell. Son of a Blacksmith of this Place [Putney], rais'd from the Anvil and Forge to the most beneficial Places, and highest Honours in the Nation, insomuch, that tho' a Laick, he presum'd to exercise an Ecclesiastical Authority over the Clergy, and assum'd an Office, which begun and ended in him. To his Advice, we owe the Destruction of Religious Houses in this Nation and the Sacriligious Alienations consequent on it. But the Justice of Divine Providence soon overtook this Favourite of Fortune, and not only despoil'd him of his upstart Honours, but of his Life, and so for some time retarded the happy Reformation began upon so bad principles.[8]

In his description of Chobham, Aubrey cannot refrain from adding: 'That sacrilegious Mover of the Monastic Dissolution, Lord Cromwell . . .'[9] And here, in 1610, John Norden (somewhat earlier than Aubrey) includes the King in his description of the actions in 1537:

Religious houses all flourished with increase, till the ripeness of their fruit was so pleasing in sight and taste unto King HENRY the Eighth, that in beating the boughes he brake downe body and all, ruinating those houses, and seazing their rich possession into his owne hands. So jealous is God of his honour, and so great vengeance followeth the sinne of Idolatrie.

We have heard that the King obtained the manor-house of Chobham two years before the great dissolution of the monasteries. It seems fair to suggest that the King, when proceeding from Windsor to Oatlands, had realised the potentialities of the house. In a letter dated September 1514, we can read:

The King went to Oatlands and there in the meads under Chertsey was killing stags holden in for the purpose, one after another, all the afternoon, although they were warned by the trumpets and made known thereby if they did enter any deer of prize . . . and on Thursdy the King lyted at Byfleet, and from there I took my leave, and from Oatlands he removes to Chobham or Woking, *I know not whether the first*, and then to Guildford, and so on to Windsor . . .[10]

So it seems that Henry had viewed the Chobham Manor house for future consideration.

'The certain other lands' as mentioned by Weever (*see above* p. 7) were, in fact, 500 acres adjoining and surrounding the grounds of the manor-house, all of which the King had enclosed by paling, thus creating a deer park: 'The Manor remained in the Crown for some time, during which the king kept it for his own use; He was at Chobham in 1538 and again in 1542'.[11] Having said that Henry VIII purchased the manor and certain other lands in Chobham, we were lucky to find a reference to the way in which one of these 'purchases' had been carried out. This reference we found in the records of the 'Court of Requests', a new court in the period:

Wolsey also encouraged the poor man's traditional right to appeal direct to the king's council; and pressure of work led to special arrangements for poor men's cases which later developed into a formal court, the 'Court of Requests'.[12]

Here are the details of a case which, although undated, must have been brought during Queen Elizabeth's reign (after 1564):

Complainant John Martyn of Chertsey Surrey joiner. Thomas MARTYN his grandfather was lawfully seised of certain customary or copyhold lands called Chalvers Lands parcel of the Manor of Chabham. He surrendered them according to the custom to Johan his wife for life with remainder of his heirs and so died.
She was admitted tenant [a manor of the King, Henry VIII] The lands were taken from her to make a park. In consideration the King granted Johan by copy of court roll of the same manor a moor

called Hellgrove and certain parcels of land called Buttyes in the said lordship of Chabham for life with remainder to the heirs of her husband [admitted 27 Henry VIII]

On death of Johan, Nicholas MARTYN her son & next heir was admitted 18 May in 1st year of the queen that now is. [1559]

On his death the complainant was admitted 12 Oct 1st year of the said queen and has held the lands undisturbed.

Now one William HEATHE of parish of Chabham Esq having the estate of Dr HEATHE late archbishop of York his brother who by patents 5 & 6 Phil & Mary purchased the manor. He has now unlawfully entered on the land. Petition is to summon William HEATHE to the Court.[13]

We have quoted this case here although the cause of the complaint refers to a later development (*see* p. 14). We have, however, felt that this was the right place to discuss this extract, because it shows that Henry VIII, despite all his might, could not and did not just command the transfer of the lands which he needed and, surprisingly, offered the tenants of the lands, who were his copyholders, a fair exchange for what he 'had taken' from the widow Martyn to complete his park. An extraordinary demonstration of the relationship of ruler and subject in 16th-century England, amazing when we think of Charles V and Francis I, the continental contemporaries of Henry VIII. As stated earlier (*see above*, p. 8) the *Victoria County History of Surrey* only mentions two visits by the King, in 1538 and 1542. By 1540, the King had already given a considerable part of the manor to one of his favourites:

John Danister, Esq. one of the barons of the Exchequer, died 28th February 1539/40 seized of an estate here, described as consisting of 6 messuages, 4 cottages, 200 acres of land, 100 acres of meadow, 200 acres of pasture, 120 acres of wood in Chobham.[14]

We can further report that: 'Sir Anthony Browne was made keeper of the manor in 1543. Christopher Heneage appears to have had a grant of it during the reign of Elizabeth'.[15] The last gentleman seems to have given his name to the present-day farm in Chobham called Heneage Farm, now a private residence.

In addition to the two personal royal visits, details of the preparations for two further visits, in 1545 and 1546, have been preserved among the papers of the family of More-Molyneux, in their manor at Loseley. Extracts from these documents are printed here as they give not only detailed costings of the operations but also names of Chobham people engaged in assisting in the work in preparing the site, in carrying goods, and a variety of local purchases. Each of the accounts begins with a brief summary of the purpose of the operation (as these are very similar we only give one as an example):

A paymente made by Nyclas Brystowe Esquire as well for the Charge of the Caryage by Lande and water of the Kyngs Hyghness Tents Hales Pavylyons and Joyned Tymber Howses from London to Hampton Court and Otland & from thence to Chobham with new Edypfyng & settyng up of the great Tymber Howse made of "Force" with recaryage of all the said Tents Hales Pavylyons and Tymber Howses by land and water from Chobham to London Eyryng [airing] and drying the same at London which had taken wett . . . As also for all manner necessaryes bought for the premyses for the span of 14 weeks that ys from the 15th Daye of July in the 38th year of the Reigne of our Soveraigne lorde Henry the eighth by the Grace of God Kynge of England France & Irland Defender of the Faythe, & in Erthe [Earth] Supreme Head under God of the Church of England & also of Irland unto the 18th Day of October next & Immedyatly Following inclusive.[16]

In one of the introductory remarks in 1545 the clerk had obviously omitted to state the King's new title 'as Head of the Church in Ireland' (which had only been introduced in 1541) and the omission was quickly added in another hand! As to the need to dry the tents at London we read that: 'the said tents had to be carried and dried at the Blackfriars in London which had taken water upon the Thames in the sudden tempest in the night from the 4th day of September'.[17]

For each group of craftsmen the reports give the names, the daily rate, the number of days (and nights in some cases) worked and the total earned – in addition to giving a brief account of the jobs carried out. We start with the 'job descriptions' (to use a modern term!):

> Tailors: working as well in Repayring of the Kyng's Tents, hales and Pavylyons and settyng up of the same as also in sewyng of Ruffs [roofs] of canvas for paynters and sewyng of Tessures and Hangins for Banketyng howses both at Hampton Court and Otlands and dryng of Tents at London by the said space.
>
> Joiners: as well as repayring of the King's joyned howses and settyng up of the same at Otlands and Chobham as also in makyng of pynakles for the great howse of "Force" there and helpyng of the makyng up of a gate to the sayd howse at Otlands.
>
> Carpenters I: as well in mendyng and makyng of poles as also makyng of stake for the same tents.
>
> Carpenters II: workyng upon the newe tymber Howse made of 'Force' at Chobham with caryage and provysions for the same begynyng the 5th Daye of September and endyng the 28th of September next followyng. [It should be noted that this group worked for 23 days as against the 14 weeks of all the other craftsmen.]
>
> Glayzers: in repayryng of the hornes wyndows in the joyned howses.
>
> Cordwyners ⎱
> Sawyers   ⎰   [No description is given as jobs seem obvious.]

In addition to these craftsmen there is also one set of:

> Labourers: cuttyng bowers lodyng the same makyng of Stakes and hedgyng abowte the King's Lodgyng at Chobham.

Four 'Officers' are shown to be in charge:

As Master Sir Thomas Cawerden	[@ 4s. a day]
as Controller John Barnard	[@ 2s. a day]
as Clerke Thomas Phillippe	[@ 1s. 6d. a day]
as Yeoman John Brygys	[@ 2s. a day]
as Groome Thomas Hale	[@ 1s. 6d. a day][16]

We thought it best to show the costings in tabular form:[16]

| | | Totals | | | Average | |
Occupation	No	Days	Pay	Pay/day	Pay/man	Days
Tailors	85	2,219	1,823s.	9¾d.	21s. 6d.	26
Joiners	36	1,279	743s.	7d.	20s. 7d.	35
,, apprentice	7	457	238s.	6¼d.	34s.	65
Carpenters I	13	623	394s.	7½d.	30s. 3d.	48
,, II	46	970	781s.	9½d.	17s.	21
Glaziers	7	94	78s.	10d.	11s. 2d.	13
Sawyers	14	234	149s.	7½d.	11s.	17
Cordwainers	2	58	68s.	14d.	34s.	29
Labourers	47	309	167s.	6d.	3s. 6d.	7
Officers	5	54 ea	52s.	see above	see above	
	261		£224 13s.			

Some additional remarks giving more detailed information will aid understanding of this table. Most of the labourers were Chobham men and all the others had apparently come from London. Many of their names could also be found on a similar report of the expedition in 1545, so we assume that they were on the permanent payroll of the Master of the 'Office of the Royal Tents, Hales, Pavillions and Timber Houses' situated at the Blackfriars in London.

The number of days worked by each man varied between 25 and 79 and the pay of individuals also varied, viz. the headman-tailor was paid 12d. per day with the rest getting from 7d. to 9d.; the head joiner received 12d. per day and the others in his craft 7d. or 8d.; the chief glazier had 10d. per day and the other glaziers between 6d. and 8d. The head of the carpenters, Henry Hothorn, was paid 12d. per day and local purchases of timber are shown as 'obtained for Hothorn'; other carpenters received only 7d. and 8d. per day.

The term 'joined houses' and their transport between Blackfriars, Oatlands and Chobham seems to point to some kind of 'prefabrication', a very early example of what we think of as a 20th-century invention!

We can, of course, only guess what impression the 'invasion' of a number of Cockney men had made on the village: of the 261 men mentioned, 42 were Chobhamers (most of the labourers), of the rest some 30 tailors never got as far as Chobham and the 46 carpenters came for only three weeks so that around 150 men stayed in Chobham for some considerable time. We have no documentary evidence of the size of Chobham's population in 1546, but the best basis for a rough

2. An old example of the prefabrication of the timber frame of a house.

estimate are the musters in 1583 which lead us to a figure of about 400 in 1583 and a somewhat lower figure for 1546, say 375. One can only guess the reaction of the locals, especially the female half!

In addition to the upheaval created by the presence of the craftsmen we ought also to point to the coming and going of all the carts bringing supplies from London and Oatlands and from other villages in Surrey. Here are the details of carriage-duties:[16]

1. Carriage of tents and joyned houses with other necessaries from the Waterside to the park at Oatlands at 2d. the load; men from 11 villages in West Surrey took 72 loads, among them six men from Chobham   12s.

2. Land carriage of tents from Oatlands to Richmonte and thence to Oatlands again – 2s. 4d. the load 'to & fro'   16s. 4d.

3. Tents from Oatlands to Hampton Court, at 8d. the load   2s.

4. Poles from Haling beyond Croydon to the Blackfriars in London, taking 2d. for every mile & load; 16 loads   £1 1s. 4d.

5. Tents & joyned houses from Oatlands to Chobham at 9d. the load, men from 56 villages, 11 from Chobham, 192 loads   £7 4s.

6. The foundation of the 'Joyned' houses and the great timber house from Oatlands to Chobham at 9d. the load – 65 loads, carried by men from 17 villages – seven from Chobham   £2 8s. 9d.
7. Day carts – 75 days at 12d. a day   £3 15s.
8. Various timber goods taken from different places to Chobham   18s.
9. Carts carrying the said stuff from the waterside unto the Office at the Blackfriars   15s. 2d.
10. Water carriage of the same tents and joyned tymber howses from Otlands to London   £5 10s.
11. Land carriage of the sayd tents and joyned tymber howses agayn from Chobham to Otlands to be conveyed home agayn unto the Blake Fryars at 9d. the load – 72 loads [62 by Chobham men]   £2 14s.
12. Dewe to William Wormyngton for his riding Charge by the space of five days in provydyng for cartes for the carriage of the sayd stuff at 12d. the day   5s.

Total cost of carriage   £26 1s. 7d.

The final pages of the account give details of local purchases:

1. A variety of timber purchased from various sources   £12 2s. 5d.
2. Dewe to THOMAS ATFELDE of Chobham for two lodes 14 feet of Tymber, three lodes of joysts taken at his house & his labour for lodyng of the said tymber   £1 14s. 6d.
3. To John Spong of Chobham for purchase of two lodes eight feet of okyn [oaken] tymber ready sawyn to frame delivered at Chobham Park takyng five Shillings for every lode so done   11s. 6d.
4. Purchase of Byrchyn [birchen] Bowghes [boughs] from four 'men' at 4d. the lode   8s.
5. Purchase of Ewe [yew] bowghes from Chobham people:
   a/ John Stevenson
   b/ John Emott
   c/ Elyzabeth Mylton
   d/ Bartholomew Skyte   3s. 6d.

Total of local purchases   £14 19s. 11d.

Ironwork and its carriage; and other provisions:

1. Dewe to William Turker of Chertsey, smith, for nine pairs of hinges 11 pairs of hooks wayng 100 lbs at 2d. the lb   16s. 8d.
2. Dewe to Thomas Spore for ink and paper by him layd on at sondrye tymes   2s.
3. To William Porter of Weybridge for half a dozen Bylletts to make tent stake of hym bought and delyrd at Otlands   2s. 3d.
4. To John Mathin and William Porter as above   2s. 3d.
5. To N. Kendall, wax chandler, for 14 lbs of Wax, spent at the Blake Fryars in searyng of the newe Canvase for the covyryng of the Joyned Howses & the Howse of 'Force' joynyng to the sayd Joyned Howses taking for . . . lb so wrought   £3 13s.
6. Dewe to Jasper Arnold, Basketmaker, for 14 great . . . for tent stake at 10d. the pair   11s. 8d.
7. Dewe to Jane Dowsett of Kyngston for six doz of candells spent in workyng by nyght at 1d. the lb   9s.
8. Dewe to Robert Wykynson, Turner, for Tent Stakes at 2s. the . . .   £3 10s.
9. Dewe to Sir Thomas Cawarden, knight, for 16 lodes of poles at Holingbrook beyond Croydon takyng 10s. for 28 lodes so done   £8
10. Dewe to Wyllyam Sharpare, Smyth, for theyr parcells folowyng of hym bought and delyvered at London viz. various Brodes   10s.
11. Dewe to John Alard, glasyer, for ten Lantern Horne at 2s. the ten for 2 lb of powder 12d. for 2 lb of lead ready cast 6d. for resyn 1d.   £21 7s.
12. Dewe to John Lyle, cordwayner, for thread and wax by him bought and delyvered at Chobham   1s. 6d.
13. Dewxe to Thomas Chappell, upholsterer, for these parcell Following of him

bought and delyvered at London viz. nine yards of reade saye at 9d. the yd. and for six pairs of browne lyars at 4d. the pair 2s.,	8s.	9d.
14. Dewe to William Hobson, haberdasher, for these parcells following of him bought and dyed at London . . . for 10 butte of threade at 2s. 4d. the butt 23s. 4d. for one doz of Whartells 6d. for besyng thread 14d.	£1 5s.	
15. Dewe to John Sturgyon, ironmonger, of London bought of him and delyvered at London, viz. english sprygge, leather trashe, lantern Horn for mending & repayryng windows, etc	£8 3s.	10d.
16. Dewe to Thomas Blake, smyth, for joynts with bolts, corners of the long galerys mending the old joynts, hoopes for tents, great wire for the frame of the tymber howses etc	£26 13s.	7d.
Total of various provisions	£75 16s.	6d.

The total expenditure for the expedition amounted to no less than £341 11s. In the report for the 1546 expedition we found the following note which refers to Chobham people:

> To Barthylomew Skyte and Alyn Lye constables of Chobham for horses by them provyded and delyvered by days for caryng and fetchyn of dyvers and sonndre necessaryes from London Chertsey Stanes Wyndsor, and other places by the space of 14 days at 4d the day – 4s 8d and gyven in reward to the sayd Constables for theyr paynes takyng duryng the sayd tyme 3s 4d and to Peter Frimlyeman for one horse by the space of 10 days at 4d the day – 5s unpayd as before . . .[17]

The lists of Chobham people mentioned in the records as employed provide some problems: the whole expedition took place at harvest-time, when every farmer would be very busy in his own fields, whilst, on the other hand, the wages paid by the London people do not appear to have been attractive enough to entice farmers to leave their own work, so it is perhaps permissible to argue that a farmer called upon to do 24 days work such as labouring, and earning for these days only 12s. in all, would have sent a labourer in his own place. (There are three persons viz John Stevenson, John Spong and Henry Rogers, whose names are shown every time some work or other had to be done.) Unfortunately, we have no contemporary records to distinguish between farmers and labourers, but even a charge of 12d. for a whole day's work with a cart and 9d. for a load taken from Oatlands to Chobham (which, of course, meant first an empty journey to Oatlands) was not such as to encourage a farmer to attend. Of course we must not forget that a call by his Majesty's delegate would not easily be refused. It might be useful to compare these charges with the craftsmen's wages (from 6d. to 9d. per day for all and 10d. to 12d. per day for the foremen). It is possible that in a later chapter when we discuss together all records for the years before 1654 (the start of the extant register books), that we may come to more definite conclusions about individual persons.

To end this most extravagant report we must, however, admit that we have not found proof in any record of Henry VIII's reign that he really did visit Chobham in the last two years of his reign (1545-46) and the preparations may have been in vain. After all, 1545 was the year of the *Mary Rose,* and:

> In 1545, Francis, King of France, made strenuous efforts to invade England, and on the 16th day of October, in that year, an order is sent by the King, Henry VIII, for the raising of 400 men in the County of Surrey.
> From the Hundred of Godley: XXVI men, whereof iiij Archers, XVI Bilmen.[18]

Mr Neville Williams in his *Henry VIII and his Court* (1971) says, on page 149:

> In 1546, or possibly the year before, Henry began using a special chair or 'tram' with shafts back and front, something akin to the later Sedan chair, in which he was carried from room to room when his legs were weak.

We mention this here, because we found in the Loseley Papers the bill of William Greene, 'the Kyngs coffermaker' for making this chair, amounting to 'xxx s and j d.'.

Finally we can quote:

> By the end of 1546 it was plain to all that his death was drawing very near. The King had made his usual progress in August and September, but after staying in his various palaces in and near London, he returned to Whitehall on 3 January 1547 a dying man.[19]

For our purpose, however, it was a worthwhile effort.

We must apologise for this rather voluminous interruption in our story of the manor house in Chobham and take it up again, now, after the death of King Henry.

> The Manor Place, commonly called Chobham Park, was sold in July 1558 by Queen Mary to Nicholas Heath her Chancellor, Archbishop of York for £3,000. The land was inclosed by a pale, whence it was called a park, and is marked as such in Norden and Speed's map of 1610.[20]

To appreciate the enormity of the purchase price we can quote: 'And all this at a time [1603] when a total landed income of £3,000 was considered ample to support the dignity of a peer'.[21]

We shall find later (*see below* pp. 17-18) that in the year 1557, the year before the Queen's death, that she issued a writ under the Privy Seal to provide herself with badly needed financial assistance. Queen Elizabeth confirmed the grant to the Archbishop, who, however, refused to take the oath of allegiance and abandon the Catholic faith. In consequence he was deprived of the benefice of York and, in 1564, the possession of the manor-house and park was nominally conveyed to his brother William.

This is the William Heathe who 'unlawfully entered the lands' which John Martyn had inherited from his father. This alleged trespass (*see above* p. 8) was apparently illegal as the copyhold lands which Henry VIII had granted to the family were not part of the area which the Archbishop had purchased and which was, later, conveyed to his brother William. (The case suggests the possibility that John Martyn had in fact returned to the land which had been in his family for at least three generations and, thus, entered the paled park.)

We now return to the Archbishop's story:

> As for Hythe he seems before this time to have had his liberty of dwelling at large, and might be gone to his Seat at Cobham in Surrey, where he lived and died at full Ease, Quiet and Safety, and as handsomely as most Gentlemen in England. For Cobham (according to a particular of that Manor which I have seen among Sir Michael Hick's Papers) was situate Twenty Miles from London, four miles wide of Windsor held in Sokage. It contained Five Hundred Acres of Land, Meadow, Wood and Pasture. The Wood and Timber valued at Eight Hundred Pounds. A Fair House, Garden and Orchard. The whole Ground Paled about. It was rented at 180[L] a year. The Price of the Purchase 3000[L]. It was now Sir Francis Lee; formerly Mr. Hethes, the heir and Successor of Dr. Hethe. This was that grave Man's easy retirement in his old Age.[22]

These are the remarks of John Strype written in 1711. John Aubrey added this in 1719:

> At this House in Cobham Park was a Consecrated Chapel us'd by this truly Apostolical Archbishop, until his Death, about the ninth Year of Queen Elizabeth, who paid so high a Regard to his Piety and Learning, that she visited him once every Year during his life.[23]

Although there is a plaque in the Tower of London stating that Archbishop Heath died there in 1579, there exists a letter (in the Loseley Papers) which gives the year as 1578 and implies that he died in Chobham. To bring the Archbishop's story to a conclusion, we hear again John Aubrey:

> In the Church, on the North Side of the Chancel, under a large blue Marble Grave-stone, lies buried the Body of Dr. Hethe, Archbishop of York, Lord Chancellor of England, and twice Embassador to the Court of Rome, but depriv'd of his See some Years before his Death. On a Fragment, of a Brass Plate, that was formerly fix'd on a Stone, near the last mentioned, is this mangled Inscription: Here lyeth William Heeth of Chabham, . . . COUNTYE of Surrey Esqr. Who died the XIV . . . Nov in the year of our Lord God MCCC . . .[24]

The Brass plate is still in the church as is the dark marble slab in front of the altar.

It was William Heath's son Thomas, who conveyed the manor-house and park in 1606 to Sir Francis Leigh (or Lee) although Christopher Heneage appears to have had a grant during Queen Elizabeth's reign (*see above* p. 9). In the Lay Subsidy List of 1570/1 'Christopher Heneage, gent', is assessed at £10 for lands as the biggest landowner in the village. His wife was buried in Chobham on 29 March 1588 so we can assume that the couple had been living there.

In 1614 King James I granted the Manor of Chobham to Sir George More of Loseley (the son of Sir William – *see below* p. 18) whose family already owned the manors of Bisley, Bagshot and Woking, but in 1620 all these manors were granted by the King to Sir Edward Zouch:

> Sir Edward, on the feast of St. James then next, and every heir-male of Sir Edward on that feast next after they should succeed, should carry up the first dish to the King's table at his dinner, on that day, wheresoever he should then be in England, and at the same time pay 100[l.] in Gold in the King's Mint, in lieu of all wards and services whatsoever.[25]

This Letter Patent dates from 13 November anno 18 (1620); Aubrey, writing in 1673, says:

> In Process of Time this Estate was granted by King James I to Sir Edward Zouch in Tail Male, with Remainder over to several others of the Family of Zouche, in Tail Male, of which Limitation James Zouch of Woking, Esq. Lord of this Manour [Chobham] and Patron of the Vicarage, is the only Heir Male surviving, and has no issue.[26]

The purchase by the Archbishop had only covered the manor-house and the Park as formed by Henry VIII; the advowson and rectory i.e. the great tithes, had remained with the Crown. Manning and Bray clarify the position of Chobham:

> Queen Mary had sold the park to Nicholas Heath, Archbishop of York. But the Manor and advowson of the vicarage remained in the Crown till King James I. In his 18th Year (1620) he granted the same with the Manor of Bisley to Sir Edward Zouch. The reversion in fee remaining in the Crown.[27]

Although there is no evidence that the Zouch family took a special interest in their Chobham Manor, they are remembered in the area in various ways:

> Sir Edward Zouch Knight and Lord of this Manor loved this church and Parish, spake for us to Kings, as much as in him has inlarged our Common.[28]

So goes an entry in the parish register of Bisley! The Chobham churchwarden in 1683 made the following entry:

> Item. Pd for Beere & Tobaccow at Edward Stympsons for the Ringers for the first time Mr Zouch came over 0.4.6[29]

This was, of course, James, the grandson of Sir Edward Zouch. Sir Edward died in 1634; his tomb, in (Old) Woking Church adds to the date of death: Knight Marshal of England 1622. His son James succeeded him but died very soon, in 1643. James's eldest son, Edward, likewise enjoyed only a rather short time as Lord of the Manor, dying in 1658, when his youngest brother, another James, succeeded him. This James died without male heirs in 1708. Aubrey, again, can add something to our knowledge of the Zouch family:

> Here has been a Chauntry, to which some Lands and Houses, called FREEBARNS, formerly belonged. Dorothy, Sister of James Zouch, Esq.; and late wife of Mr. English, was interred here about eleven Years since.[30]

Aubrey who finished his *Natural History of the County of Surrey* in 1719, seems in this entry to point to the last James Zouch. It might be a pleasant interruption of serious historical endeavour to recount a rumour which persisted a hundred years after the death of the last of the Zouch family; John Shore, later the second Lord Teignmouth, recalls in his memoirs:

> The aspect and associations of the Hermitage [this is now a modern housing development] buried

in the depth of a dark wood were yet more spectral. There lived, more than a century since [he writes about his stay in Chobham around 1808] a wealthy coachbuilder named Zouch, a man of ill-fame, who might be seen at night, a headless trunk, driving a coach and four through the gloom of his dense plantation. The occupants of this house were a gardener and his wife, and the former singly on his becoming a widower. He professed scholarship, had picked up some Latin, and was fond of a chat with us. [Mr. Shore was a student under the vicar of Chobham.] When asked if he was not afraid to thread the mazes of his wood in the dark, he replied: 'No, I have reasoned thus with myself: If Master Zouch is in heaven, he would not wish to come back; and if in hell, the devil would not let him'.[31]

There is no proof whether this story refers to the last Zouch nor, in fact, whether it is just a locally made-up story.

The reversion of the Zouch estates remained in the Crown and in 1672 Charles II granted it to the Trustees of the Duchess of Cleveland and for such children as she might have by the King. Thus when the male line of the Zouch family failed in 1708, the Duchess's son came into possession but sold it to John Walter in 1715. And to end the story of the manor of Chobham, John's son Abel inherited it in 1736, obtained an Act of Parliament in 1748 to grant him the freehold and, finally, sold the whole estate in 1752 to the Onslow family who are to this day the Lords of the Manor of Chobham.

Before we interrupt the connection of the reigning monarchs with Chobham, we can report a number of instances where the royal hand reached down to our parish; this requires a rather long introductory explanation: we start with a report taken from Hall's *Chronicle of the History of England* issued in the 13th year of Edward the Fourth (1474):

The King, preparing for a war with France, conceived a new device in his imagination, by which engine he might covertly persuade and entice his rich friends to give and grant him some convenient sum of money towards his inestimable charges and incredible costs; which thing if they did not willingly assent to, he then would impute the greater ingratitude or the more unkindness: whereupon he caused his officers to bring to him the most rich persons one after another, and to them he explained the cause, the purpose, and the necessity of the war begun, etc.

King Edward had called before him a widow, much abounding in substance, and no less grown in years, of whom he merely demanded what she gladly would give him towards such great charges? 'By my troth', quoth she, 'for thy lovely countenance thou shalt have even 20 l'. The king looking scarce for half that sum thanked her, and lovingly kist her. Whether the smell of his breath did so comfort her stomach, or she esteemed her kiss of a king so precious a jewel, she swore incontinently that he should have 20 l. more. The king, willing to shew that his benefit was to him much acceptable, and not worthy to be put in oblivion, called this grant of money a BENEVOLENCE. Notwithstanding that many with grudge and MALEVOLENCE gave great sums towards that new-found Benevolence. But using such gentle fashions towards them, with friendly prayer of their assistance in his necessity, so tempted them, that they could none otherwise do than frankly and frely yelde and gave hym a reasonable reward.[32]

This is how a modern historian views this issue:

King Edward IV was said to know the names and fortunes of everyone of any standing all over the country. This knowledge he employed to obtain large loans and gifts which freed him from dependence on the subsidies granted by Parliament.

There was a good deal of subtle policy, but he achieved the extraordinary task of freeing the Crown from its burden of debt.[33]

The reader might feel that this excursion into old history is rather extravagant but there are a number of instances when Chobham people were involved in such 'BENEVOLENCE'; their names present nearly the only lists we have of inhabitants before 1654 (when the extant parish registers will provide them). The only reference we could find of Henry VIII's efforts is the following:

Among the Commissioners appointed to arrange and collect the Benevolence which the king, by advice of his Council, had decreed in 1544 towards the defence against the French king, the name of Sir Thomas Cawarden appears with others for Surrey. [In the war against France, Thomas Cawarden had to furnish soldiers.][34]

We felt that the following explanation of the various financial demands on citizens will clarify the issue:

> The richer subjects of the Crown contributed also to forced loans, which were not meant to be repaid, and to 'benevolences', which were theoretically free gifts. The 'privy seals', which the government issued in 1542, were really royal bonds in blank which commissioners in the shires were authorised to fill in and present to persons who lent to the king; along with the blanks and with instructions for the use of discretion, the Commissioners were given lists of persons to be approached and information as to their assessment in the subsidy books.[35]

In the Loseley Papers are copies of letters sent by Queen Mary and James I to their 'rich' subjects which read as follows:

> By the Queene Trustie and wellbelovd, we grete you well, and let you wit that, knowinge the fidelitie and faithfull good will you bere towards the suretie of our parson, and defence of your contrey, the savegard wherof we daubt not but you do so much tender as you will not faile to do your possible endevor towards the mainten'nce and defence of the same. We understanding your habilitie, have appointed to take of youe by waye of lone the some of twentie pounds, to be repaid againe unto you between this and the feast of the Nativitie of our Lord God, which shalbe in the yere a thowsand fyve hundreth fiftie-eight at the furthest. Wherfore our pleasure is you shall cause the said some of twentie poundes to be furthwith uppon receipt herof delyvered unto our trustie and wellbeloved John Skynner, esquier, to our use, whom we have appointed to receive the same at your hands. And this our

The Loseley Manuscripts.

MANUSCRIPTS,

AND

OTHER RARE DOCUMENTS,

ILLUSTRATIVE OF

SOME OF THE MORE MINUTE PARTICULARS

OF

English History, Biography, and Manners,

FROM THE

REIGN OF HENRY VIII. TO THAT OF JAMES I.

PRESERVED IN THE

MUNIMENT ROOM OF JAMES MORE MOLYNEUX, ESQ.

AT LOSELEY HOUSE, IN SURREY.

" Now come tidings of weddings, maskings, mummeries, entertainments, jubilees, embassies, tilts and tournaments, trophies, triumphs, revels, sports, plays: then again, as in a new-shifted scene, treasons, cheating tricks, robberies, enormous villanies in all kinds, funerals, burials, deaths of princes, now comical then tragical matters." Democritus to the Reader, Burton's Anatomy of Melancholy.

NOW FIRST EDITED, WITH NOTES,

BY ALFRED JOHN KEMPE, ESQ. F.S.A.

LONDON:

JOHN MURRAY,

ALBEMARLE STREET.

1836.

3. The title page of Kempe's book, describing in great detail the Loseley Papers.

letters of Pryvie Seale, subscribed by the said John Skynner, confessinge the receipt of the said some to our use, shabe suffycent to bynd us and our heyres to repay and answer the said some, unto you or your assignes, at the day before appointed. And because we make our full accoumpt of the receipt

of so much money at your hands, we require you in no wise to fail us herein. Given under our Pryvey
Seal at our mannor of St. James, the XVIIth daie of September, the fourthe and fifthe years of our
raine. [1557] Received of William Moore, by way of loane to the Quenys Majestyes use, the sayd
some of XX li. P. me Joh'em Skynner To our trustie and wellbeloved William More.[36]

There is no documentary evidence to show the response of William More (the receipt in
the last sentence of the appeal was, apparently, already written in the demanding letter)
but the queen died in the following year (1558) and we know that he had to wait for his
knighthood until 1576, when Queen Elizabeth granted that honour to him.

Again, the death of the reigning monarch in 1558 gives us a chance to break into our
reports of royal demands for financial help and we can report a further development in
Chobham:

Queen Elizabeth granted the Rectory [i.e. the great tithes] to William Haber and Richard Duffield
in fee, 4 February 1565; they sold it to Owen Bray of this place [Chobham].[37]

As we are going to meet Owen Bray several times in our story, we had better establish his
position in Chobham:

John Danister, a baron of the Exchequer, died seized of the manor of Aden in 1540. His daughter
Anne, then aged two, afterwards married Owen Bray, second son of Sir Edward Bray of Shere. (*See
also above* p. 9)[38]

However, we must now return to Royalty and the new Queen's new idea of overcoming
her financial problems:

We have not met with any lotteries on record before the time of Queen Elizabeth, when they appear
to have become a common mode of raising money for the purposes of the State. The documents at
Loseley are perhaps the only original illustrations extant of the lotteries of that period.[39]

Here are details of the Lottery in 1567:

A verie rich Lotterie Generall, without any blancks, contayning a great number of good prices, as
wel of redy money as of plate, and certaine sorts of merchandizes, having ben valued and priced by
the comaundement of the Queenes most excellent Majestie, by men expert and skilfull; and the
same Lotterie is erected by hir majesties order, to the intent that suche commoditie as may chaunce
to arise thereof, after the charges borne, may be converted towardes the reparation of the havens and
strength of the Realme, and towardes such other publique good workes.
The number of lots shall be four hundreth thousand, and no more; and every lot shall be the summe
of tenne shillings sterling, onely and no more.
The Prices. Whosoever shall winne the greatest and most excellent price, shall receive the value of
five thousande poundes sterling, that is to say, three thousande pounds in ready money, seven
hundred poundes in plate gilte and white, and the rest in good tapissarie meete for hangings, and
other covertures, and certain sortes of good linen cloth. Second great price. 3.500 £, i.e. 2.000 £ in
money, 600 £ in plate, the rest as above. Third great price: 3.000 £ i.e. 1.500 £ in money 500 £ in
plate, the rest as above. 4th. 2.000 £; 5th. 1.500 £; 6th. 1.000 £ and 7th to 12th prices between 200
£ and 700 £ each; further 13 prices at 100 £ each; further 24 prices at 50 £ Each; 60 prices at 24 £ 10
s each; 90 prices at 22 £ 10 s each; 114 prices at 18 £ each; 120 prices at 12 £ 10 s each; 1150 prices
between 3 £ 10 s. and 8 £ each; 8.500 prices at between 25 s. and 50 s each and, finally, 19,418 prices
at 14 s and 15 s. each; and all the rest shall be allowed for every adventure at the least 2s and six
pens in ready money.[40]

In addition to the prizes themselves there were many extra items of value so that against a
total of £200,000, prize money of about £100,000 was to be distributed in about 30,000
special prizes.

It is well worth quoting a substantial extract from the following proclamation by the
Lord Mayor of London:

By the Maior of London. Whereas a very rich Lotterie generall hath now lately bene erected by the
order of our dread Soveraigne Lady, the Queenes most excellent Majestie, and by hir highnesse

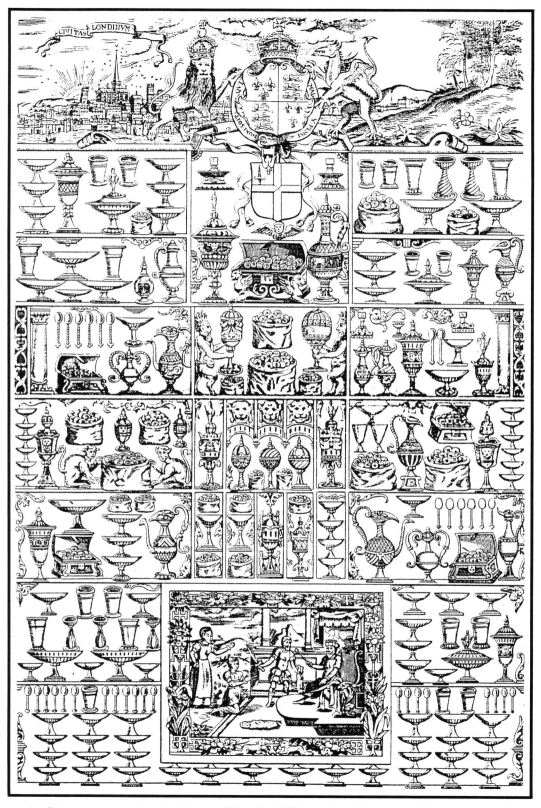

4. Prizes represented on the Lottery Chart for 1567, captioned 'A very rich Lotterie generall without any Blankes'.

commandement since published within this hir highnesse Citie of London, the 23rd daye of August, in the 9 yeare of hir Majesties most prosperous raigne, together with the prices, articles, and conditions concerning the same, as by the Charte of the sayde Lotterie more playnly appears. In which Charte among other thyngs it is comprised, that hir Majestie and hir sayd Citie of London wil answere to all and singular persons, havyng adventured their money in the sayd lotterie, to observe all the articles and conditions, contained in the same from poynt to poynt inviolably. Nowe to avoyde certaine doubtes since the publication of the sayde lotterie, secretly moved concernyng the answering thereof, wherein though the wiser sort may finde cause to satisfie themselves therein, yet to the satisfaction of the simpler sorte, the Lorde Maior of the sayd Citie, and his brethren the Aldermen of the sayd Citie, by the assent of the Common Councell of the same, doe signifie and declare to all people by this proclamation, that, according to the articles of hir Majesties order conteined in the sayd Charte so published, every person shalbe duly aunswered accordyng to the tenour of hir highness sayde proclamation.[41]

The proclamation was further supported by the Earl of Leicester and Lord Burleigh (as Lords of the Privy Council) in their letter to:

all and every the Quene's Majestie's Justices of the Peace, Treasurers, and Collectors of the Lottery, and to all Mayors, Sheriffs, Bayliefes, Constables, and to all others her highness officers, ministers, and subjects, spirituall and temporall, as well within corporations, liberties, and fraunchises, as without, in the Counties of Kent, Sussex, Surry, Southehampton, and the isle of Wight, and to every of them.[42]

It appears that the Lottery did not find the quick support expected:

After our heartie comendations, whereas yt hathe pleased the Quenes Majstie to cawse a very riche and general lottery to be erected and set forthe, to be redde and published within her Citie of London, at tymes prefixed in the same, and furtherance therof hathe apointed sondry officers, and, as it shuld seme, eyther of their negligens or by some sinister disswasions of some not well disposed persons, ther doth want a great nombre of the said lotts not yet present to performe the seame, contrary to her highnes expectacion; for which causes it hath pleased her Majestie to apointe her loving subject John Johnson, Gent. Bothe to understande in whome the former defaulte and lacke have bene, and the cawses therof, and so to take the accompts of the Treasurers, collectors and doers therof, and also to take further ordre for the speedier collection of the same, according unto certeyne instructions assigned for the better service therin to be done.

To whome we requier you and every of you to be ayding, helping, counciling and assisting, to the uttermost of your power, for the accomplishment therof, as you tender her highnes favor, and will aunswere to the contrary. So fare you well, at the Courte the 12th daie of July anno 1568.

Your loving Frends, R. Leycester. W. Cecil.[43]

Thirty-two Chobham men reacted to this reminder, 'adventuring' together £6, of which Owen Bray, Gent., purchased one whole lot at 10s. and the other 31 parishioners together bought 18 lots in amounts from 2s. to 6s. 8d. each in line with the proclamation:

every man putting into the lottery according to his ability some one lott, or more, some half a lott, some 2s. 6d., some 12d. some 3d., some 2d. or more or less according their haviours and power, and the same put into the lottery under one posye, in the name of the hole parishe.

These mottoes, devices or posies were publicly proclaimed at the drawing, whence came the term in use at the time, 'reading the lottery'.[44]

The names of the 31 Chobhamers were:[45]

6/8 each:	Henry Feilde of Millwards	3/- each:	Henry Feild of Valley Greene
5/- each:	Thomas Stileman		John Wye
	Henry Carter		H. Hedgefeilde
	John Taylor	3/4 each:	John Clark
	Thomas Spong sen	2/6 each:	Richard Burchett
	John Beedle sen		Richard Emmett
	John Beedle jun		William Woods
	John Beacham		George Martyne
	Widow Porte		Richard Heald

4/- each:	Henry Boughton		John Shrubb
	John Bagford	2/- each:	Owen Hudson
	William Wheatley		John Phillips
3/- each:	John Woods		Bartholomew Luff
	Arthur Norwood		James Hunter
	Henry Taylor		Thomas Woods
	Edmund Brookes		

. Queen Elizabeth is said also to have used the same method as Queen Mary but we have not found any documentary evidence. In the following letter sent out by her successor, James I, we find a reference to earlier Privy Seals which would have included some of the Queen's, too. We could not find any statement of the financial result of the 'Grand Lottery' but there is evidence that the Queen had to return to direct taxation as granted by parliament:

> In theory, direct taxation was exceptional, though under Elizabeth, with inflation biting, it tended to become the rule.
> The subsidy was rather substantial: 4s. in the £ on land and 2s. 8d. in the £ on personal property. The money of the subsidies seems to have been paid willingly enough and, during the Spanish War of Queen Elizabeth, direct taxation became regular and annual. In 1589 Parliament voted a double subsidy, in 1593 and 1597 treble subsidies, and in 1601 a quadruple subsidy.[46]

The earliest Lay Subsidy which we could find dates from 1570/71.[47] Forty-five inhabitants of Chobham are listed, divided according to whether they paid on 'lands' or 'goods':

Lands	£	Goods	£
Christopher Heneage, Gent.	10	Henry Hedge	11
Thomas Wye	7	Henry Rogers	10
William Bullen	6	Walter Atfelde	7
Agnes Woodes jun.	5	Henry Lee	7
Thomas Brodhurste (the vicar)	3	John Wapshott	6
Widow Edmeade	2	William Chanell	6
Richard Edmete	1	William Woodes	6
Joan Hales, widow	1	Thomas Butt	6
Thomas Birchett	1	Henry Atfelde	5
John Paine, jun.	1	Thomas Prichett	5
Heirs of Ambrose Birchett	1	John Sherbert	5
John Bekonsfelde	1	Robert Norwoode	4
John Rempnant	1	Thomas Millest	4
John Woodes, jun.	1	John Phillipp	4
John Hiller	1	Richard Cowper	3
Richard Broksted	1	John Edsawe	3
John Marten	1	Thomas Taylor	3
Henry Wye	1	John Holte	3
	52	Thomas Spong	3
		Thomas West	3
At 4s. in the £	£10 8s.	George Wapshott	3
		John Atfelde	3
		Roger Shrubbe	3
		William Atfelde	3
		Robert Millest	3
		Thomas Lane	3
			125
		At 2s. 8d. in the £	£17 3s. 9d.

Total £27 11s. 9d.

5. The first page of the Muster List dated 27 January 1583, showing the types of arms and the names of the mustered men.

We have now mentioned the Spanish war, and we must interrupt our 'financial' investigation to use the lists of musters contained in the Loseley Papers; 'England prepared for invasion by training the militia in the counties'.[48] A Muster List dated 27 January 1583 mentions the names of 108 Chobham men, distinguishing their respective weapons:[49]

Pike men selected	11
Bill men selected	8
Bill men of the best sorte	17
Bill men of the second sort	52
Archer selected	12
Archers of the second Sorte	3
Gunners	5
Total	108

Needless to say that the village is still named as 'Chabham' in this document. A second list which does not give a date, just showing 'temp. ELIZ.', contains 82 names; strangely enough the names are not identical with those of the 1583 list. This second list is said to be about eight years earlier than the first-mentioned one.[50]

Pykemen	1
Pykemen selected	3
Bylmen of the best sorte	15
Bilmen selected	2
Bilmen of the second sorte	19
Archers of the best sorte	9
Archers selected	5
Archers of the second sorte	12
Carpenters	1
Laborers and Pyoners	15
Total	82

We shall give the names of all these men in Chapter Five.

Again we were lucky to find among the Loseley Papers details of the Subsidy of 1593: 'Parliament had granted four subsidies in 1601, which would continue to be collected into 1605.[51] Here are the details of the 1593 subsidies which were collected by five commissioners for the County of Surrey – Chobham people contributed a total of £23 4s.

The Certificate of Sir Wylliam More and Sir Thomas Browne, Knights, George

More, John Reader & Lawrence Stoughton Esquires, Commyssioners of our Soveraigne Ladie Queene Elizabeth amongest other assigned within the County of Surrey for the execution of the Act of Parliament of the graunte of the first subscidye of three entyre Subscidies graunted to our saide Soveraigne Ladie in the Fyve and Thirteth yere of her Majesties Raigne for the payment of the said first Subscidye & uppon the saide Commyssioners severinge of themselves lymitted unto the Hundreds of Wokinge Blackheath & Wotton Godley Godalmynge & Farneham in the saide County all such persons as are taxed with the saide Payment of the saide first Subscidie within the Hundreds aforesaide & all the Towneshipps & other places within the same with the serall somes of money whereat the saide persons are taxed to the payment of the saide first subscidie made the twenteth Day of October in the Fyve and Thirteth yere of the Raigne of our saide Soveraigne Ladie Queene Elizabeth [1592].

In Witness whereof we the saide Commyssioners to this Certificate conteyninge Tenne Prests in parchment have sett our seales the Day & Yere above wrytton.[52]

The document also shows the names of 47 inhabitants of Chobham who were taxed on the basis of 4s. in the pound of the value of 'lands' and 2s. 8d. in the pound on the value of their 'goods' (i.e. personal property). Their names and assessments follow here:[53]

Lands	£	Goods	£
Nicholas More, gent.	9	Henry Lee	8
Thomas Wye	8	John Rogers	7
John Sawyer	4	William Woods	6
William Beard	2	Robert Norwood	6
Richard Emmott	2	William Stenton	5
Henry Spong	2	John Bedell	5
Thomas Edwards	2	Henry Phillipp	4
John Hywood (the vicar)	1	Thomas Taylor	5
John Broxesed	2	Thomas Thetcher	4
John Felde	1	Henry Atfelde	4
John Payne	1	Henry Feild, jun.	4
Henry Hall	1	Thomas Lane	4
Thomas Daborne	1	William Attfeild	4
Thomas Martyn	1	Richard Shrubb	4
Richard Broxesed	1	Richard Edmead	4
William Hillier	1	Christopher Feld	4
Henry Wye	1	John Wheatley	3
Henry Payne	1	Henry Rason	3
Henry Rempnant	1	Roger Shore	3
John Bullen	1	John Warner	3
Henry Woods, jun.	1	Richard Hall	3
		John Hoult	3
	44	Henry Woods	3
		Thomas Cobbett	3
At 4s. in the £ = £8 16s.		Richard Mylton	3
		Lawrence Dubbes	3
			108
		At 2s. 8d. in the £ = £14 8s.	
		Total £23 4s.	

In addition to this list of 1593 a further three lists, dated 1589, 1594 and 1595, with their rolls of taxed persons in Chobham, have been used in our report of the families of Chobham and their members; to these rolls of the time of Queen Elizabeth were added rolls of 1622 to 1624 (James I) and of 1628 to 1642 (Charles I).

Trustie and welbeloued, wee greete you well : Although
our subiects the least doubt of our vnwillingnes to throw
desire to auoide it in the whole course of our gouernment : Yet
vpon you (in no sort to be eschewed) as wee shall be forced p...
meanes, oe to want without great preiudice. In which consi...
how much wee found the Crowne exhausted by the accidents of f...
of our daylie expence euer since wee came into this Kingdome, ...
that as our necessitie is the onely cause of our Request, So you...
may further adde one thing, which is no lesse notorious to the
hath beene affourded you, notwithstanding more extraordinarie o...
euer lighted vpon any King of this Realme. A matter wh...
seruice and fidelitie in the highest points wee haue had so elere...
fourme of Subsidies offered to Princes in Parliament, caried
vour to eschew by all the wayes wee can. You shall therefor...
you, howsoeuer the omission in the former time to repay some ...
should be kept, wee haue perswaded our selues that you will no ...
engage that word yet neuer broken to any, which now wee doe ...
which werequire therefore it, that within twelue dayes after the
George More Knight, whom we haue appointed to be our C...
and twenty day of March which shalbe in the yeere of our Lo...
you, which, with the hand of our said Collector testifying th...
the repaiment thereof, and shall be an immediate warrant to our E...
        Giuen vnder our Priuie Seale at our Palace of W...
Ireland, and of Scotland the eight and thirtieth.

6. James I's letter sent 'under Our Privie Seale' to Sir George More in 1604. The loan was
to be repaid by 24 March 1605.

By the King.

...e nothing more against our minde then to be drawen into any course that may breede in
...rthers vpon them, Hauing already published both by our speeches and writings, our great
...our Estate at this time, in regarde of great and vrgent occasions falne and growing dayly
...to disburse greater summes of money then it is possible for vs to prouide by any ordinary
..., seeing no man of any indifferent iudgement or vnderstanding, can either plead ignorance
...warres, and inward rebellions, Or on the other side doth not obserue the visible causes
...hinke it needlesse to vse any more arguments from such a King to such Subiects: But
...d dutty must be the chiefe motiue of your ready performance of the same. To which we
...us, that since we came to this Estate, no one meanes or other of extraordinarie helpe
...e of large Expence, one falling on the necke of another without time of respiration, then
...we make not mention as proceeding from the coldnesse of our peoples affections, of whose
...But rather as a circumstance the better warranting this course, seeing the ordinarie
..., it now that inconuenience of burthening the poorer sort of our people, which we doe endea-
...rstand, that in this consideration, and in respect of our opinion of your good minde towards
...n regard of vnexpected violent necessities, might make a doubtfulnesse now that promise
...neasure our Princely resolution by the precedent accidents, nor euer doubt of vs when we
...giue for repayment of whatsoeuer this Priuie Seale of ours shall assure you. That
...t hereof, you will cause the summe of twentie fiue pounds to be deliuered to Sir
...e in our Countie of Surrey: The loane whereof, we doe desire to be vntill the fourt
...1605. For assurance whereof, we haue directed these our letters of Priuie Seale vnto
...t of the same summe of ————— wch shall binde vs, our heires, and successors, for
...er to pay the same vnto you, vpon the deliuerie of this our Priuie Seale into our said Receipt.
...nster the last day of July, in the second yeere of our reigne of England, ffrance and

James I had to return to the issue of Privy Seals:

A proclamation dated 16 July [1604] contained writs under the privy seal for a forced loan. This was a practice well established under Elizabeth, but far from popular, especially since latterly hers had not been repaid.[54]

There is a letter preserved in the Loseley Papers which we reproduce here; although it is on the lines of that of Queen Mary, it contains a number of sentences which warrant a further lengthy transcript.

By the King. Trustie and wellbeloved, wee greete you well. Although there be nothing more against our minde then to be drawn into any course that may breed in our subjects the least doubt of our unwillingnes to throw any burthens upon them, having already published both by our speeches and writings, our great desire to avoide it in the whole course of our government:

Yet such is our Estate at this time, in regarde of great and urgent occasions and growing dayly upon us (in no sort to be eschewed) as we shall be forced presently to disburse greater summes of money then it is possible for us to provide by any ordinary meanes, or to want without great prejudice.

In which consideration, seeing no way of any indifferent judgement or understanding, can either plead ignorance how much we found the Crowne exhausted by the accidents of forreint warres, and inward rebellions,

Or on the other side doth not observe the visible causes of our dayly expence ever since wee came into this Kingdome, Wee thinke it needlesse to use any more arguments from such a King to such Subjects: But that as our necessitie is the onely cause of our Request, So your love and duety must be the chiefe motive of your ready performance of the same.

To which wee may further add one thing, which is no lesse notorious to the Realme, that since wee came to this Estate, no one meanes or other of extraordinarie helpe hath beene affourded us, nothwithstanding more extraordinarie occasions of large Expence, one falling on the necke of another without time of respiration, then ever lighted upon any King of this Realme.

A matter whereof wee make not mention as proceeding from the coldnesse of our peoples affections, of whose service and fidelitie in the highest points wee have had so cleere proofe.

But rather as a circumstance the better warranting this course, seeing that ordinarie fourme of Subsidies offered to Princes in Parliament, caried with it now that inconvenience of burthening the poorer sort of our people, which wee doe endeavour to eschew by all the wayes wee can. You shall therefore understand, that in this consideration, and in respect of our opinion of your good minde towards us, howsoever the omission in the former time to repay some loane, in regard of unexpected violent necessities, might make a doubtfulnesse now that promise should be kept, we have persuaded ourselves that you will no way measure our Princely resolution by the precedent accidents, nor ever doubt of us when wee engage that word yet never broken to any, which now we doe hereby give for repayment of whatsoever this Privie Seale of ours shall assure you.

That which we require therefore is, that within twelve dayes after the receipt hereof, you will cause the summe of *twentiefive pounds* to be delivered to *Sir George More Knight*, whom we have appointed to be our Collector in our Countie of *Surrey*.

The loane whereof, we do desire to be untill the foure and twenty day of March which shalbe in the yere of our Lord God 1605.

For assurance whereof, we have directed these our letters of Privie Seale unto you, which, with the hand of our sayd Collector testifying the receipt of the same summe of *xxv £* shall binde us, our heires, and successors, for the repaiment thereof, and shall be an immediate warrant to our Exchequer to pay the same unto you, upon the deliverie of this our Privie seale into our sayd Receipt.

Given under our Privie Seale at our Palace of Westminster the last day of July, in the second yere of our reigne of England, France and Ireland, and of Scotland the eight and thirtieth [1604].[55]

We have put in italics the words in this letter which were obviously left open to be filled in when the addressee had been settled. (This seems to be a very early example of an official, 'printed' document with spaces left out of the 'print run' to be inserted later by hand!)

This letter had been sent to Sir George More as collector and the amount quoted (£25)

appears to show that the letter had been sent to Sir George for 'onward-transmission' to the addressee. Sir George's response to the royal letter is shown in the following document:

> 22nd February 1604/5 2nd year of the reign of King James. Received by me Sir Francis Egioke knight one of the tellers of his majesty's Exchequer of Sir George More knight collector of the money lent by privy seals in the county of Surrey, the sum of two hundred and twenty Pounds of current English Money for the King's majesty's Use
>
> Examined skynner   signed J Wardour[56]

The date shows without doubt that the collection in Surrey had been quite successful; unfortunately we do not know whether any inhabitant of Chobham had been concerned in it.

Here is an example of King Charles I using a 'new' method:

> In 1631, with the endorsement of the Court of Exchequer, men worth £ 40 a year in land or above were fined for not assuming the honour of knighthood.[57]

And here are the names of seven men from Chobham and their responses:

> Henry Field of Valley Green says he has not above £30 p.a.
> Henry Feild of Milwards says he never had above £20 p.a.
> William Wheatley says he has not full £20 p.a.
> Richard Emott did not appear.
> Henry Spong says he has not above £20 p.a.
> John Bedle says he will stand to his plea in the Exchequer.
> John Beacham stands to his plea in the Exchequer.[58]

It is not surprising that this effort proved less than successful as parliament, under James I, had in 1607 'called for the abolition of "distraint of knighthood" which obliged men owning land worth more than £40 to assume this honour'.[59] There are other instances of the growing difficulties in the King's financial efforts:

> Opposition to such exactions known as 'benevolences' developed among the gentry, while merchants had already been alienated by industrial and commercial monopolies conferred on courtiers and by imposition.[60]

This note refers to the year 1615 and here is yet another:

> The King tried to collect further 'benevolences' to pay for his foreign policy, but in January 1621 was compelled to seek aid from a new Parliament.[61]

In the Loseley Papers is yet another example of a royal copy of the method introduced by Edward IV; this time, however, by Charles I:

> A Certificate of the names of such persons within the Countie of Surrey as maie be thought able to furnishe his Majestie with severall somes of money by waie of Loane and what somes they maie severally spare then whose family did lend to his Majestie being rated at a third parte lesse then their was at that tyme.[62]

The list of names with the 'allocated' sums begins with:

> Sir George More of Loseley, Knight ....50 £

then, among others:

> Owen Bray of Chobham, gent ....10 £
> Richard Lumley of Chobham, gent ....10 £

Although the document is undated, it is said to be of 1626.

The same year, 1626 (2 Charles I), is also given to yet another list of subscribers in the Godley Hundred which show the signature 'Ed Zouch'; if the date is correct this must be Sir Edward, the first of the Zouch family as lords of the Chobham Manor. Although the amounts set out and the division between subscribers by 'land' and 'goods' points to a parliamentary subsidy, in fact for 'goods' the charge is £2 for £3, rather higher than normal.

We feel that the list is worth quoting as it shows 34 Chobham people assessed on either 'lands' or 'goods' (with only the last valued). The list is headed thus:

The names of all those parties who have subscribed their names with the somes agreed to be lent to his Majestye.[63]

Lands:	£	Goods:	£	£	s.	d.
Henry Atfeild	4	John Beedle, the elder,	7	4	13	4
John Beedle, jun	3	Henry Spong	7	4	13	4
Henry Feilde	3	Richard Emott	6	4	–	–
John Bagford	2	John Beacham	5	3	6	8
John Wye	2	Widow Porte	5	3	6	8
Henry Taylor	2	John Taylor	4	2	13	4
Rodger Feild	2	Thomas Stylman	4	2	13	4
George Martin	2	James Hunte	4	2	13	4
Henry Carter	2	Henry Boughton	3	2	–	–
William Wheatley	2	Owen Hudson	3	2	–	–
Arthur Norwood	2	George Stylman	3	2	–	–
John Woods	1	Richard Burchett	3	2	–	–
William Woods	1	John Clarke	3	2	–	–
John Shrubb	1	Richard Roall	3	2	–	–
Edmond Brockhurst	1	William Woods	3	2	–	–
John Phillypps	1					
Thomas Woods	1			42	–	–
John Norwood	1					
Bartholomew Luffe	1					
Henry Pain	1					
	35		Total	£77	–	–

Comparing the tax levied on this occasion we find that for 'goods' the charge is now 13s. 4d. in the pound; if the charge on 'lands' was now in the same proportion to the 'goods' charge as before, it now amounts to £1 in the pound (perhaps that is the reason why no values are shown!) The signature of the new lord of the manor raises the suspicion that perhaps his influence has something to do with the higher rates now charged.

Here ends one of the reasons for providing examples of royal efforts to obtain financial assistance (apart from their purely historical interest) as from 1654 our parish registers provide the source for further demographic studies. We add, however, in addition to those recorded in the Loseley Manuscripts which presented such a rich source of exciting goings-on, the last instance of such efforts when King Charles II, in 1661/2, requested a FREE AND VOLUNTARY PRESENT in which he, contrary to his grandfather's advice to exclude from his privy seal the 'poorer sort', addressed his appeal to gentlemen, farmers and even labourers; the list of contributors, on the other hand, gives us a chance to add to the names on the 'Hearth Tax' lists of 1664 their occupations which, on the tax list, is only shown with non-payers.

Here are the names of contributors from Chobham:[64]

£	s.	d.		£	s.	d.	
0	–	–	Anthony Thomas, gent	–	2	6	Thomas Emmett, hus
1	10	–	William Hill				Richard Edmund
			Joshua Chandler				Henry Hale, hus
1	–	–	William Beauchamp, yeo				James Martin
			Henry Atfield				George Goring
			Richard Emett				John Phillip, hus

£ s. d.		£ s. d.	
– 15 –	John Biddle		John Slyfield, hus
	George Stillman		William Spong
– 10 –	Henry Attfield, gent		Henry Wye, hus
	John Hudson, yeo		George Worsley
	William Pigg	– 2 –	John Attwood
– 6 8	Henry Taylor, yeo		William Berriman, lab
– 6 –	Christopher Woods, hus		John Hard, hus
– 5 –	Henry H Attfield		Henry Smither
	Jane Bagford, widow		Roger Spong, lab
	William Appleby		William Spong, lab
	Robert Corfe, hus	– 1 6	John Beauchamp, hus
	William Lee		Robert Davis, lab
	Barth. Luff, innholder		John Hamon, shoemaker
	John Norwood, tanner		John Peto, hus
	John Shrubb	– 1 –	John Child, hus
	Thomas Shrubb, hus		William Feild, hus
	Alice Spong, widow		John Hiller, lab
– 4 –	William Burchett		William Patfall, hus
– 3 –	Thomas Wood, hus		Robert Luff, lab
– 2 6	John Cobbett, hus		Henry Savage, lab

Total present from Chobham £25 11s. 2d.

Abbreviations: yeo : yeoman; hus : husbandman; lab : labourer.

All that remains to be said now about the manor-house of Chobham is that: 'The old house called Chobham Park was pulled down and the park broken up in the early 18th century'.[65] One part of the old house is now a family home. This might be the right moment to quote a much later description of this site, as found in 1895 by C. R. B. Barrett:

> Returning, I passed through the fields to Chobham Park, now a farmhouse, and built out of a small portion of the outbuildings of the ancient mansion. Chobham Park was originally a doubly-moated house, and was of great size and magnificence. From the time of Edward the Confessor till the spoliation the estate belonged to Chertsey Abbey. When seized by the Crown it remained royal property till sold in the reign of Mary to Archbishop Heath, the price paid being no less a sum than £3,000. Record remains that the moats were dug by De Rutherwyke, Abbot of Chertsey, and that they were filled by means of a channel cut from a large piece of water known as 'gracious Pond'. But in these days the pond is drained and the moats filled in. According to Manning, at the west end of the present house in his day there was some remarkable glass – spoils, no doubt, from the old mansion. This glass shewed a park with gate and palings, a subject possibly intended as a rebus on the name of Abbot Parker, who resigned his Abbacy in 1529. One quarry had the cypher I. L. above a crown, and on another was scratched with a diamond: "Elizabeth' N'nsuch – Quall sempre – fui Tal esser – Vo Quo." But the glass is no longer at Chobham Park, and the most diligent enquiry on my part failed to trace its whereabouts at the present time.[66]

(For the Queen's visits *see also* p. 14.)

After this excursion into the future we have to return to 1841, when E. W. Brayley can give this report on the site we discuss:

> The mansion stood on one side of the road leading from Chobham to Chertsey, where was afterwards a farm house. The park was divided into separate farms; which became the property of Mr Revel, whose daughter conveyed the estate by marriage to Sir George Warren, who died in 1801, and through his daughter, it passed to Viscount Bulkely, who was the owner in 1811. It is now the property of Sir Denis Le Marchant, Bart. (so created on the 23rd August 1841), by whom, together with Chobham Place and several large farms in the parish it was purchased about three years ago. About one hundred acres are attached to what is still called Chobham Park which is tenanted as a farm by the Daborns.[67]

Brayley's statement tells, in a rather condensed manner, the story of much of Chobham's land: after the end of the Chertsey Abbots' rule the royal Lords of the Manor opened the parish to wealthy gentlemen who wished to become 'landed proprietors' putting at the same time local men in practical charge as their tenants. The pulling down of the manor-house thus ended a history of nearly 500 years.

The parish constables in Henry VIII's last year (1546).

Chapter Three

Other Manors and Important Sites

The sad fate of the chief house in Chobham was, fortunately, not shared by buildings on other sites in the parish but on others which had been mentioned in Rutherwyk's cartulary, the original buildings were replaced by newer ones in Queen Elizabeth's time:

> The period 1550 to 1660 has been described as the golden age of cottage-building, for beside the new timber-framed farmhouses rose new cottages to replace the decayed, chimneyless hovels of the medieval village; Records indicate that this rebuilding reached its peak between 1580 and 1640.[1]

Of all these sites in Chobham the most important is the Manor of Stanners and Ford which lies near the Eastern border of the parish:

> The early history of the Stannards estate is at present blank until it appears suddenly as a manor in an admission in June 1308 of the right of John de Ham and his wife Aline. It passed with Ham for some time and in 1319 was said to be held by them. It is possible that it is to be identified with the manor, which, until the failure of their male line in 1255, was held by the de Bagshot family, hereditary foresters of Windsor Forest in 1255. A number of deeds concern the conveyance to the Abbey of land called Hessle by a man who had obtained it between 1235/55 from Geoffrey de Bagshot. The Bagshot estate was clearly a manor since in making this grant Geoffrey could release suit due to his court. This estate was noted 'Stanor' in 1482/3.
>
> Rutherwyk's first act here in 1319, was to effect an exchange with John de Ham and his wife Aline, in which he conveyed to them an estate called Bradwaysland which his predecessor had acquired in 1275. In the deed of exchange this manor is mentioned. There is considerable obscurity about the fate of the Bagshot lands after their partition in 1255 so it is possible that it was their Chobham manor which became Stannards.[2]

This extract from the Surrey Record Society's report and comments on the early days of Chobham shows that even expert antiquarians could not quite pierce the darkness of the Abbey's cartulary but we have tried here to summarise these early records.

Before his death, in 1255, Geoffrey de Bagshete (Bagshot) held land in the 'vill of Chabeham', called Hessle. He had given part of this land to John de Hessle and another part to Ralph de Brudeford; Hessle's part was also subsequently given to Ralph at which point in time the name 'Stanors' appears. All these changes took place under the Abbot Alan (1223-1261). We have no knowledge about what happened to this land under the next two abbots but under John de Rutherwyk, whom we have met before:

> The manor of Stannards, Stanyors or Fords was held of the abbey of Chertsey with the manor of Ham, next Chertsey by John de Hamme and Alina his wife in 1307.[3]

We shall find that, in future, the fate of Stanners was often linked to that of Ottershaw (a part of Chertsey parish). We continue:

> During the reigns of Edward II (1307-27) and Edward III (1327-77) it was held, under the de Hammes, by a family of the name of Ford, whose name became attached to that of the manor of Stanners and Ford. It seems to have remained united to that of Hamme for some time.[4]

The fate of this subordinate (under the abbot of Chertsey) manor now becomes very complicated as the owners changed often. We take up the story again in 1687, when we hear that it was owned by Francis Swanton who is said to have sold it to Nathaniel Cocks, whose burial in 1694 is entered in the Chobham Register. In 1721 his widow and daughter conveyed:

7.   Fishpool Cottage, an example of a building which replaced an old cottage in Queen Elizabeth's time.

8.   Buckstone Farm, an old building beautifully maintained and improved.

the manor or lordship or reputed manor or lordship to John Martin who, in 1728, sold it to Thomas Woodford, the sale including two farms known as Forde Farm and Coxhill Farm, a common called Mynefield Green and other lands. Thomas Woodford's son Thomas inherited his father's estate and sold the manor of Stannards and Fords to Thomas Sewell, whose son and heir sold it in 1795 to Edmund Boehm, the owner of Ottershaw Estate.[5]

This extract requires a certain amount of clarification and addition; we have seen that by the time when the sale to Thomas Woodford, senior, took place, the manor had already been divided i.e. the southern part of it had acquired alone the name of 'Forde farm' which, in later documents, appears also under the name of 'Bonseys farm':

Thomas Woodford by his will devised this estate to his eldest son the Rev. Thomas Woodford, who in April 1761 sold it to Thomas Sewell Esq. a Counsel of eminence at the Chancery Bar, afterwards knighted and made Master of the Rolls. He married to his first wife Catherine Heath daughter of Thomas Heath Esq. of Stanstead Nonfichet in the County of Essex. After her death he in 1773 married Mary Elizabeth Sibthorpe, daughter of Conningsby Sibthorpe of Canwick in the City of Lincoln Esq., by whom he had one child who died an infant in the lifetime of Sir Thomas. After buying Ottershaw Sir Thomas pulled down the old house and built a new one on higher ground. He died in March 1784 intestate, leaving Thomas Bailey Heath Sewell Esq., his eldest son and heir. This gentleman married Lady Elizabeth Birmingham, daughter of the Earl of Louth, from whom he was divorced in 1779. He was Lieutenant Colonel of the Surrey Fencible Cavalry raised in 1794, at the time when the French threatened an invasion of this country. In 1795 Ottershaw and other lands to the amount of 300 acres, and the manor of Stannards and Forde in Chobham, was sold to Edmund Boehm Esq. This gentleman has very much enlarged his property there, and made great plantations. The ground surrounding the house is now extended to the road from Chertsey to Guildford.[6]

Mr. Boehm's property was sold in 1820 after his bankruptcy and it was acquired by Mr. James Fladgate, who had been the tenant of Stannards and Forde since 1780.

The second subordinate manor in the parish was that of Aden, about which Manning and Bray had this to say:

At the North end of Chobham-street is a good house, which, with the mill and 40 acres of arable and meadow, is called in the deeds, 'The manor of Aden'.[7]

Here again is the *Victoria History of the County of Surrey*: 'a John Ardern held land in Chobham in 1331'.[8] And again:

I have a deed without date wherein is a Fine and recovery by John de Pentecost of 5 acres in Chobham from John de Ardern and Agnes his wife [Ardern is the local pronunciation of Aden].[9]

We have been able to establish that John de Pentecost's name dates this last entry to the second quarter of the 14th century and so it refers to the same fact as the previous quotation.

To this we can add the following from *Bisley Bits*:

The tenancy of the manor was sold by the son of Geoffrey de Lucy in 1294 to Sir Henry de Leybourne, who in turn made a grant of 'certain lands in Busselagh' to one Hugh de Smerhull. He very shortly afterwards decided to dispose of what had been granted to him, and, accordingly, sold it in 1305 to 'Amicia of Chabeham' and her son Thomas. The years of 1314 and 1315 were times of sore famine. The crops failed, prices ran so high that many perished from hunger, and the nobles made matters worse by turning adrift the retainers whom they had clothed and fed and who had lived with them in their castles. This condition of things prompted Amicia and her son Thomas to part with their interest in Bisley, and they made a free grant of it to John Arderne and his wife Agnes. This portion of the parish of Bisley is entirely separated from the rest and is described as 'Bisley Detached'.[10]

This quotation from Bisley records, in addition to mentioning the Ardern family, states so many interesting details of general interest, that it seemed to have been worthy of being reprinted in full. Here is a further extract from the same source:

The old house at Scott's Farm – a house of considerable proportions, and formerly the residence of

9. & 10.   Front and back view of Stanyards Cottage, part of the Stannards and Ford estate.

the Campions – has long since been replaced by a comparatively modern structure [*Bisley Bits* was written in 1892!].[11]

It would appear, then, that the site of Scotts House dates back at least to the 14th century (*see also below*). To establish the family of the Arderns as a leading Surrey family we can add that 'John Arderne was the grandfather of John Arderne, Sheriff of Surrey in 1409'.[12]

We have, above, mentioned the Campions, Scott's Farm and 'Bisley Detached'. The Ordnance map of 1872 shows Scotts Grove on the border of the area marked as 'Bisley Detached' so that we feel it not to be out of order if we quote yet once more from the Bisley documents:

> William Brooke Citizen and wax chandler of London gave unto the Bisley parsonage for ever, Four Marks, and four pence, a yeare out of his tenement at Fleet Bridge. [1450]
>
> 18 Edward IV [1479] Isabella Manory widow daughter and heir of Nicholas Atte Broke, late of Chobham, granted to William Campion Citizen of London and others, all her tenements in Chobham, Bysley, Chertsey and Horsull Co. Surrey.
>
> Isabell Champion widdow and one of the daughters of the said Brooke gave unto this church [i.e. Bisley] for ever one Mead in Chobham called Brachmead. [1517][13]

11. Brook Place, formerly called the Malthouse, as it was rebuilt in 1656.

In an earlier quotation (*see above* p. 5) we have shown that the Brooke family had lived in Chobham for about one hundred years prior to these donations to Bisley. It is however, not certain whether they lived in Brook Place; 'Brook Place, called Malt House on the old ordnance map, is a small, square, and picturesque 17th-century building, now a farm-house'.[14] We have shown in the previous chapter how the actions of King Henry VIII altered the direction of Chobham's development; we hear: 'In the account given in pursuance of the Act of 26 Henry VIII [1534-5], there were the following Lay Officers: . . . John Danister of Chobham, Under Steward'.[15] In another document we read that Danister was put in charge of collecting the rents and other income of Chertsey Abbey before the final dissolution.

But now more about John Danister:

> John Danister Esq., one of the Barons of the Exchequer, died 28th February 1539/40, seized of an estate here, described as consisting of 6 messuages, 4 Cottages, 200 acres of land, 100 acres of meadow, 200 acres of pasture, 120 acres of wood in CHOBHAM; of Ottershaw in Chertsey, lands in Bussheley and Talworth. A manor or tenement called Hill Place and a messuage called Twytcham, 60 acres of land, 70 of meadow, 60 of pasture and 40 of wood in Horsell. On the day he died, he executed a deed by which he conveyed the estate in Horsell to his trustees for his bastard son Robert and the heirs of his body, the rest to himself and Ann his wife for their lives, remainder to the heirs of their bodies. Ann was his daughter and heir aged 2. [10 June 32 Henry VIII (1541)][16]

We can continue:

> John Danaster, baron of the Exchequer, died seized of the MANOR OF ADEN in 1540. His daughter Ann, then aged two, afterwards married Owen Bray, second son of Sir Edward Bray of Shiere. Their son Edward had a son Owen, whose daughter married a Mr. Sear, and their daughter married Mr. Johnson.[17]
>
> Mr. Johnson, an attorney, had no legitimate issue, but some of his family sold this estate to General Broome, of whom it was purchased by Mr. Chappell, a stationer in London, who, about 1808, sold it to the Rev. Mr. Jerrom, who now resides in it [1811] and succeeded to the Vicarage of Chobham on the death of Mr. Cecil in 1810.[16]

With the arrival of General Broome, we have reached the period of the extant Land Tax records, which enable us to give further details about Brook Place. (In the lists, General Broome is stated as Colonel!) The lists confirm the change of ownership to Mr. Chapell in 1783, and to the Rev. Charles Jerram in 1806. By the time these records begin, i.e. 1780, the old manor of Aden had been split up: Brook Place was the part which Owen Bray's bride inherited, and the site of the original manor-house, now called Chobham House, was the property which General Broome had kept for himself. Perhaps this will clarify matters:

> The [old] house was rebuilt on another site, and is now called 'Chobham House'. The mill, which was part of the estate, was sold separately in the 19th century.[17]

Owen Bray, whose arrival in the village has just been mentioned, we have heard of before as the first lay impropriator of the Chobham rectory (*see above* p. 18). We have also heard that, in 1567, he 'adventured' one whole lot in the Queen's Lottery. His son Edward is shown in the Lay Subsidy List of 1589 assessed at 21s. 4d. which must have been for some considerable value of land (if we compare that in the same subsidy Thomas Heath, nephew and heir of the Archbishop of Chobham Park, is assessed at 26s. 8d. for the old manor-house and 500 acres of land!). 'Gent.' is shown as both their occupations. Owen's grandson, another Owen, is shown as 'father of Dorothy' on the occasion of her burial in 1587. An indenture of 1616 notes him in a land transaction with Richard Lumley whom we had met from his response to King Charles I's request for a loan in 1626. The second Owen's wife, Sence, – as she is spelled in the Bray family tree and in our 1616 document – was buried in Chobham on 23 March 1667, a 'widow named Samitia alias Sencia'. To go yet one generation further, we find that Edward, the first Owen's great grandson, was born in 1608 and is still alive and busy in 1651.

Two quotations might help us here:

> In 1648 this house [Brook Place] was the property of Edward Bray, a descendant of the Shiere family, who paid composition for his estate as Royalist. It belonged to the manor of Aden, but was NOT the Manorhouse.[18]

The Bray family were connected with Chobham in old times, and I find an Edward Bray compounding for his estates on June 20, 1649. Bray compounded, though he was not sequestrated, fearing as he avers, 'that he would be questioned as to things he had done in the first war'.

Chobham must have been very Parliamentarian or politically colourless, for the only other inhabitant who compounded was one Gabriel Young.[19]

Brook Place shows, on a panel, the inscription 'W. B. 1656'. This must be the date of rebuilding the house. 'It would therefore appear that there was an earlier house that was pulled down during the Commonwealth and rebuilt by W. B. 1656.'[20] In old documents the house was referred to as 'Malthouse'. It is, of course, tempting to link the initials on the house to the Bray family which had owned and lived in the house, but the family had left the village before that date. (They are not shown in the list of householders in the Hearth Tax returns of 1664.) Edward, the last of the Bray family to live in Chobham, had by this time sold his estate to William Beauchamp (hence the initials 'W. B.') just as his father, the second Owen, had passed their grant of the rectory shortly before his death to Sir Thomas White of Farnham.

This seems to be the right place to quote another note from Manning and Bray about the rights to the rectory, i.e. the great tithes:

Queen Elizabeth granted it to William Haber [or Harber] and Richard Duffield, in fee. 4th Feb. 1565; they sold it to Owen Bray, of this place. 10 Nov. 1638, he and his son and heir apparent Edward Bray, conveyed it to Sir Thomas White. He was of South Wanborough, Hants. From him it descended to the Woodruffes.

In Nov. 1687, Sir George Woodruffe and George his son and heir apparent, suffered a recovery, and in December following conveyed it to Philip Beauchamp. In 1811 it was possessed by several persons. Sir William Abdy had the West End tithes, Lord Bulkely had the East End, Mr Woods of Chobham had part and several owners of lands had purchased the tithes thereof.[20]

Having described the story of the subordinate manors of Chobham we can now proceed to yet another site which goes back as these to the late 13th century; the estate which in old records was given the name of its owners, the Pentecost family.

Agnes Prioress of Bromhale and the Convent of the same place greeting – know all of you that we have given to Pentecost of Fremesham all that land in the manor of Chabeham in the place which is called Fremesham.[21]

This entry in the Chertsey cartulary is dated A.D. 1258. This is the oldest record of the family's name but we find them in a number of property transactions as either witnesses or partners: Richard is mentioned between 1309 and 1312, his son John from 1325 to 1348 and Stephen, John's son, between 1348 and 1373.

We have up till now not claimed the title of 'manor' for the estate of the Pentecost family but there is yet another extract which seems to enable us to do so:

Stephen Pentecost greeting – whereas John son of Walter atte Brigge of Chabeham and Robert son of the same John hold of me – one messuage and part of a half virgate of land – as appears in the COURT of John Pentecost my father held at Fremesham on Wednesday next after the feast of St. Lucy the Virgin in 22 Edward III (1348).[22]

We can add here that the *Victoria History of the County of Surrey* states:

Chobham was divided into tithings, Stanners, Pentecost, and the Forest Tything, lying east, west and north respectively, but the modern division is practically into hamlets.[23]

This entry points to the fact that around the Pentecost estate a kind of hamlet had developed before it could be called a tithing. But from a variety of old documents we were able to extract the story of what happened to this part of the village after the failure of the Pentecost family. The oldest part of the Pentecost farmhouse did not, as at present, face north to the Bagshot Road but originally faced west towards a lane which in a deed of 1659 is called

Pentecost Lane which, on the map of 1872, leads towards the south and to the present Beldam Bridge. Also, in an abstract of title dated 1622, we find: 'to a Farm called Pentecost alias Millwards in Chobham of Mr. John Attfield, the son of Henry Attfield'.[24] This refers to Henry Attfield who in various documents dating from 1567 onwards is described as 'of Millwards' to distinguish him from another Henry the owner of 'Velley Green' and yet a third H. A. who assumed the Christian name 'Hedge' from his property called 'Hedgelands'.

We can add here how local inhabitants pronounced unusual words: 'Millwards' is shown as 'Millards' in the burial entry of John Attfield's wife Constance in 1667; the word 'Pentecost' proved too much for Chobham men so they called the farm at first 'Pankhurst' which gave rise to 'Pankers' at John's death in 1675 and this was followed by 'Pancras'. The strangest change, however, is the local name for a part of the Pentecost estate now known as 'Pennypot'. Investigations into the Attfield family activities were made even more difficult as in many documents the name is often 'Field alias Attfield', for example Henry Field of Hedgelands was shown as 'Henry alias Hedge' Field on his death in 1683.

After this digression, we can now say that the Pentecost estate had been divided: in the Land Tax Lists of 1790 the old name of Pentecost is revived and its owner is, from 1780, Richard Collier; another part is owned by Lady Abdy and its tenant is James Collier, the son of Richard. Richard died in 1800 and James took over his father's part of the farm, too, but died in 1810. His widow, née Sarah Fladgate, acted as heir for one year then remarried, after which her second son, another Richard, took over; he is listed in the Census of 1851 as resident in 'Pancras'.

The next site we should discuss is 'Chobham Place' about which Aubrey reports as follows:

> In the Parish, on a Hill, is a pleasant Seat, and neat-built House of Brick, of the aforementioned Anthony Thomas Esq., vulgarly called Radium; Rhedum in Welsh signifies a Fearny Place which agrees with the nature of this Place. From the top of this House (which is flat and leaded) is a very large Prospect, viz. over all the Flat of Surrey and Middlesex, Bucks, Oxon, Hertfordshire, St. Albans, Box-Hill; Easterly Farnham and Hindhead 25 Miles Westerly, the Valley and Meadow that run by the Ruins of Newark Abbey. In the Garden here, and in the Heath, over against the House, are found Pebbles of Hardness next to a Diamant, but of Lustre and Clearness inferior. Here is a most salubrious air, blue Mist arising in the Valleys, but scarce over in all the Year come nigh this House. About a Bow-Shot from this House, in Valley Wood, is a ston'd Well, the Water whereof has a rough Taste, and with Powder of Galls, turns to a Purple colour, which comes from the Iron. It very rarely freezes in the hardest Winter, and when it does, the Ice not so thick as two leaves of paper.[25]

But we must now leave Aubrey's romantic outpourings and return to our business of describing the history of this house:

> Chobham Place was the seat of Anthony Fenrother Esq. about the time of Queen Elizabeth. His daughter and heir married Samuel Thomas Esq., their son Sir Anthony Thomas was engaged with others in draining East, West and Wildmore Fens near Boston in Lincolnshire. Anthony the grandson of this gentleman, dying a bachelor in 1701, was succeeded by his brother Gainsford Thomas (deriving his Christian name from his mother, a daughter of Erasmus Gainsford of Crowhurst in this County, Esq.) This gentleman was also a bachelor and by his will dated 1719, and proved in 1721, devised the estate to William Abdy Gent., Henry Thomas Fellow of New College, and to his Cousin Sir John Hare, in trust for his sister Ann Thomas, a lunatic, and if she should not recover and have issue, in trust for Dame Mary Abdy, widow of Sir Anthony Thomas Abdy of Felix Hall in Essex, and to her sons Sir Anthony Abdy, Bart., William Abdy and Charles Abdy, and their heirs male in succession. He directed that the pictures of Fenrother and his decendants, the Thomas's, should remain as heir-looms. He gave some charities to the poor of the Parish. Lady Abdy was daughter of Dr. Millward by a daughter of Sir Anthony Thomas and died 1744 at the age of 86. Her son Sir Anthony Thomas Abdy died before her without male issue; whereupon her second son William who

had succeeded to the title, succeeded to this Estate. He had three sons, of whom Sir Anthony Thomas Abdy the eldest inherited the Title and Estate. This Gentleman was a Barrister; was elected a representative for Knaresborough in 1763 and in the ensuing Parliament. He died without issue in 1775, and his next brother the Rev. Stotherd Abdy having died before him without issue, his youngest brother William, a Captain in the Royal Navy, inherited this Estate. He died 21st July 1803, leaving his son and heir, who became the seventh baronet. In 1809 he sold the house and park to the Rev. Inigo Jones, who took possession but died in October in that year, after a few hours illness. He left a widow and three young children.[26]

I feel that a family tree of the Thomas and Abdy families will simplify this most complex story, to which we can again add something from our research of the Land Tax records; in 1780 Lady Mary, widow of Sir Anthony Thomas Abdy, held, presumably as part of her dower rights, the most valuable of their possessions, viz. the Pancras, Gratious Pond, Home and Shrubbs Farms, whereas her late husband's younger brother, Sir William (the sixth baronet), was shown as owner of the big house and two minor farms, though after the death of his mother in 1792, he was shown as owner of all properties of the family. We shall have to say more of this later when we talk about the will of Gainsford Thomas, and the fate of the Abdy estates after 1809.

In the sale to the Rev. I. Jones were included the house and the Home Farm, whilst the other farms were kept by Sir William with his old established tenants. All that remains to be said now about this most important site is that: 'The house was sold by the Rev. Jones to Sir Denis Le Marchant after letting the house to Samuel Thornton'.[23] We shall hear more about Mr. Thornton and his family later. The house, at the time of the 1851 Census, was let again by its new owner.

Before we leave the story of Chobham Place we must stop for a moment in the church to inspect the two floor slabs offering in Latin the story of the Thomas family. And as we are now talking about this family it might be the right place to add something about the origin of the Thomas's fortune:

> The inhabitants of West Holland and Sibsey made a long tale of their sufferings. They say that, for time out of mind, they have enjoyed free common for all their cattle and rights of turbary and other profits in the East and West Fens, and because of this multitudes of people have been induced to live in these unwholesome parts. But lately the covetous eyes of the . . . Thomas fell on their land. He declared that the fens were harmfully surrounded, and ten years ago managed to get himself appointed chief undertaker for draining the land. The first commission gave him permission to drain only the East Fen, and thereupon he and his confederates, 'more interested to add to their estates by getting great shares out of the West Fen and other grounds, which were rich and good grounds, than to advance public good by improving bad grounds', produced a second commission which acted in an illegal fashion and granted them all they asked.[27]

This vague condemnation of some 'Thomas', referring to the acts of the Thomas family in the Lincolnshire Fens, is no sound evidence of the connection. Having said this we must now refer to our description of the history of Chobham Place (*see above*, p. 38) and to the will of Mr. Gainsford Thomas which we mentioned earlier (*see above*, p. 38). On page seven of this very voluminous document we read:

> and the heir of Sir Anthony Thomas knight or otherwise in East West and Wildmore Fens on the North and the North East side of the River Witham near Boston in Lincolnshire which lands were drained by the said Sir Anthony Thomas and partners . . .
> And upon this further trust That the said Dame Mary Abdy or her heirs shall grant and convey five hundred acres of the said last mentioned premisses To the use of the said William Abdy and his heires
> And five hundred acres more therof To the use of the said Henry Thomas and his heires
> And five hundred acres more to the use of the said Saint John Hare and his heires and the residue thereof I do devise to the said Dame Mary Abdy and her heires.[28]

So the Lincolnshire property of the Thomas family must have amounted to no less than 1,500 acres; it is not surprising that the family in all the one hundred and thirty years of their residence in Chobham was never concerned with purchasing land in the parish (with the exception of three cottages which Mr. Thomas devised to the churchwardens of Chobham for the use of the poor).

During their long occupation of Chobham Place the members of the family had taken some interest in the happenings in the village as many of them acted as J.P. Their reputation had by 1680 reached beyond the village borders:

> The petition asked the bishop to arrange for such persons as he thought fit to inspect the state of the church, and an inspection was carried out on 28 May 1680 by Anthony Thomas of Chobham, White Titchborne of Frimley (a well-known family at Frimley Park) and Andrew Lamont rector of Bisley.[31]

So reports Mrs. Marie de G. Eedle in her *A History of Bagshot and Windlesham* (we quote again from this volume – *see* p. 41).

Again, we must quote the will of Mr. Gainsford Thomas:

> And give and devise forty shillings a year to the Churchwardens of the said parish of Chobham and their successors forever to be employed for teaching a Child or Children of the poor Inhabitants of Chobham to write read and cast accounts and do hereby charge my said estate at Chobham with the payment thereof.
>
> And I appoint the process of five pounds (the gift of Mrs Mary Hope deceased mentioned in the Will of my late father) to be imployed for teaching Girls to read English being the Children of the poor Inhabitants of Chobham.[28]

Before we proceed to describe the inns and other sites of interest in the parish, we must first mention two sites in the north or north-east of the village where small cottages were transformed by their owners into very attractive gentlemen's seats. (They may, in fact, have formed the nucleus of the above-mentioned Forest Tithing which was to lie in the North.) These were Hyams and Westcroft.

> Hyams. A villa residence upon a very verge of the wilds of Chobham. It is remarkable for the beauty of its position commanding a pleasing view of the Surrey Hills, and the finely wooded country that intervenes. The flower garden and pleasure grounds are extensive and laid out with great taste. The house contains many fine family portraits by Titian, Sir Peter Lely, Zuechero, Hogarth, etc. This place has gradually expanded from a cottage on the moor to its present state, under the superintendence of different proprietors, amongst whom Lord Lennox, the Hon. Sir Augustus Foster, the Dowager Lady Granville and the present proprietor, the Right Hon. Lord Vaux of Harrendon.[29]

We shall hear later about his Lordship's actions in Chobham.

In 1823 G. and C. Greenwood in their *Surrey Described* mentioned 'Highams: a neat villa residence of Ch. Terry Esq.'.[30] In the 1851 Census we find living in Highams Lodge: Lord Vaux d'Harrowden and his wife Caroline, their two daughters and son, a governess, a butler, footman, coachman and four female servants: one cook, a lady's maid, a housemaid and a kitchenmaid. (The staff gave seven different counties other than Surrey as their birth places.) About the house we can report that Mr. Ch. Terry sold it to T. E. Allen Esq. in 1827; Lord Lennox-Sussex purchased it sometime after 1839 and reformed the house to its present shape.

We must now proceed to our next house: Westcroft Lodge. This cottage was purchased in 1792 by John Farhill, Esq., who proceeded to transform it for his own use. He had to sell the renovated house in 1803 to John Bradbourne, Esq., who lived in it for some years before letting it between 1813 and 1833, when he finally decided to sell to Thomas Dyer, Esq. Dyer lived there for seven years before letting it in 1840, and selling it in 1842 to Thomas Fielder, Esq., who resided in it at the time of the 1851 Census when his household consisted of him and his wife Mary, two young women who are entered as 'constant residents', one gardener, a cook and housemaid.

It is perhaps of interest to quote what Mrs. Eedle has to report in her history of Bagshot and Windlesham about the owners of Westcroft:

Woodlands was built not long before 1796 for John Farhill of Chichester on 43 acres of land called Woodlands, which he had bought in 1788. In 1798 Woodlands was acquired by John Bradbourne and it was to remain in this family until 1824, when it was sold to James C. Fyler of Monksgrove, Chertsey.[31]

This is yet another instance of the 'late' links between Chobham and its neighbouring parishes, such as we have seen earlier with Bisley parish.

But now we have to point our eyes towards other sites where existing houses of apparently Elizabethan style had followed earlier housing, as they were mentioned in the Abbey's cartulary in the 14th century. One of these is the present-day Larkenshaw Farm which originally was called Lorchon's Haw:

1332: The same Abbot [John de Rutherwyk] purchased from John Payn . . . one garston which now John LORCHON holds.[32]

And yet another entry:

1422: I, John Lorchon of Chabeham have given . . . Which I have and hold in Chabeham which tenement is situated between the tenement lately of Frebarn Petrisfield on the northern part and the tenement of Thomas Grappe on the southern part. To hold for ever.[33]

Another entry names the farm:

1475: The lord John May Abbot of the Monastery of St. Peter of Chertsey and the Convent of the same place greeting . . . and also one curtilage called Lorchoneshaw by rent and service yearly . . .[34]

The farm became part of King Henry VIII's park and thus the property of the Archbishop Heath and his family until the end of the 16th century. After a break in our knowledge we find it in 1826 as part of properties of the Rev. Bertie tenanted by James Fladgate, who by 1839 had become its owner.

The name Foghelbroke is still used today for a farm in Chobham:

1340: John de Rutherwyk Abbot and Convent grant that a certain pasture called Holehurst which pasture John Atte Hurst and Laurence Fogelbroke hold at farm.[35]
1357: The Lord John de Benham had one cottage which a Margaret de Foghelbrok formerly held. And also certain bondmen to wit John de Foghelbrok John Atte Hurst and others.[36]

We were unable to trace any later records of this farm.

Next of the old sites and farms is the Washford Farm near Beldam Bridge:

1327: I Margery daughter of Hugh de Wassheford of Chabeham have given to John son of Richard Pentecost and Alice his wife all that my meadow which I lately acquired from Richard my brother and which lies in Chabeham between the meadow of Walter de Bradle called leymead on one part and a moor of Maud de Langehurst on the other. To hold for ever.[37]

We have lost the story of this farm until 1834 when we see James Watts as owner and Jonathan Miles as tenant. However, Edward Draper, yeoman, leaves in his will dated 1803 his freehold Washford to his son James whom we can follow afterwards.

The last site to be mentioned here is now called Sandpithall, and was formerly Grapes Farm. It was given as an abutment in the charter of John Lorchon made in 1422,[33] and also in a charter of 1453:

1453: Brother John Hermondsworth Abbot of the Monastery of St. Peter of Chertsey and the Convent greeting know that we have granted one curtilage with a half virgate of land called Eyreys late of Thomas Grappe formerly of William Stanore at Chabeham.[38]

Space dictates that we should stop now although the List of Antiquities as issued for the N.W. Planning Area contains for Chobham a large number of buildings dating back to the

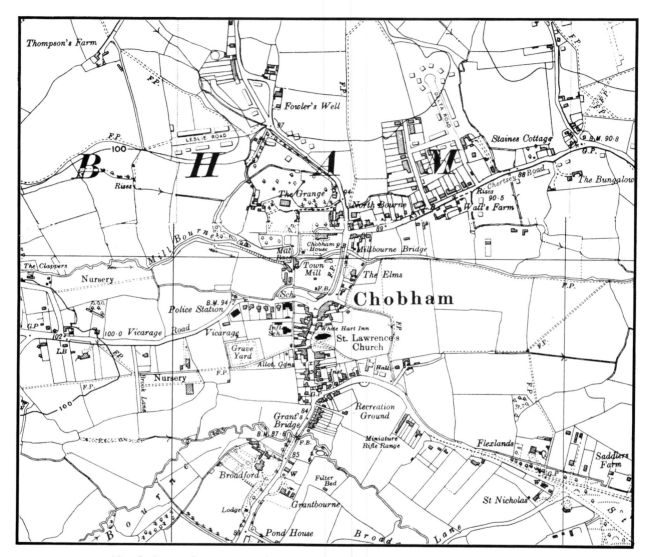

12. Ordnance Survey map of 1944 showing Chobham and its immediate environs.

15th and 16th centuries. These we shall try to say something about when we come to talk about the men who lived and worked in them.

But before we close this chapter there are still the inns of Chobham to mention. Strangely enough, neither Aubrey, nor Manning and Bray, nor Brayley, nor the *Victoria History of the County of Surrey* discuss the inns of Chobham. As an introduction to this theme, we have to fall back on an article in the *Woking Review*:

In the days before there was a Woking Town, Chobham was the shopping centre for people who lived at Old Woking. The Chobham Corn Exchange, famous for miles around and its week-end market, reputed to have been far better than that at Guildford, attracted people from a wide area. It was probably because of its importance a century ago that it had so many public houses in its short main street. It had, not so many years ago, more public houses in one street than Woking had in its town centre.[39]

Yet another piece from the same source:

Prior to attending church in olden days Chobham residents used to hold a pig auction in what is now the rose garden of the White Hart Inn, an ancient hostelry, which was built in 1550 on a framework of ship's timbers. There is a widely held belief that the original inn on the site dates from 1380 when Chobham was part of the Great Windsor Forest. The story claims that Richard II fell off his horse while pursuing a white hart and decided that four public houses should be built locally named after his quarry.

The pub was probably a posting house for hundreds of years for a barn in the yard had stables for six horses. The fittings of an ostler's bell can be seen on one of the exterior walls and a few letters of the words are still legible. Also on the outside of the building can be seen bricked-up windows where a landlord 200 years ago avoided window tax. The chimney of the lounge had to be swept from the neighbouring churchyard through an aperture in the wall.[39]

The Land Tax lists show the names of owners and occupiers of the *White Hart*; between 1780 and 1792 there were no less than six owners but only two publicans; in 1792 William Knight purchased the inn and owned it until 1809 when John Parfit took over – in that time no less than seven men ran the inn. The *White Hart*, however, has a place in the village's history as an entry in the appendix to Manning and Bray states:

List of Town's and Tradesmen's Tokens during the 17th century. The right of making these copper Tokens was given by Patent to individuals, who sometimes made a very great profit thereof; for the intrinsic value of these tokens was in no degree equal to their nominal value. The Patentees pledged themselves, however, to take these back for something less than their nominal value, but it is not probable that they were ever returned to them in any great quantity.[40]

Mr. J. L. Weston of Woking, in whose collection of local items of interest is one of these tokens, describes it as follows: 'Obverse: William Luffe – centre a hart couchant; Reverse: Chobham – W-A-L'.

This token was issued at a time when records of events in Chobham had become varied. In the register books we find entries sufficient to allow reconstruction of a complete family tree of the Luff family. Sarah Stelman, in her will of 1756, mentions her family's link with the Luffs and the list of contributors to the 'Free and Voluntary Present to Charles II' of 1661-2, also mentions the Luffs; in the Hearth Tax lists of 1664 two Luffs are shown:

1. The Free & Vol. Present:	Bartholomew Luff, Innholder
	Robert Luffe, lab.
2. Hearth Tax:	Robert Luff – two hearths
	Bartholomew Luff – six hearths
3. Parish Registers:	Bartholomew died 1666 – wife Alice
	William – wife Alice
	son William bapt. 1676, bur. 1728
	grandson William bapt. 1700, mar. Mary Stelman 1728
4. Wills:	Mary Stelman had a sister Sarah, bapt. 1717 bur. 1756

The token must have been issued after 1666 (the death of Bartholomew) who ran the *White Hart* and whose brother William apparently had taken over from him, and who issued the token with his wife Alice. This William's son William is described in Sarah's Stelman's will, where she gives '£10 to my kinswoman Ann Luff, daughter of William Luff, the elder, late of Chobham, Barber & Chirurgeon' and, finally, 'to my second cousin Mary Luff

13. One of Hassell's drawings of Chobham (1824) showing the *White Hart Inn* and also the lychgate and the stocks on the churchyard wall.

14. The *Sun Inn* on the west side of the High Street.

daughter of William Luff the younger, late of Chobham, Barber & Chirurgeon'; the last mentioned Mary Luff was the daughter of William and Mary (married 1728) so was really a niece and not second cousin to Sarah Stelman.

We realise that all this effort has not made our story more fluent, but we have shown that, by collation of all available documentary evidence, we can clear up some rather complicated problems with assurance.

But now we have to turn to the other, no less famous and important inn, the *Sun*, on the west side of the street; but before we do that, we ought to say that whilst the *Sun* was used by the Overseer of the Poor dealing with the west side of the parish, the *White Hart* was the choice for the east side. The story of the *Sun* is neither as romantic as that of the *White Hart*, nor is the house as old. It is stated to be 'early 18th century'. The Land Tax lists show in 1780 that the inn was owned by John Whitborn, Brewer from Ripley, and between that date and 1809, when his son Robert took over, six publicans ran it. In 1827 Mr. Henry Harris bought the inn and James Squires ran it for him. In the 1841 Census James Squires is shown as an innkeeper, living in the High Street with his wife and daughter, a female servant and a manservant. In 1851 he had apparently retired, as he is shown as retired victualler with his wife and a young man, who is shown as the 'Governor of Union's son', living in Brook Cottage.

Apart from these rather less interesting details we have to look at the *County Herald* which for 7 August 1846 states:

> The return grand match between the Gentlemen of Chobham and Odiham was played on Little Heath. At the conclusion of the match the players sat down to a most sumptuous dinner at the Sun Inn consisting of fish soup, poultry and every delicacy of the season, Pines, melons etc. being included in the dessert, the whole of which reflected great credit on mine host, Mr. Squires.[41]

We shall have to come back to this dinner when we talk about the period after 1800. But here is another entry in the *Herald* of two years later:

> A match at Little Heath between eleven players of the South East side of Chobham Street and eleven of the North West side. In the first innings the N. West side scored 66 and the S. East 53; in the second innings a most terrific thunderstorm came over the ground raining in torrents with hail and the lightning and thunder were truly awful; as soon as the rain ceased everyone resorted to his home drenched in wet and the pencil of Cruikshank might well have been employed on the occasion to sketch the scene. The players having changed their garments repaired with their friends to the Sun Inn where mine host Squires provided a most excellent supper. About 30 did ample justice to the repast. Mr T Hudson presided and Mr R Nix made an able Vice. R Collyer Esq., W Clarkson Esq. and other gentlemen joined the Company after supper.[42]

The *Herald*, in addition, reports that on two other occasions the supper, received with no less enthusiasm, was consumed at the *White Hart*!

> Aug 15th 1846: A Cricket Match was played on Saturday between two elevens of Chobham and Woking. The latter, at the entrance to the village [Chobham] were precipitated out of their vehicle into the road but nothing daunted, away they went with wounded limbs to try their skill but in consequence of the wet state of the weather the Match was not played out. They afterwards partook of an excellent supper at the White Hart Inn.[43]

Compare for a moment the description of Chobham in the *Index Villaris*, dated 20 May 1690, as having three seats for three gentlemen! And further:

> Report of the Overseer of the Poor, 1782:
> Paid Parson and Clerk Dinner 3s.[44]

And a similar entry from the year 1785:

> Paid Parson, 2 clerks, Bisley Officers dinner 4s.[44]

May I show off? *Tempora mutantur, et nos mutamur in illis* (after eight years of Latin lessons,

15.   The *Horse and Groom* on the east side of the High Street.

16.   The *King's Head* on the west side of the High Street.

but way back, ending in 1925). We shall try to show how this transformation developed in our last chapter.

Earlier we had mentioned that the Chobham High Street contained not less than four public houses in those olden times but have only talked about two of them: the other two were the *Horse and Groom* on the east side and the *King's Head* on the street's west side but the *Horse and Groom* has made room for a bank and the *King's Head* has been demolished and replaced by a modern outfitters not so long ago. But neither of these two inns is shown in the Census lists before 1851!

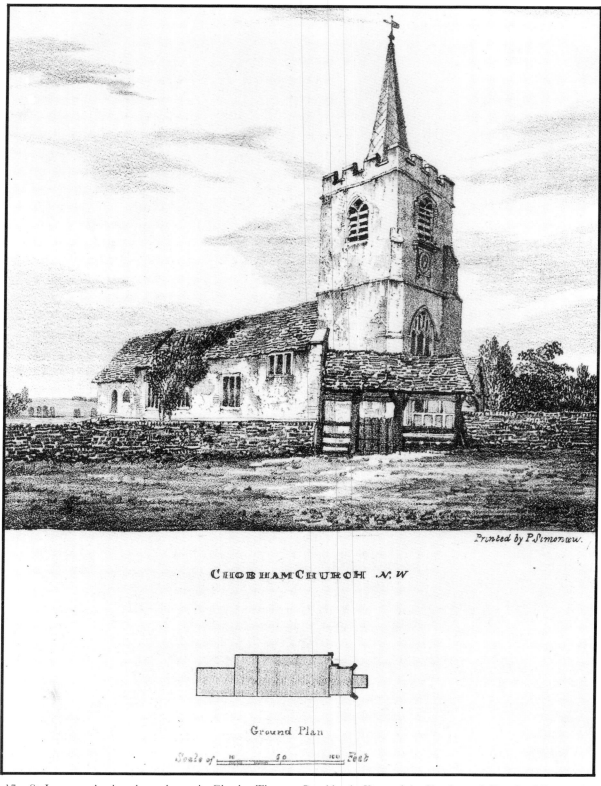

CHOBHAM CHURCH. N. W

Printed by P.Simonau.

Ground Plan

Scale of 10 50 100 Feet

17. St Lawrence's church as shown in Charles Thomas Cracklow's *Views of the Churches and Chapels of Ease in the County of Surrey, 1827.* Note the old lychgate and the adjacent stocks. The plan shows the old chancel, but the north aisle had not yet been added.

Chapter Four

Church Affairs in Chobham

Having outlined the story of Chobham's manorhouse and other important sites, we must now stop in front of the church which, in age, beats all other buildings in the parish. We know now that our church can look back on a thousand years, even if it has changed its appearance several times.

Earlier we talked about the statement in the Domesday Book which mentions both a church and 'another' chapel in Chobham. The *Victoria History of the County of Surrey* suggests that the church mentioned is Bisley church (as Bisley is not mentioned at all in the Book) and the chapel is our present-day church of St Lawrence, known in the early days as a chapel. We can quote (but we doubt the link between the two sentences):

> Some of these newer pensions represented payments for raising chapelries to the status of churches. Thus: 20s. and 6lb of wax was charged on Chobham when this happened about 1217, being reduced in 1230 to 10s. and the wax.[1]

Yet another reason for these payments (which explains the whole story) was as follows:

> The difficulty of bringing their dead to the mother-church was much felt, and their rector, Thomas, in the very early part of the century, having made an application to the Pope, the churchyard was consecrated for burials. Concessions were made by both sides, and Chobham agreed to pay twenty shillings a year and 6lb of wax in consideration of the loss to Chertsey from burial fees. About ten years later the Subdean of Sarum, who seems to have been this same Rector Thomas, obtained from the Abbot a remission of half the money payment, but an attempt of a succeeding vicar of Chobham to escape the contribution of wax was frustrated.[2]

Miss L. O. Mitchell, who was a close relative of the vicar and wrote a number of monographs on Chobham as

18. A later view of St Lawrence's church and churchyard.

19. An interior view of St Lawrence's church showing the arches on the right hand side of the main aisle; above the new arches can be seen the round openings, part of the old Saxon church.

20. The old parish chest, about 700 years old, which until the early 1920s contained all the parish registers and other documents relating to Chobham.

she found it at the turn of the century, wrote in 1908 in a pamphlet *Chobham Parish Church* (we shall return to the question of the 'other' chapel):

> We know that the Chapel mentioned in Domesday Book, and restored by Abbot John de Rutherwyk in 1307, was allowed to fall into ruin, and to-day its very site is forgotten.[3]

Although not an expert, this author spent a lot of time and effort in her search of the history of Chobham and must be accepted as reporting the state of local knowledge at her time.

The *Victoria County History*, written about the same time, gives a very detailed description of the church, yet Miss Mitchell's notes speak of her personal feeling for her village and she gives some interesting details; for example she enumerates the eight bells in the belfry and their inscriptions. Of the fourth bell she quotes: 'H. C. Vicar. R. C. and W. B. Churchwardens. 1684. W. E.'.[4] The vicar was Henry Christmas, about whom we shall hear more later, and the churchwardens were Robert Corffe and William Beauchamp. Looking up the churchwardens' accounts for the year 1683, we find:

> Item. Pd to William Eldridge towards the New Bell more than I rec'd that the
> neighbours subscribed unto   2. 0. 0[5]

Other items in the accounts for the same year refer to other expenditure on the bells:

> Item pd to Thomas Grove for mending of the Clapper of the great Bell & other
> work about the Bells   0. 13. 11
> Item pd to Francis Ewdall for a new Wheele for the second Bell and other
> works done then with the expenses   1. 7. 6[5]

Miss Mitchell has another note about yet another of the bells:

> The sixth bell, though undated, is easily recognized, as it bears the famous shield of William Culverden. This well-known London Brazier died in 1522, and thus this most interesting bell is nearly 400 years old and is one of twenty-two pre-Reformation bells found in Surrey Churches.[6]

Coming across these accounts for 1683 we found some other 'plums':

> Item. Pd to the Apparator for a Prayer Booke for the Thankgiving Day
> concerning the Plott   0. 1. 6[5]

And yet another with some local interest:

> Item. Pd for Beere & Tobaccow at Edward Stympsons for the Ringers for the
> first time Mr Zouch came over   0. 4. 6[5]

Although the Bisley Register mentions the assistance given by the Zouches to their parish, this entry is the only reference to the new Lords of the Manor of Chobham; it obviously refers to James, the grandson of Sir Edward.

This seems the right place to give a description of our ancient church, pointing out the most important items (as précis of the much more detailed story in the *Victoria County History*):

> The earlier church was a small building consisting of a chancel with a nave of about half the length of the present one, dating from the beginning of the 12th century or a little earlier. Parts of two of the early windows still remain high up in the south wall of the nave, cut into by the arcade which was built about 1180, when the south aisle was added. The Tower was built about 1450, and thus the church remained until 1866, when the north aisle was added. In 1892 the west porch was reconstructed, a few old timbers being used. In 1898 the whole of the chancel and the chapel east of the south aisle were rebuilt.[7]

Of the west porch Miss Mitchell has this to say: 'One enters the tower by an oak porch restored in 1892, and which tradition says once formed part of Chertsey Abbey'.[8] In Cracklow's *Views of Surrey Churches*, of the 1820s, is a picture of St Lawrence in Chobham which shows, in the wall surrounding the churchyard, a lychgate and stock, about which we shall hear more later. Having described the building in which the vicars officiated here now is the list copied from that in the church:

Patron	The Vicars of the Parish of Chobham		
Bishop of Winchester	William de DAGELYNGGESWORTH	31 May	1324
	Robert de NYWENHAM	was Vicar	1343
	Melo de de WODEHAM	1 Aug.	1349
Abbot of Chertsey	John Portus de HERTILBURY	8 Mar.	1376/7
	Thomas BONLITHE		
	William SMYTH	8 Jun.	1390
	Robert BRICKTSCHETE	24 Dec.	1398
	John HONYTER		
	Thomas BRIGHTYENE	8 Aug.	1452
	John LOWDYAN	15 Mar.	1453/4
	Richard HALSALL	20 July	1465
	Alan TOMSON	7 Aug.	1487
	John TRUSTRAM	27 July	1507
	Richard DOLSYNBY	30 Nov.	1510
Philip & Mary	Robert NEWMAN	28 May	1557
Queen Elizabeth	Richard OLDE	16 May	1560
	Thomas BROADHURST	12 July	1561
	John HEYWOOD	14 Sept.	1575
	Thomas TAUNTON B.A.	22 May	1595
	Philip SMITH	Died	1649
James Zouch the son	Robert FIELD M.A.	14 Apr.	1665
	Henry CHRISTMAS B.A.	14 June	1680
	William OADES	19 Mar.	1691
John Walter	Thomas WARTON B.D.	20 Oct.	1730
Abel Walter	Joseph WARTON	12 June	1746
	Alleyne WALTER	21 June	1748
	George Clarke GAYTON	30 Nov.	1779
Tr. of John Thornton	Richard CECIL	14 July	1800
	Charles JERRAM	12 Oct.	1810
	James JERRAM	21 Apr.	1834
	Samuel J. JERRAM	24 Feb.	1854
	Herbert S. ACWORTH M.A.	2 Feb.	1881

As we said earlier, the Chertsey Cartulary gives the first reference to a vicar in Chobham for the year 1207 but no further details are known about the incumbents before 1324. But even then we must wait quite a time before we know more about them than just their names and dates. Not until the middle of the 15th century can we establish that the vicars had some contacts with their congregations: five of these early vicars are mentioned in the wills of some of their flock as witnesses.

Richard Halsall (1465-1487) by William Lane in 1486
Alan Tomson (1487-1507) by John Deny in 1488
Thomas Broadhurst (1561-1575) by Margaret Martin in 1565 and John Bonion in 1565
John Heywood (1575-1595) by William Woodes in 1595 and John Newman in 1595
Thomas Taunton (1595-1649) by Henry Attfeilde in 1596, John Davy in 1598 and Robert Norrard in 1600

The Reverend John Heywood has added further to our knowledge in his will, which luckily was preserved:

8th April 1595. Wife Isabell to redeem lease from Thomas Thatcher of Chobham of land at Staines, also lease of a mead called Hale bought of one Parvis. Sister Alice Norcome. Elisabeth Manninge dau. of John Thomas Taylor and John Biddle Overseers. Wtn John Ball etc.[9]

This seems to show that the vicar was engaged, as were most of his parishioners, in farming of some kind:

The clergy were, after all, part of the village community, in a position of natural leadership; they often came from the same social origin as their parishioners; they were involved, as cultivators, as well as receivers of tithe, in the economic life of the village, and while this produced tensions, it also produced solidarities and shared interests.[10]

Mr. G. M. Trevelyan, on p. 63 of his *English Social History* (1973 edn.) makes this point even more clearly:

Sometimes the parish priest spent most of his time as a farmer, cultivating his own glebe (normally forty to sixty acres of the open field) like the peasant born that he was, and even hiring other hands.

It is interesting to note that 'a terrier of the Glebe lands belonging to the vicarage of Chobham' (undated but giving the names of two churchwardens by which it can be traced to the end of the 17th century) mentions no less than eleven plots of land covering 75 acres in all.

Following John Heywood as vicar in 1595, Thomas Taunton is thus described by our old source, Aubrey:

Thomas Taunton, The late Minister of Chobham, was 117 years old when he died, near 60 years Minister here, 10 years Schoolmaster at Lothesley, 15 years Minister at Wonersh; was a Graduate at Oxford, when Bell and Bavon were poison'd at the Assize by a Damp, which was in 1577.[11]

This entry produced one of my greatest disappointments: Mr. Taunton signed two documents dated 1639 in a rather suspiciously steady hand. On further investigation, I found that he was, in fact, at Oxford in 1577 when his age is given as 18, thus making him born in 1559 and 'only' 90 at his death in September 1649. But, on the other hand, his incumbency gives us a chance – if we add some imagination to the factual information as available – to say something about his relations with the churchwardens. We read in John Biddle's account for 1635, the oldest record still extant:

first under: A note what I have received
  It. for the old Homely booke   – 2s.
then under: Layings out
  It. For the new Church booke, A new Register
    book of Parchment   – 15s.
Item paid for the book of Homeles   – 6s. 6d.[12]

In 1635 the Minister was 76 years old and had been the vicar for 40 years; so we assume that he had used the book of homilies well and thoroughly to need a new book. He also seems to have felt the need for a new register book – all things which he asked the churchwarden to obtain for him. We ought to add here that the register book thus purchased is the one which holds the entries from 1654 onwards.

Here is a list of the register books still extant to-day:

1. Register containing baptisms and burials from 1654 to 1730 and marriages from 1655 to 1729.
2. Register containing baptisms and burials from 1731 to 1770 and marriages from 1732 to 1753.
3. Register containing baptisms and burials from 1771 to 1812.
4. Register containing marriages (in the new prescribed form) from 1754 to 1783.
5. Register containing marriages and banns from 1784 to 1812.
6. Register containing marriages from 1813 to 1837.

The list in the church does not give dates for the vicarship of Mr Taunton's successor, Phillip Smith. It is improbable that the patron, the Lord of the Manor, Edward Zouch, would by that time have had the right of advowson; according to a parliamentary ordinance dated 14 October 1644 'Ordination of Ministers' the duty to examine and ordain was given to an Ordination Commission, consisting of seven or more 'Presbyters' selected from a stated list of nominees. For this reason, and because we have not found any specific proof of Chobham's case in 1649, we have left the patron's name vacant. Smith apparently still used his predecessor's register book and not the new one, when purchased. However, on the inside cover of the new register is a leaf which, from its text, makes it look like the flyleaf of the old register; it reads as follows:

> N.B. In Mr. Taunton's Register (fol. 13) John Hywood Vicar there bury'd Apl 16 1595. – To him succeeded Mr. Taunton, Anno Dmi 1649 are these words viz Thomas Taunton Minister buried 15th September.[13]

We suggest that this entry was made by Taunton's successor, Philip Smith, who tried to enter the dates of the vicars' burials on a separate page. The next entry, on the flyleaf, shows his own death: 'Philip Smith, Vicar of Chobham was buryed ye 4th February 1664'.[13] Somebody must have transferred the 'flyleaf' from the 'old' book to the cover of the 'new' book as there is a further entry:

> Under ye Year 1680 is this Entry viz Mr Robert Field Vicar was buried Jun 7th.[13]

Now we come to read the 'new' register book, which on the first page says:

> April the 21st 1655. John Towers of the parish was approved and sworn Register of the Parish of Chobham in the said County according to an Act of Parliament to that purpose made & provided, by us Justices of the peace for the said County whose names are underwritten. S. Rous. L. W. Rawlins. John Westbrooke.[14]

We conclude that the new vicar carried on his normal duties at baptisms, burials and marriages until 1655, when the newly appointed 'Register' took over entering births, burials and marriages in his new book – perhaps the vicar retained HIS book. At first, the new 'Register' also entered marriages, but by November 1656 Mr. Rawlins, the J.P. whom we have met already, added to each marriage entry the words: 'by me, L. W. Rawlins', continuing this practice until 1658. Thus we can say that Mr. Smith had officiated from 1649 to 1654 and again from 1659 onwards. The last entry made in the handwriting of John Towers is dated May 1659, yet there is another puzzling entry:

> Surrey: Wee whose names are hereunder written Justices of the peace for this County wee Allow and approve George Stileman & William Beauchamp Churchwardens for the parish of Chobham for this yeare or followinge. They beeing duly chosen by the Parish as ordered to an Ordinance of Parliament in Craft made & provided – Witness our hands & Seales the 27th day of Aprill 1659 H. M. Weston, L. W. Rawlins.[15]

This appears to be the last of the annual appointments of churchwardens which the J.P.s had taken over from the annual Easter visitation, as performed by the archdeacon or the bishop's registrar.

We have already heard that the vicar Philip Smith died early in 1664 to be followed by Robert Field, the rector of Woking. The story of the advowson has become quite complicated. In 1649 this right was held by Edward, the grandson of Sir Edward Zouch (the Lord since 1621) and eldest son of James who had died in 1643 after he had appointed Robert Field as rector in Woking in 1637. Edward's younger brother, another James, moved Mr. Field from Woking to Chobham in 1665. The new vicar sets another puzzle: his wife died in 1660 and her burial is entered in Chobham, as are also the baptisms of their seven children, born between 1654 and 1674, part of which time he was still rector of Woking.

The next vicar was Henry Christmas whom we have already met when we talked about the bells, but whose stay in Chobham ended rather abruptly. His wife bore him two children, in 1688 and 1689, but both the last born and the mother died on the day after the baby's baptism. The vicar resigned in 1691. He was followed by William Oades, whose sudden resignation in 1730 presents us with yet another puzzle.

Here is the text of an injunction apparently issued by the archdeacon's office; probably issued after a local visitation by the bishop's registrar:

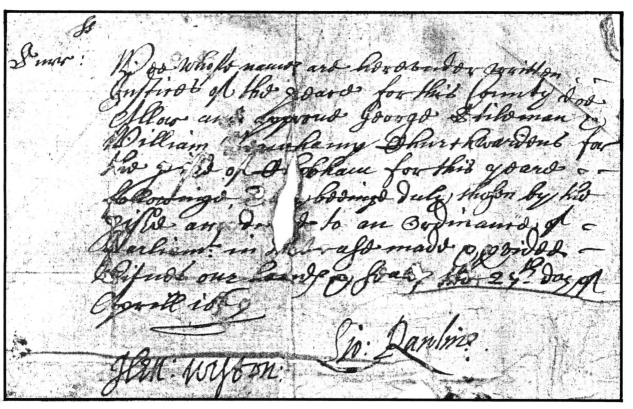

21. A document dated 1659 in which two Justices of the Peace appoint the churchwardens for Chobham. Before 1649 this had been the duty of the diocesan meeting at Winchester.

Chobham. A bason for the offertory to be bought.
A Napkin to cover the Elements to be bought.
A Table of Degrees of marriage – to be hung up in the church.
A Linnen cloth to cover the Elements to be provided.
Cushion for the Pulpitt to be mended.
Middle Isle of Church to be cleared.
Pavement in the Porch to be mended.
Copings of the Church wall to be made good.
Aug. 26. 1712. A Certificate to be made – that these Defects are amended, and returned into the Office of Registrar, on or before the first Court Day of Hilary Term, next.
Ri. Harris, Registrar.[16]

Mr. Oades was the first vicar whom we can identify as having entered parish matters in the register book as he signed some of the entries. He was the first vicar who refers to the consequences of the 1678 Act of Parliament for 'Burial in Woollen':

January 1718. Memorandum yt this day I issued forth my certificate to Owen Hudson Churchwarden yt I had not received a legal Affidavit concerning ye Interment of Mr John Woodman, whom I buried ye 24 of January last past. Witnessed my hand William Oades.

No Affidavit brought to me, but ye five pound paid, and given to the poor because buried in Linnen.[17]

Yet another:

22 October 1729. Memorandum yt this day I issued forth my certificate to Henry Clifford and Daniel Heather Churchwardens yt I had not received any Affidavit concerning ye Interment of William Spong whom I buried in my Churchyard ye eleventh day of this Month.

Witnessed my hand William Oades.[17]

The Act of 1694 instructed clergymen to collect a duty on every marriage, burial and birth (other than paupers – the births also to include those who had not been baptised in the church):

August 9th 1698. ye exakt Account of the Marriages, Births and Burialls with their duties particularly belonging to them punctually inserted in the Register by virtue of the Act made this last sessions of Parliament and commence the first day of August last.

Christenings 1698	– 2 –	each	3
Marriages 1698	– 2 –		1
Christenings 1698	– 2 –		1
Burialls 1698	– 4 –		2[18]

Here is another entry which shows how much this vicar cared for his community:

Memorandum that February 15th 1725/6 Whereas the Reverend Mr William Oades Vicar of this Parish has given Twenty Shillings Towards the Cieling of our Chancel. We do acknowledge his said Gift is his Voluntary Contribution purely out of regard to his neighbours who have seates in or near the said Chancell that they may be kept warm in the time of Divine Service and that the House of God may be more beautified. Witness hereunto our hands and names – W. Beauchamp Impropriator. Arthur Seare, Henry Rogers, Churchwardens.[19]

Yet the Rev. William Oades resigned in 1730. Although there is no documentary evidence, we feel justified in linking his action to the fact that the Manor of Chobham had changed hands. The new owner, Mr. John Walter, who came from Busbridge in Godalming, had been elected as Knight of the Shire in Parliament in 1722, having purchased Bisley, the Manors of Woking and Bagshot, and had appointed Dr. Warton as vicar of Basingstoke in 1725. When Woking became vacant, Dr. Warton was given this living too and, in 1730, he exchanged Woking for Chobham. Throughout all this time he remained vicar, and head-master of the grammar school, in Basingstoke. Our new vicar was rather different from his predecessors, as becomes clear when we read in the little book *The Father of the Wartons* by D. H. Bishop:

Thomas Warton, the Father of Joseph and Thomas, junior, was born at Godalming, Surrey, in the year 1688. From 1717-24 fellow at Magdalen, proceeded to AB 1710; MA 1712, BD 1725. He was Professor of Poetry at Oxford 1718-28; Vicar of Basingstoke, Hants 1725-45. He held also the living of Woking 1727-30; and that of Chobham 1730-45.[20]

How must the former Professor of Poetry have felt in the rather secluded atmosphere of Chobham? Yet he seems to have taken matters in hand almost immediately, as we read:

August 15 1731. At a Publick Vestry then holden by the Vicar & Parishioners (after usual Notice given) It was unanimously Resolved that a Vestry Room be made at ye West End of ye South Isle for the Payment of ye Poor & to transact all Parish business in by ye Parishioners in Vestry assembled. T. Warton Vicar, Henry Lee, Henry Slyfield, John Spong, Will Beauchamp, Robert Emmett, John Spong, Thomas Woods, William Bayley.[21]

The payments up till then had been made in the two inns, the *Sun* for the Westend and the *White Hart* for the Eastend which was, apparently, not good enough for the new 'refined' vicar who, though non-resident himself, acted, again, to ensure orderly administration in his 'new' parish:

Thomas Warton Vicar of Chobham does hereby Nominate publish and declare Henry Hathwell to be Parish Clerk of Chobham in the Room of Wm Harvest Deceased. And the same Henry Hathwell is henceforth entituled to and singular the Dues and profits in any wise belonging to the Office of Clerk of the said Parish pursuante to the Canon in that Case provided.
Given under my seal published in the Parish of Chobham aforesaid the First Day of June in the year of our Lord 1740.
Witness R. Vincent curate John Turner Churchwarden
    Rich Chittey John Street.[22]

It seems that, on Dr. Warton's advice, the quite-new Lord of the Manor moved the incumbent of Bisley (also his manor) to act:

Bisley 15th June 1740 – Humphrey Field was chosen Clerk of the parish of Bisley in the room of Henry Hathwell removed to Chobham by Thomas Gayton M A Rector of the said parish. John Stedman, William Goodman Churchwardens.[23]

The family of the new clerk had been resident in Chobham for some 200 years (here the name was spelled 'Hartwell') and he had, apparently, been called to Bisley by the rector. Henry H., shown in his will as husbandman in 1785, died at the good old age of 80 in 1788. That he was accepted in Chobham is shown by the fact that he was asked to stand as witness in two wills, in 1753 and 1766. (We ought to add here, that Humphrey Field who replaced Henry Hathwell as clerk in Bisley had also been a resident of Chobham.)

The new parish clerk took his new appointment very seriously:

The Communion Linnen plate and other things belonging to the parish Church of Chobham Delivered to Henry Hathwell the Parish Clerk this Ninth Day of June in The Yeare of our Lord 1740, are as follows:

> One Silver Cup
> One Silver Plate
> One Puter Flagon
> One Puter Dish
> One Puter Basson
> One Table Cloath
> Two Napkins
> The Surplice
> The black buriall Cloath.[24]

Miss Mitchell, writing in 1908, has this to say about the first five items:

The interest of the church plate centres round the chalice, or rather the beautifully embossed base of the same. A careful examination shows that the cup is not of a uniform date; the base is of different workmanship and thinner metal than the bowl, which has been set into it. The date of the bowl is, of course, fixed by the hallmark stamped upon it, 1562. It is, in fact, an Elizabethan bowl of ordinary type, ornamented with strapwork bands and hour-glass curves, common in that period. The exquisite base, with its original design and skilful workmanship, points to an earlier date, and may be considered one of the few remaining bits of pre-Reformation church plate surviving in the county. The alms basin appears to be the oldest made of pewter in the county. It is inscribed 'Chobham Church in Surrey, 1712'. The flagon is a pear-shaped vessel, unlike the usual eighteenth century tankards. It was presented by Sir Anthony Abdy, Bart., in 1767. The largest piece of church plate is a handsome two-handled cup, made in 1787, and presented by Samuel Thornton in 1857.[25]

Obviously, the last two items mentioned by Miss Mitchell could not have been in the church in 1740.

Now we must return again to Dr. Warton, the vicar. No further trace of his presence can be found in any of the books during the 15 years of his vicarship; he was followed by his son Joseph, who only lived to hold the post for two years, until 1748. Joseph Warton was followed, in 1748, by Alleyne Walter, perhaps a relative of the Lord of the Manor, and, although there is no proof that he really lived in the village, he is the first incumbent after a long break who actually made entries in the register book. This was the new register book for marriages, introduced by Lord Hardwick's Marriage Act of 1753, which asked the officiating minister to sign each entry.

We must now return to the resignation of Mr. Oades in 1730. Yet another entry in the register book demands an explanation: '1732. The Register so far is imperfect; the Register Book was not delivered to me Mid 1732 R. V.'.[26] Although there is no proof for the suggestion, perhaps the resigning vicar had taken the Book with him, returning it, then, to Mr. Richard Vincent who had been the perpetual curate in Horsell since 1727, also Mr. Walter's possession. According to the register books in Bisley and Chobham, and the visitation records, he performed the vicarial duties in the three parishes by alternating services in the three churches:

> Chobham: 30th January 1752. Ann daughter of Mr A Spooner was born in Horsell but as there were no prayers at Horsell she was baptised in this church. R. V.[27]

Yet another entry in the Bisley book:

> Bisley: 9th March 1735
> James Wopshott and Ann Fledger both of Chobham were married March ye 9th by virtue of a Licence by Mr Vincent.[28]

Mr. Vincent carried out his duties as a vicar would have done:

> August 31st 1752. Memorandum That I this day issued forth my certificate to John Stedman, and Richard Chittey, Church-wardens, that I had not received any affidavit concerning the interment of Ann Thornby, a stranger, whom I buried in this church-yard ye 16th day of this month. R. Vincent.[29]

This refers, as we had shown with Mr. Oades, to the Act of 1678. The situation in Chobham became now rather complicated! Mr. Alleyne Walter, the vicar from 1748, entered his name in the new book from 1754 onwards until 1759, whilst Mr. Vincent is shown in the visitation book as curate from 1742 to 1746 and signing marriage entries from 1758 to 1772. No less than 13 names are entered by officiating ministers (signing as 'curate') between 1755 and 1780 while one Coriolanus Coplestone is shown every year from 1761 to 1768, followed by three 'odd' actors, when the new perpetual curate in Horsell, Francis Scourfield, took on the mantle of Mr. Vincent. He is shown continuously between 1775 and 1792, although in the visitation records Thomas Till is shown as curate at Chobham from 1781 to 1783.

The Rev. Alleyne Walter left the vicarage at Chobham and the rectory of Bisley in 1779 when his successor, in the church lists in both parishes, is shown as appointed by Abel Walter, the son and heir of John Walter, who, however, had sold both parishes in 1752 to the trustees of the Onslow family. It is possible, of course, that the Walters had kept the advowson to themselves. The new vicar was Mr. George Clarke Gayton. He remained vicar for 21 years, in which time his name is found in the marriage register twice and local rate lists show him as residing in the village from 1785 until 1788, when his house is shown as 'empty'. During his incumbency no fewer than 12 different 'curates' signed marriage entries; of these, however, Thomas Till is shown as curate in the visitation records between 1781 and 1783, and Henry Hammond equally between 1798 and 1800. As we have used the visitation records to such an extent, we ought also to add that the Church in general must have made a very great effort to improve the work of their parish priests by adding curates in many parishes where a rector or vicar had previously worked on his own. The records show that in the Archdeanery of Surrey the number of curates had increased from 22 in 1785 to no less than one hundred by 1800. (Chobham being one of the parishes in the Deanery of Stoke.)

We have reported on this most complicated subject of parish ministers from all available documents because the frequent changes in the vicarage and in Sunday services must have made the job of the churchwardens in these seventy years more difficult. Quite apart from the ever-increasing complications of their normal duties, they had to attend the annual Easter visitation meetings at which the outgoing and incoming wardens were confirmed and their annual accounts approved whilst in nearly every entry the name of the incumbent is shown as 'absent' or 'excused'.

We have now discussed the church and its incumbents at some length so that we feel it is the time to consider Nonconformist efforts before we close this chapter. It is known that there was a Baptist chapel at Burrow Hill in Chobham for some considerable time but no records have survived. What we have been able to find were the records of births noted in the Baptist chapel erected by Henry Bartholomew (of Chertsey) in 1806 in the Westend; the births cover families resident in Chobham, Bisley, Walton, Horsell, Shepperton, Windsor, Bagshot, Windlesham, Frimley and Worplesdon. The birth entries are more useful than those in the Church of England in that they show not only the father's surname but also the mother's maiden name and the names of her parents. (Two burials of children are also noted.) One entry says that the Westend chapel was founded about 1796.

We have to wait for the results of the religious census of 1851, however, before we can give the full picture of religious life in our village; the census mentions the various places of worship and their attendances on the Sunday services in the morning, afternoon and evening and the numbers attending Sunday Schools.

1. Church of England: in addition to St Lawrence's church, the Church of the Holy Trinity, Westend is also mentioned.
2. Baptists: four different places are mentioned and one chapel of the Biblical Christians.

The attendances were:

			a.m.	m.	p.m.
Church of England	Adults		320	320	0
	Sunday School		86	133	0
Other	Adults		188	167	130
	Sunday School		32	34	0
Totals	Adults		508	487	130
	Sunday School		118	167	0
			626	654	130

Grand Total = 1,410

a.m.: morning service   m.: midday service   p.m.: evening service.

We have made it quite clear that the Rev. Gayton as vicar of Chobham had very little influence on his flock since he was so seldom there, so it would seem right to say that, paradoxically, his death was to change the life of the village considerably. In the visitation lists we found the entry: 'G. C. Gayton, vicar, dead'. But in order to understand why we want to stress the importance of this happening and to appreciate the changes to come, we have to go back about fifty years. John Thornton, a Russian Merchant, i.e. dealing with the Baltic trade, had, with a few friends who shared his views, formed what became known as the 'Clapham Sect'. Contrary to the ideas of John Wesley, the group believed that the church's teaching and the behaviour of the parish priests required a thorough revival from within. Mr. Thornton conceived the part he, as a layman, could play was in purchasing advowsons which would enable him to present the living, when it became free, to a selected man of his and his group's convictions. John Thornton not only expected others to live 'a good life', he devoted as a principle half of his considerable income to his religious ideas. He insisted that his whole household joined in daily prayers so that his eldest son Henry as well as the youngest, Samuel, found it natural to continue their father's work after his death in 1790. At the same time it was, of course, necessary to find young men to fill these vacancies when they became available and an Evangelical Ordination Fund enabled a steady if small number of devoted and promising young clergymen to study under the Rev. Simeon at Cambridge. It was not only the job of their teachers to prepare them in the right ways but we know that John Thornton tried to satisfy himself that the students felt a serious and unselfish call to their chosen vocation. Before his death, Thornton had been able to purchase 11 livings – his son Henry mentions in a letter an amount of £2,500 as the price of one – and created a trust for the future selection of candidates.

22. The Rev. Richard Cecil, vicar of Chobham from 1801 to 1810 after his appointment by the Thornton Trust. His evangelical leanings were suspected by his congregation but he proved a very able and popular preacher.

The new vicar chosen by the trustees for Chobham and Bisley was the Rev. Richard Cecil, who, at the age of 52, was well known and respected as a favourite preacher at St John's Chapel, Bedford Row, in London. Here he had gathered round himself a congregation of more or less refined people who assisted him willingly in his efforts to make the Word of God a real part of the daily life of his parish. In addition to his well-admired sermons, he introduced some practical measures of aid to poor parishioners. He arranged that the sacrament monies, collected three times a year, were kept in the hands of a treasurer and were distributed by him and three other gentlemen of the congregation on the recommendation of seatholders. Apart from such annual distribution on St Thomas's Day, he kept small sums which were sent during the year to persons found in need, accounting for them at the annual settlement. In Chobham, the new vicar was to introduce this scheme within months of taking up his duties.

The reputation of the new man had, of course, preceded him and it is reported that there was general alarm, that a ringleader of the 'Methodistical Class' was coming to disturb the peace and good neighbourhood which the villagers had hitherto enjoyed. One of the leading lights in the village suggested that, after giving the new arrival the due civil reception, he would retreat to the neighbouring churches. Mr. Cecil's sermons proved quite contrary to these fears; he is said to have put down his ideas on preaching and that 'The hearers in church should be treated as rational and feeling creatures, but upon a bold and palatable Ground'. Described as a 'delicate, highly cultured man who had never passed through the school of adversity and who met no rough experience in his ministerial work', it is, perhaps not surprising, that he remembers that: 'when I first came to Chobham, as I was sitting in the vestry – on hearing the noise and uproar of the boys, and the people in the gallery talking aloud to each other – I burst into tears'.

The Rev. Cecil was to be resident in Chobham only for three months each summer so that the appointment of a capable curate had to be settled quickly. Within his first four years in Chobham no less than three men were appointed and confirmed. It was then, in 1805, that he heard that a young man whom he had recommended to Simeon at Cambridge had proved an excellent choice: Charles Jerram was to become Cecil's curate later that year.

Chapter Five

The People of Chobham and their Families

We have several times mentioned the year 1654 as the beginning of those reliable and interlocking records of the village's inhabitants, the parish register books, which survive from the rousing times of the Commonwealth era, the product of the actions of parliamentarian forces in Chobham. Unfortunately, the earlier book or books have disappeared so that records of the older families before then have to be sought as by-products of the various affairs in which local residents had been involved. This was, of course, the reason why we gave such a lot of space to the various examples of royal and parliamentary financial demands and other interruptions of the routine of village life.

In extracting from all these lists the names of families concerned, we were surprised to find many of the leading families of the 18th and 19th centuries already mentioned in nearly every list from 1545-6 onwards. In reading the old names two difficulties had to be considered: first the variety of spelling surnames caused by the fact that the name was entered as heard or understood by the clerk, who was often unaware of local pronunciation, and, as in all old documents, the problem of deciphering the old-fashioned handwriting.

In this chapter we shall try to present, first the trees of families whose members we found engaged in covering the villages's main official duties such as the posts of Churchwarden (marked as CW) and Overseer of the Poor (marked as OP) with the year the offices were performed. We must, however, point out that we have found the names of very few of these officials before 1730, i.e. only 76 of the actual two hundred who, at two a year, must have held office. This shortcoming will result in many instances where a farmer, in consideration of his standing in the village, especially in the early years, would certainly have been elected by the vestry but who was not recorded as being so. Then other families will be discussed.

We had constructed our family trees originally just to show register entries, thus covering the 200 years from 1654 to 1851, or some six to seven generations. It was possible in a few instances, however, to increase this number to some ten generations by adding information extracted from the documents of the previous one hundred years, back as far as 1545-6. Unfortunately, none of the early lists give wives' maiden names (if recording their names at all) neither do many of the early register entries unless the marriage itself had been entered; in most other instances childrens' baptisms and burials, and wives' burials, only show the father's or husband's name.

To conclude this introduction, we must admit that our most ambitious intention was to cover at least 10 generations on each tree by going back as far as 1545. Ideally, and with complete trees, we could have expected 512 surnames for the earliest set of parents – a number which clearly exceeds the total of resident families in Henry VIII's time. (In an attempt above at estimating the population in 1545, we arrived at a figure of around 375 people, perhaps seventy-five to a hundred families.) This leads us to the conclusion that literally every family in the parish in 1851 (i.e. the 'old Chobham families') was somehow related to every other such family.

Apart from giving the name of the family (with variations of spelling) and the Christian names of its male members (who are the only ones to maintain the family name) and their in-laws of both sexes, where known, we shall also give a brief account of their homes and

other details where available. At the same time we shall also try to estimate the size of the
population whenever we have enough information to do so.

We start our report by adding to an earlier quotation from the Domesday Book (*see above*
p. 4):

> The Abbey (of Chertsey) holds Chobham itself . . . In Lordship 29 villagers, 6 smallholders and 3
> slaves; Odin Holds 4 hides, and Corbelin 2 hides.

Would it be correct to say that these 38 households contained at least around one hundred
persons? Perhaps it will be of interest to compare this with the other villages in the Abbey's
Hundred of Godley: 'Chertsey holds 59 men and a smithy; Thorpe holds 36 men; Egham
holds 57 men'. In a valuation dated 1535 Chobham is shown as fifth in value of the Abbey's
manors, after Chertsey, Egham, Thorpe and Cobham (the last was not part of the Godley
Hundred).

The earliest list of residents' names appears in a tax list of 1331/2[1]; in size-order it reads:

Robert de Stanore	34d.	Thoma Fokelbrok	12d.
Johanne of Arderne	32d.	Johanne ate Groue	12d.
William Bradele	29d.	Thoma le Marshal	12d.
Robert Bartelmew	18d.	Johanne Totenhale	12d.
Beatrice Brok	16d.	Robert de Hale	8d.
Willelm atte Brugg	12d.	Gilbert in la Lane	8d.
Agneta de Forde	12d.	Thoma de Stone	8d.

The *Victoria History of the County of Surrey* mentions a few of these names in an old story:

> A dispute arose in 1343 concerning land in 'Stanors' which John de Totenhale claimed to have
> received from Alice de Ford and Ralph. It was adjudged that John, being illegitimate, could not
> inherit this land which therefore became escheat to the Abbey. It was afterwards claimed by Agnes,
> a daughter of Ralph and Alice.[2]

John and Agnes are both shown in the above tax list and we have already identified 'Stanors'
and 'Arderne' as the names of the two early subordinate manors; the families of 'Brok' and
of 'Fokelbrok' have also been mentioned earlier.

In our attempt at showing names of families and their members we must now make a
very long interruption before we reach further records: we have been unable to find the
necessary details before the arrival of the Tudors as kings but even then about one hundred
years had to pass before our sources enabled us to present a systematic and reasonable
answer to our questions.

The first of our family trees to be shown is that of the residents of Chobham Place, i.e.
the 'Thomas' and 'Abdy' families. When we described them earlier (*see above* pp. 39 and
40) we said that a proper tree would be helpful to distinguish between the different
'Anthonys' and 'Thomases'. We realise, of course, that these families were not villagers in
the true sense; but as they represented for a very long time the only 'permanent' gentle
families in the area and, as such, their members were frequently called upon to act as
Justices of the Peace in village affairs, we felt it right to include them here.

We have also heard that the Thomas family never acquired land in Chobham but
concentrated its efforts on the large acreage which Sir Anthony had obtained in Lincolnshire.
The last of the Thomas male line, however, Gaynesford, showed his concern for the
wellbeing of the village when, in his will of 1721, he left not only a sum of money for the
poor inhabitants and three cottages to be used by the churchwardens for housing poor
families, but also provided an annual sum for teaching of children of the poor 'reading,
writing and casting accounts'. In 1734, Sir William Abdy, as the will's executor, issued
highly critical instructions specifying those children who should in future benefit after he
had heard that the daughter of a churchwarden had benefited.

And When the last four have taken their Turn the
Names of Three Children out of each And shall be
enterd within the Parish Book And the Masters and
Mistresses shall pursuant unto these directions
receive and Teach them accordingly as the Vacancys
Shall arise and so from time to time make new
Entrys of Six Children as before as often as the
preceedent List shall be answerd in Order that
the Children of the Poor Familys may have a due
Rotation of being instructed by Mr Thomas Gift

Wm Abdy

July 23 1734/

23. In 1734 Sir William Abdy set down his strong views on the use of money left by Gaynsford Thomas for the teaching of *poor* children. He felt it was wrong that the daughter of a churchwarden had been chosen to benefit from this bequest.

24. Hassell's drawing of 'A Mansion' – probably Chobham Place, the home of the Thomas and Abdy families.

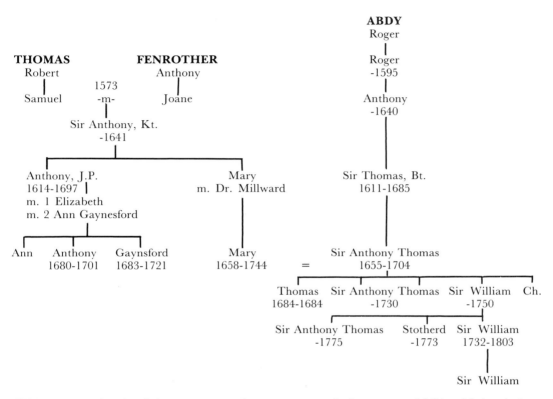

This seems to be the right moment to show our appreciation to our old friend John Aubrey who, in 1673, pointed out the link between the Thomas family and Chobham Place: 'In the parish, on a hill is a pleasant seat [Chobham Place] of the aforementioned Anthony Thomas Esq.'.[3] He made this note having started a 'short pedigree' of the family after copying the Latin inscriptions of the two 'flat Marble Gravestones' in St Lawrence Church, which are still there today. In addition to these two sources we must also mention the 'Heralds' Visitation of Surrey' of 1662/3 which shows a full and detailed tree with the signature of Anthony Thomas.[4]

It will be of interest to show here details from the 'Visitation' which we could not include in our earlier report on the house. Samuel Thomas, *armiger*, Master Gunner of England, married Joan, the daughter and heiress of Anthony Fenrother, armiger, alias Fenrotter, of London. Their son, Sir Anthony, Kt., married the daughter of Sir William Ayloffe of Essex, Kt. and Bt. (this was the man who drained the Lincolnshire fenlands). Their son, Anthony, was appointed J.P. and their daughter, Mary, married Dr. Millward; it was their daughter, Mary, who in marrying Sir Anthony Thomas Abdy, brought the Abdy family from Essex to Chobham. (The Abdy baronetcy dated from 1641.) Mary, now Lady Mary Abdy, was the main beneficiary of Gaynsford's will so that, after the earlier death of her husband, her sons became the heirs. Her husband, the second baronet, was followed by his eldest surviving son, Sir Anthony Thomas, who died without children so that the title came to the youngest son William, who in turn was followed by two of his sons, another Anthony Thomas and, finally, William as the sixth baronet. This last-mentioned Anthony Thomas was a solicitor in London who by his will left his library to be auctioned; the auctioneer's catalogue is still in the British Library and witnesses the wide range of his interests. In this will, dated 1775, Sir Anthony Thomas introduced to Chobham the family of Mumford, one of whose members, Samuel, was to take a leading role in the running of the village. We shall hear more about him later.

We have given these two families a lot of space but in the continued absence of the Lords of the Manor we feel they can rightly be called the squire's family as they occupied Chobham Place for nearly 250 years. We feel we do not exaggerate their importance when we say that their presence would have presented to the farming community a steadying influence, especially in the years when the vicars were non-resident.

Here we ought to mention the other family which can be claimed to be of gentle origin: the Bray family whose links with the village were forcibly broken as we have already described (*see above* pp. 36-7). Here, again, the repetition of Christian names makes a fully set-out tree valuable; this is mainly based on *The Visitation of Surrey* in 1623[5]:

> Sir Edward Bray Kt. (He was brother of the Lord Bray.) His second son was
> Owen Bray Married Ann, daughter and heiress of John Danister, one of the Barons of the Exchequer (*see above* p. 18). His eldest son was
> Edward Bray Married Susan daughter of John Dotley of Merton, Oxon. His eldest son was
> Owen Bray Married Sense daughter of Wm. Blackwell of London. His eldest son was
> Edward Bray (15 years old in 1623)

It was the last Edward who had, as we have said before, (*see above* p. 37) to pay a fine as a royalist and sell his house, Brook Place, in 1651. We have spoken of Brook Place before, but here we want to say that Manning and Bray were, in our view, mistaken in stating that the inscription on a panel on the house: W. B. 1656, refers to a William Bray, making him a descendant of Edward Bray. We have shown earlier that W. B. were the initials of William Beauchamp who we know owned the house at that time.

Returning to the Bray family tree we ought to explain why we showed it in such detail; we wanted to point to their difference in social standing when compared with the residents of Chobham Place — their brides were without exception of non-gentle descent.

With these two families we have exhausted our 'stock' of gentle families, yet there is another house which could claim to have been the home of another such family: Castle Grove House. The building shows, on its gable, the date 1643 but we were unable to find its inhabitants before 1783, when the vicar is reported to have lived there for a few years. But, as we have earlier mentioned that the *Index Villaris* of 1690 rated Chobham as the seat of three gentlemen, we feel, without definite proof, that this might have been the third gentleman's residence.

Brook Place can still be considered as a gentleman's seat inspite of the departure of the Brays in 1651. We find that the son of William Beauchamp (the W. B. of 1656), Phillipp, is called 'Gent' when his childrens' baptisms were entered in the register and he also calls himself 'Gent' in his will of 1739.

Before we set off to show the family trees of the farming men of Chobham, we ought to explain a few points:

1. In cases where the number of surviving sons renders the tree somewhat unclear, we have set before the first member of the *new* generation a capital letter.
2. Whenever the date of baptism or burial is based on circumstantial rather than documentary evidence we use a sign (X).
3. Similarly the sign (X) is used to show that the link between generations is based on circumstantial and not documentary evidence.
4. We have italicised the surnames of brides where known and the Christian names of sons who are detailed in the next generation.

25. Brook Place showing its attractive Jacobean features.

The size of this chapter requires an explanation: we must admit that the amount of information shown up through the very detailed method of writing up the trees surprised us. We feel, however, that the many enquiries we had from local family historians, and from abroad as well, justified such extravagance. Moreover, in addition to this reason we found, when writing the trees, that a number of interesting and perhaps important conclusions and observations came to light.

Going through our records we were rather surprised by the large number of cases where the first-born child of a marrying couple was born well before the 'expected' time. Are we correct to suggest that in this way the birth of many a 'base-born' child was prevented? We must admit that even today a farmer (on the Continent) will permit his son to marry only after having had proof of the bride's ability to have children. We have found some instances where such children had been accepted in the single mother's family as one of their own children but in other cases the child was included in the father's will, so providing for it.

We feel that this statement refers to a rather important fact and have, therefore, attempted to extract from our records a properly constructed report. This entailed:

1. The division of all known marriages in Chobham into fifty-year periods,
2. The extraction from our family-cards of all the families where the dates of marriage and of baptism of the first-born child are shown,
3. The calculation of the time-difference between these two dates and, finally,
4. The calculation of the proportion of the extracted marriages in which the first child was born 'early'.

The analysis produced the following figures:

50-year periods	1650-99	1700-49	1750-99	1800-49	Total
Totals of Chobham marriages (A)	111	119	323	420	973
Number of extracted marriages (B)	66	85	212	203	566
Number of 'early' baptisms (C)	10	18	90	72	190
Percentage B÷A	58.5	71.2	65.6	48.3	58.2
Percentage C÷B	15.1	21.2	42.4	35.4	33.5

To sum up, we extracted nearly sixty per cent (58.2) of all marriages which presents a sound basis for our calculation; our analysis, therefore, fairly confirms our initial 'superficial observation' i.e. that in one third of all marriages in Chobham the first child was born 'early'.

Another point which struck us was the often large number of children born in wedlock and the short intervals between births. It was not surprising to find that many a mother died soon after a baby's birth, often the last of a number of births.

Yet another point should be commented on. In a number of cases where a mother had died the widower remarried too soon (according to our 20th-century morality) yet looking at this in *their* circumstances we could argue that the father, if in work, being out all day had to find somebody to look after his young children, so that he remarried as soon as was reasonably and decently possible.

Apart from these general observations and conclusions we ought also to say something on how we chose the families to be included here. As our fundamental intention has been to show which of the nearly 100 different family-names provided the officials to run the village's affairs, basically, therefore, we chose any family whose members had held office. We start with names mentioned in Henry VIII's time, still present in 1664 and living in the larger houses i.e. those with four or more hearths; some of the families were enumerated in the 1851 Census, three hundred years later.

There were 21 of these families, to which we added nine more who arrived in the village in Queen Elizabeth's time, a further five who arrived during the reign of James I, seven more mentioned for the first time under Charles II and, finally, five others found after 1700, making a total of 47 families who, within the 200 years from 1635 to 1851, provided members to serve as parish officials. Seven further families, although never reaching posts of responsibility in the community, bring our total to 54, but, before we close our list of the families which we mean to call the 'old families of Chobham', we ought to add a further nine, some of whom appear once or twice in the list of parish officials and which we would have liked to present in tree-form had it not been for the lack of space: i.e. the Baigent, Goring, Dakins, Fenn, Hampton, Loveland, Stevens, Sturt, Turner and Underwood families. So in all, we have mentioned no fewer than 63 families in our report. Our criteria for including a family was whether it was one of the more important, i.e. longest-lasting families, rather than one with a more transitory existence in the village.

We have also promised to name the homes of our families. With regard to farming families we have quoted the farm which a family at some time or other was known to have occupied. The result of this, of course, was that we recalled farms which to-day are only known as names of streets.

With regard to occupational terms used in the farming community, we ought to warn that the terms (as shown in old documents) such as 'yeoman', 'husbandman', or 'farmer' should not necessarily be taken to determine the householder's standing as we have found that any of these terms may mean that he was a 'free-', 'copy-' or 'lease-holder' or a tenant of a resident or absent owner.

The Census of 1831 enumerated a total of 55 farmers and it was sheer coincidence that we were able to link nearly every one of them to one of the trees shown here. In the Index we give a list of *all* known farms with references to the occupiers we could trace. But the Census also enumerated 78 members of trade or handicraft occupations. Of these, no fewer than 42 were shown to have lived in the High Street. Of the tradesmen here, 12 were shopkeepers and publicans, there were another five in the Brimshot and Burrow Hill area, one more shop in Fellow Green and the *Jolly Butcher Inn* in the Westend.

The remainder of the High Street was occupied by 32 craftsmen. Among them four had followed their fathers in their crafts and houses, another three lived in the houses which their fathers, though working in different crafts, had occupied, and only a further four were shown as living in the same houses 30 years or more. Three widows still occupied the houses their husband-craftsmen had left them. This left eight houses occupied by newcomers to the village among the craftsmen in the High Street. From their ages at arrival in Chobham, we conclude that the rents demanded for such houses made it impossible for young craftsmen of local descent to afford them, so that outsiders could take such opportunities; the three public houses which were owned by outside breweries also found non-villagers as publicans. The only farmer shown as living in the High Street in 1831 had changed his trade to 'bricklayer' in 1841. We found two documents which confirm that Chobham attracted craftsmen from other villages:

> To the Churchwardens and overseers of the Parish of Chobham and to the Rest of the Inhabitants of the said Parish: whereas James Cobbett cordwainer and Mary his wife of the Parish of Worplesdon is desirous with his wife and child to go and reside in the Parish of Chobham in this County as being a place of more advantage & proffitt in his Industry. Wee therefore the Churchwardens and overseers of the poor of the said parish of Worplesdon pursuant to an Act of parliament entituled Act for the better releife of the poore of this Kingdom Doe hereby Owne and acknowledge the said James Cobbett to bee an Inhabitant legally settled in our said Parish of Worplesdon and doo hereby promise for ourselves and our successors, that if att any time hereafter these James Cobbett his wife or child or children shall become chargeable to the said Parish of Chobham, that wee will receive him and them into our said parish agane.

And here again is another letter, this time dated and signed:

> To the Church Wardens & Overseers of ye Poor of ye Parish of Chobham in ye County of Surry or to Either of them. Gentlemen, The bearer James Read served his Apprenticeship with Robt. Elward a Cordwainer in Bridgewater Gardens in our Parish of St. Giles Cripplegate, London, Therefore beg yr favour that you will let him and his family live in your Parish un molested there being a Standing Order in our Parish not to grant any Certificates. Your complyance with this will very much oblige, Gentlemen Your most humbel servant Saml. Rossell, Curate – John Hammond, Thos. Lavin Churchwardens Wm Lovejoy, Wm Budgen Overseers. – London, August ye 1st 1740.

James Reed is shown in the Chobham Register Book as having married Margaret Hone on 19 October 1740 and a boy, William, was baptised on 8 January 1741.

We have also discovered another statistical point from our records. Our notes show the value of estates of Chobham testators as proved at the Archdeaconry Court of Surrey between the years 1766 and 1856. In these 49 cases, which range from £20 to £800, the average works out at £244. We must, however, mention that two outstandingly large estates, one of £2,000 (William Grove, 1808) and £3,000 (Morris Burchett, 1839) have not been included in the above figures. But individual farms were generally between 20 and 50 acres though, as time went on, some farmers managed to purchase several farms to increase their holdings. Only three farms, all owned by the Abdys, were larger than 100 acres.

Beauchamp alias Beacham

A – **John I** (152X-159X) Mentioned in the Chobham Park building lists of 1545-6. Wife unknown, had two sons and three daughters: *Thomas, William,* Mary *Thatcher,* Alice *Beedle,* Elizabeth *Spong.* He adventured 5s. in the Queen's Lottery in 1567. His son was:

B – **Thomas I** (   ) Only known as mentioned in his brother's will. His brother was:

William I (155X-1621) Yeoman, his will, dated 1610, was proved 1622. In the Muster List of 1583 a 'Bilman of the beste sort'. He gave £5 in his will to the poor of Chobham. His son was:

C – **John II** (157X-165X) Executor of father's will; wife Joan, one daughter Jane, two sons *William* and *John.* In the 1626 subscription list assessed at £5 for goods. His eldest son was:

D – **William II** (159X-1676) Yeoman. *CW 1659-61*; rebuilt Brook Place 1656; in 1661 gave £1 as his Free & Voluntary Present to the King. In the Hearth Tax list of 1664 assessed on a house of six hearths; wife Jane, two daughters: Elizabeth, Jane; four sons *William, Esra* b. 1657, *Phillipp* b. 1662, John b. 1664, who died three weeks old, Elizabeth b. 1666, died in childhood, Elizabeth b. 1670, Jane b. 1672, died 15 years old, *John* b. 1675. Jane (the mother) died 1679. His younger brother was:

John III (160X-1671) Husbandman. Wife Margery who died six months after her husband; daughter Ann who died a baby in 1662. In 1661 gave 1s. 6d. as the Free Present to the King and in 1664 his house was valued at one hearth.

The eldest son of William II was:

E – **William III** (165X-172X) Husbandman. *CW 1682/83, 1710.* Wife Mary, five children: *William* b. 1701, Joan b. 1703, married William *Edmead* 1725, *Joseph* b. 1706, married Jane *Chittey* 1740 at Windlesham, Richard b. 1708, died three years old, *Richard* b. 1711. He signed, in 1725, Mr. Oades' gift (*see above* p. 56) as impropriator. The next brother was:

Esra I (1657-17XX) No further details: his next brother was:

Phillipp I (1662-1733) Gent. Wife Alice, nine children: Elizabeth b. 1701, Ann b. 1703, died five months old, Mary b. 1707, Sarah b. 1708, died at age 11, *Phillipp* b. 1710, *Anthony* b. 1712, Jane b. 1713, married Brian *Harding* 1738. In his will dated 1729 (proved 1734) Phillipp left only 1s. to his eldest son Philip (perhaps because the boy had married – against his father's will? – when he was only 17½) and all his estate and rights as impropriator to his second son Anthony and appointed him, together with his widow Alice, as executor. To his two married daughters, Elizabeth and Ann he gave one gold ring each of one guinea value ('in remembrance of me') but to his two unmarried daughters, Mary (aged 22) and Jane (at age 21) £500 each, which amount was to be reduced to £50 if they should marry without their mother's consent. Among his property, he mentioned the Malthouse in Chobham and other land owned in Bisley. His next brother was:

John IV (1675-1719) Yeoman. Married twice: first wife was Ann who had one son *John* b. 1700; his second wife was Elizabeth who bore four children: *Martin* b. 1702, *John* b. 1704, *Daniel* b. 1705 and Elizabeth b. 1707.

The eldest son of William III was:

F – **William IV** (1701-17XX) No further details. His next brother was:

Joseph I (1706-1783) Maltster. *CW 1751*. Married Jane *Chittey* 1740; two children: *William* b. 1741 and Mary b. 1743. His next surviving brother was:

Richard I (1711-1789) Wife Hannah; both buried in Chobham in the same year. No children.

The eldest son of Phillipp I was:

Phillipp II (1710-17XX) Married Ann *Wye* in 1728 (he aged 17½, she just over 18 years old) at Farnborough, Hants. No children. His next brother was:

Anthony I (1712-1786) Yeoman. *CW 1737/8. OP 1740*. Quoted as witness by three other yeomen in their wills of 1753. Wife Margaret/Mary; seven children: Mary b. 1735, married Thomas *Towndrow* from Twickenham, Elizabeth b. 1737, *Philip* b. 1742, *Anthony* b. 1748, James b. 1750, *George* b. 1752 and William b. 1755.

The only son of John IV's first wife was:

John V (1700-17XX) No further details. His eldest half-brother was:

Martin I (1702-1784) Carpenter. *CW 1760/1*. Married twice: first (1729) wife Ann *Alexander*, no children. Second wife Elizabeth; five children: Elizabeth b. 1745, Ann b. 1747, *Martyn* b. 1748, *Moses* b. 1749, Sarah b. 1754 married James *Stevenson* 1781. His next brother was:

John VI (1704-17XX) No further details. His next brother was:

Daniel I (1705-1777) Wife Ann, nine children: Ann b. 1737, married John *Mills* 1759, *Henry* b. 1740 died a bachelor 1821, Jane b. 1742, *William* b. 1744, *Daniel* b. 1747, Richard b. 1749, Mary b. 1753, Mary b. 1756, *Joseph* b. 1758.

The eldest son of Joseph I was:

G –   **William V** (1741-1827) Yeoman *CW 1778/9, 1793. OP 1795, 1800*. Maltster. Married twice: first wife Catherine *Collyer* who died 1807; second wife Sarah *Collyer*, née *Fladgate* 1811. No children.

The eldest son of Anthony I was:

Philip III (1742-1815) Married Ann *Capron* of Twickenham. No children. His next brother was:

Anthony II (1748-1805) Attorney-at-Law in Guildford. Wife unknown; one son Anthony Thomas b. 1782, who died 1795. His next brother was:

George I (1752-1813) Yeoman. *OP 1777*. Wife Diana; two children: *Philip* b. 1785, Elizabeth-Mary b: 1787, died 20 years old. His next brother was:

William V. Minister, Church of England.

The eldest son of Martin I was:

Martin II (1748-18XX) No further details. His next brother was:

Moses I (1749-1819) Carpenter. *OP 1785*. Wife Elizabeth; one son *John* b. 1785. Rebuilt the (burnt-down) Workhouse in 1795.

The eldest son of Daniel I was:

Henry I (1740-1821) Died a bachelor. No further details. The same applies to his next two brothers:

William VII (1744-18XX) and

Daniel II (1747-18XX) His next brother was:

Joseph II (1758-1834) Wife Sarah; four children: *William* b. 1791, Henry b. 1793, died four months old, Ann b. 1795, married William *Ridger*, and Mary b. 1797.

The son of George I was:

H –   **Philip IV** (1785-18XX) No further details.

The son of Moses I was:

John VII (1785-1840) Sawyer. Wife Mary; seven children: *George* b. 1813, Mary b. 1816, *William* b. 1819, Caroline b. 1821, *Frederick* b. 1823, Emily-Maria b. 1824 and Sarah b. 1827. In the 1851 census, after his death in 1840, his widow's occupation was Farmer/Annuitant although at the birth of his last child he was described as 'Labourer'.

The only surviving son of Joseph II was:

   William VIII (1791-184X) Journeyman-carpenter. Wife Mary; four children: *Walter Louis* b. 1825, *Leopold Percival* b. 1827, *Alexander William* b. 1830 and Malvina Frances b. 1833.

The eldest son of John VII was:

   George II (1813-18XX) No further details, the same applies to his next two brothers:

I –   **William IX** (1819-18XX) and

       Frederick I (1823-18XX)

The eldest son of William VIII was:

   Walter Louis (1825-18XX) No further details. His brother was:

   Leopold Percival (1827-18XX) Wheelwright. Married Mary *Evans* 1850. Their daughter *Mary Ann* was baptised in 1843 as 'illegitimate', but in modern times her birth would have been legitimised by the subsequent marriage of her natural parents.

J –   **Mary Ann** (1843-18XX)

   This brings this family tree to ten generations. We want to mention one more point before we go on to another family. We found in the Spage Register of Wills proved in the Archdeaconry Court of Surrey the following entry: John BECHUNT: will dated 7 September 1488 (which mentions his son John). We suggest that, in the local dialect and under the existing conditions, this name could have been taken down for the misheard 'BEAUCHAMP'. In this case we are presented with a further two generations beyond 1520 if we assume that John B., the father, was baptised in 145X and his son about 148X in which case the son could have been the father of our John I Beauchamp.

   The next family of yeomen of Chobham are the Biddles. Although they disappeared from the village by the middle of the 18th century they were the writers of the two oldest churchwardens' reports and, in addition, the names of John senior and junior appeared about 1600 in a large number of farmers' wills as witnesses or overseers.

Biddle alias Beddle, Beddell or Beadle

   Nicholas (15XX-158X) In the will of 1595 of the widow Elizabeth Woods, Nicholas was shown as 'deceased' but his children *John* and Margaret were beneficiaries. His son was:

   John I (154X-163X) Yeoman. *CW 1635*. Adventured 5s. in 1567 in the Queen's Lottery where his son, *John* jun. was also shown with the same amount. (Perhaps we are right in suggesting that father John put the money up for his boy.) In the Muster List of 1583 he was named as 'Archer select'. In 1626 assessed at £7 for landed property. He had two sons, the elder of whom was:

   John II (156X-163X) Listed in the Muster List of 1596 (J. B. jun.) and assessed in 1626 at £3 for land. His brother was:

Daniel I (157X-165X) Yeoman. *CW 1639*. In his account for this year he detailed the costs of repairing the church. In the Lay Subsidy list of 1641 assessed at 21s. 4d. Wife not known; three children: *John, Sampson* and Susanna.

John III (162X-1676) Yeoman. Married Frances *Hall* 1664. Five children: Frances b. 1666, *Daniel* b. 1668, Anna b. 1670, John b. 1672, died aged 12, Frances b. 1675. (The first Frances died aged seven days.) At the burial of young John, his mother was shown as 'Widow Biddle'. In 1662 he gave 15s. as his Free & Voluntary Gift to Charles II. The Hearth Tax of 1664 named him as living in a house with three hearths. His second brother was:

Sampson I (163X-170X) Wife not known; six children: Anne b. 1664, Sampson b. 1666, John b. 1667, died two months old, Henry b. 1668, died 10 months old, Susanna b. 1671, Mary b. 1678, died age twenty-one. Sampson was also mentioned in the Muster List of 1675. The son of John III was:

Daniel II (1668-174X) In the report of the churchwarden for 1732 he was named as 'gent' as he was also described in an indenture of 1728. The CWs' reports name him until 1741, when the name Biddle suddenly disappears.

We know, however, from the Land Tax list of 1780 (as we have said before) that the farm had been bought by a newcomer to the village. There is also an old will dated 11 March 1596 which is headed 'Allan Biddle of Windlesham, yeoman'. We include this here because Allan was mentioned several times 'as of Chobham' in the King's works at Chobham Park in 1545.

Allan (152X-1595) In his will, he named his wife Ideth, also three daughters: Ann, Elizabeth and Joan, and Henry, son of Joan, are named. As the name of the boy's father was not given, perhaps the boy was illegitimate and kept the name 'Biddle'. Henry Biddle was shown in the Lay Subsidy List of 1589 as living in Guildford, assessed at 5s. 4d. but no longer appears in later lists.

We said that the name Biddle disappeared from Chobham records in 1741 when we find that 'Daniel Biddle, gent.' was the last entry of the family. We know, however, that the home of the family, (still known today as Biddle Farm) had been purchased by the Rev. Ralph Price before 1780. The new owner did not come to live in the village and William Lee became his tenant at the farm. William was followed by his cousin Richard in 1781 who in turn handed over to his son Richard to be followed again by his younger brother, another Richard.

Attfield alias Field

The next family to be introduced is the Attfield clan. This family presents us with a double problem. The first was the fact that in many an old document and in the Register Books it was never clear whether an entry under the surname 'Field' does or does not refer to an 'Attfield', e.g. an entry like this: 'Henry Attfield of Millwards alias Field'. Here we should quote Mrs. Eedle's comment:

> The Attfields, an important yeoman family, appear in Windlesham by the middle of the 16th century, but there were also Attfields in Chobham and other neighbouring parishes.[7]

The other difficulty was the large number of the family's members recorded in early documents whose relationship to each other and to the next generation can only be worked out by complicated guesswork. However, the earliest entry for this family was found in the will of John Deny, dated 4 October 1488, as witness. The problem now arising was how to link this John to one of the next set of Attfields whom we found in the reports on the work at Chobham Park in 1545-6. A further complication presented itself by the existence of documents relating to three Henry Attfields at the same time, which give ample evidence of their activities but again did not give information as to their relationship with each other nor to their ancestors.

John I (145X-152X) Acted as witness in the will of John Deny of 1488. His son (X) was:

John II (151X-158X) Assessed at £3 for goods in the Lay Subsidy list of 1571. Mentioned in the Chobham Park work report of 1545-6.

Henry I (152X-1596) Husbandman. The second member in the Chobham Park work report of 1545-6. Adventured 6s. 8d. in the Queen's Lottery of 1567 when he was called 'of Millwards'. Assessed at £5 for goods in 1571. In his will, dated 1596, he called his wife Elizabeth, his two sons *Henry* and *John* and three daughters Rose *Tucker*, Elizabeth *Harris* and Joan (apparently unmarried but called 'Field'). His wife died six years later and her will mentions one son *Henry* and three daughters Rose, Elizabeth and Susan.

We accept Henry I as the first recorded owner of the 'Millwards Farm' which we know (from later documents) to be a new name for the Pentecost Farm of the 14th century. (*See above* p. 38).

Henry II (155X-161X) Elder son and executor of his father's will and was ranked as a 'Bilman of the beste sorte' in the musters of 1583. In an abstract of title he covenants his farm to his son *John*.

John III (1610-1675) *CW 1667/8*. His wife was Constance *Pickering* whom he had married in Farnborough in 1647. Aubrey found two gravestones to the couple inside the church, an honour which points to the family's standing in the village. As his Free & Voluntary Gift to the King in 1661 he gave 20s. In the Hearth Tax list of 1664 his house was shown with five hearths. In the Muster List of 1675 'Widow Field' was shown under 'persons to finde arms'. In the parish register was an entry 'Henry son of Mr John Field', baptised 1655, who was buried four months old. His brother (X) was:

Walter I (1612-1656) Again had a gravestone inside the church as Aubrey reported but we have not found any other details.

John III's surviving son (X) was:

John IV (164X-17XX) *CW 1681*. In the muster list of 1684 'persons to finde arms'; had two sons: *John* b. 1679, William b. 1687, who died in the same year. In both baptismal entries the father was shown as 'Mr. John Atfield' (again showing the family's standing in the village).

The entries up to now all related to the richest of the three Henrys, who farmed at Millwards, alias Pentecost Farm, popularly pronounced Pankhurst and then 'Pankers'. But now we must switch to the second Henry 'of Velley Green' which we take to mean 'Fellow Green', in the Westend of Chobham and adjoining the old Pentecost estate in the west.

Henry III (153X-1596) Adventured 3s. in the Queen's Lottery in 1567, where he was called 'of Velley Green'. In the Muster List of 1583 'Bilman of the beste sorte'. His grandson (X) was:

Henry V (160X-1676) No details. His son (X) was:

Henry VI (162X-1693) Married Mary *Spong* 1663; six children: Elizabeth b. 1664, died a baby as also did Elizabeth b. 1666, Henry b. 1668, Mary b. 1670, died a spinster 1689, John b. 1673, died three years old, and Elizabeth b. 1681. In the Hearth Tax list of 1664 his house was assessed at four hearths and in the Muster Lists of 1675 and 1684 he was mentioned under 'persons to finde arms'. Henry's last will, of 1683, shows a variety of bequests amounting to a total of over £200 (to relatives and friends) 'to be paid out of my freehold lands after my decease'. He does not, however, mention his son Henry as he nominates his wife as executrix. Among the beneficiaries were, amongst others, his uncle Robert with eight children as well as his uncle Humphrey with three children and five grandchildren.

Earlier we had spoken of three Henry Attfields who lived at the same time: they all died in 1596! Fortunately we can distinguish the next Henry as he assumed (or was given) a second Christian name

'Hedge', so called after his property 'Hedgelands'. An entry in 1567 (the Queen's Lottery list) calls him 'Henry Hedgefields', an interesting compromise! To start this line of the family we may quote the will of 'Henry Hedge of Bagshott, in par. of Windlesham, yeoman'. We accept him as of Chobham as he also says 'goods in my house at Chobham in my daughter's custody'. Apparently he had moved to Bagshot as in 1545, he was listed as a helper in the Chobham Park work accounts. A further clue was given in the Bishop's Transcript of 1587 of Chobham entries: 'Elizabeth, daughter of John Hedge'! This John could have been the son of Henry of Bagshot, leading us to his grandson (X):

> **Henry Hedge Field** (of Hedgelands) (162X-1683) His wife was Susan who bore him three boys: Hedge b. 1655, died 1660, John b. 1659 and another Hedge of whom we only found the burial in 1665. Perhaps this was a difficult birth as mother Susan was buried six months after her son. We can add: the Lay Subsidy list of 1571 quotes Henry Hedge of Chobham assessed at £7 for goods. In the present for the king in 1661 he gave 5s. and in the Hearth Tax List of 1664 the only 'undefined' Field's house was marked as three hearths.

There are still quite a number of this family whom we were unable to fit in the trees we had quoted. Six members were mentioned in the Chobham Park work accounts: in addition to Henry I and John II we found the brothers Allen and Nicholas, Thomas who supplied oaken timber to the king's carpenters, and Walter. Again, in the muster list of 1583, we found no less than 10 members; in addition to the three Henrys they were John sen. and John jun., Owen, Christopher, Nicholas, William and James. As we have said before, Henry VI, in his will of 1683, made gifts to his uncle Robert and his eight children, and his uncle Humphrey with three children and five grandchildren. To continue, we must quote the will of George Stellman of 1665 where he mentions five more members: Pearce (who lived in 1664 in a house of two hearths), Walter, Richard, John and William; yet a new name is that of Reuben whose house in 1664 had four hearths. 'William, son of Owen' was also mentioned in 1587.

In the parish register book we found the burial of Henry John Attfield dated 13 August 1829; on his gravestone in the churchyard we read 'H. J. A. died 13 8 1829 aged 64 – as a tribute by his brother'. A further line gives a clue: 'also Henry Gude his nephew died 1840 aged 35'. We found that Richard Gude of the Ford in Chobham, was H. J. A.'s half-brother.

Finally, a request of Richard Attfield dated 1858 addressed to Sir William Abdy asked for the grant of a new lease of Burrow Hill Farm to his sons James and Henry.

To show the Attfield family in a reasonably sound way has proved very difficult indeed and our next family has not been any easier. But the Lee family is, in contrast to both the Beauchamp and Attfield families, still active today in the village's affairs.

Lee alias Lye

A –   **Allyn** (149X-156X) *Constable* in 1545-6 who provided horses for the King's work at Chobham Park. His son (X) was:

B –   **Henry I** (152X-1605) Yeoman. In two wills of Chobham men (1595) and another of a farmer in Bisley (1598), appointed as overseer. In his own will of 1605 (proved 1607 and preserved in the Herrington Register), he left 10s. to Chobham church, £10 to the poor of Chobham, further gifts to the poor of Bisley and Windlesham and a number of gifts to relatives and servants. His son *Henry* was executor, and the son's son's six children are also named. He also named the two sons of his brother William and to his wife Millicent he gave a 'meade' of three acres called Flexland. His witnesses were the new vicar, Thomas Taunton, and John Bedell the elder and younger. As overseers he appointed John Bedell the elder and Henry Spong the younger. In the Lay Subsidy Rolls of 1571 assessed at £7 for goods and the Rolls of 1589 to 1595 show him at £8 for goods, both assessments among the highest in the village.

C –   **Henry II** (155X-16XX) These dates are assumptions as his marriage must have taken place not later than 1580 in order to give time for six children to be born before 1605 (see his father's will). In the Muster List of 1583 shown as 'Archer of the second sorte'. His children were *Henry*, Susan, Agnes, Alice, Katherine and *John*. His elder son was:

D –   **Henry III** (158X-16XX) The list of the Surrey Present to Charles II of 1661 shows him as giving 5s. and in the Hearth Tax List of 1664 his house was assessed on one hearth. His younger brother was:

      John I (159X-16XX) In the Lay Subsidy Rolls of 1640 assessed at 16s. This could be the John Lee whose burial in 1685 is entered in the parish register, where we found another entry 'Francis son of John Lee b. 1663'. His house was assessed at one hearth in 1664.

We have no means of continuing this line of the family and turn now to the brother of Henry I; he was:

B –   **William I** (153X-) We only know of William because his brother Henry I said in his will: '*William* and Lemuel, sons of my brother William'.

But we accept the entry in the Bishops Transcripts of 1587: 'William Lee bapt 22 Mar 1587', as being the grandson (X) of William I.

C –   **William II** (155X-) No details known but his son (X) was:

D –   **William III** (1587-16XX) In the Lay Subsidy Rolls of 1640 assessed at 16s., as was his cousin John I. In the Muster List of 1675 shown as 'Person to finde arms'. In 1664 he lived in a house with three hearths. His son (X) was:

E –   **William IV** (162X-1676) (Now at last, the parish register takes over and we have finished with our assumptions.) Married in 1659 Mary *Best* who bore six children: Mary b. 1660, died after 12 days, *William* b. 1662, and four other boys of whom we only know name and baptism: John b. 1663, Henry b. 1666, Richard b. 1668 and Thomas b. 1671. Father William died 1676. His eldest son was:

F –   **William V** (1662-17XX) *CW 1684*. We do not know his wife's name but they had three children: *William* b. 1683, *Henry* b. 1687 and daughter Mary whose baptism is missing but was buried in 1698. His elder son was:

G –   **William VI** (1683-1727) His wife was Sarah who died after her daughter Sarah's birth in 1712. William married again in 1721: his bride was a widow, Elizabeth *Goring* who died intestate in 1755 leaving James Goring, yeoman, the son of her first marriage, as administrator. Sarah, the daughter of his first marriage, married in 1729 Edmund *Moore* and died 1768. His younger brother was:

      Henry IV (1687-17XX) *CW 1732-4*. His wife was Mary who bore him seven children: *Henry* b. 1712, *William* b. 1714, Mary b. 1717 who married William *Patience* in 1742, Anne b. 1720, Elizabeth b. 1722, Rachel b. 1725 and Edward b. 1728. His eldest son was:

H –   **Henry V** (1712-1790) Bricklayer, *CW 1743-4 OP 1757*. Married Mary *Harris* in 1736 and died in the workhouse aged 79. They had five children: *Anthony Thomas* b. 1737 – the name recalls the squire's family! – *William* b. 1739, Sarah b. 1741, *Henry* b. 1744 and Ann b. 1747. His younger brother was

      William VII (1714-1787) Farmer. *CW 1775/1778-9. OP 1770, 1777*. Married Catherine *Rogers* in 1742, no children. In the Land Tax records he was shown as farming the Biddle Farm for its new owner, but retired in 1781. In his will he mentioned his brother Henry, his nephew Henry and kinsman William.

The eldest son of Henry V was:

I –   **Anthony Thomas** (1737-17XX) We have no details of him, nor of his next brother:

William VIII (1739-17XX) The third brother was:

Henry VI (1744-18XX) Married Mary *Blisset* from Horsell in 1767 in Horsell Church – no children.

We must now turn to another branch of the family. We found in the Muster List of 1583 a Richard Lee as 'Bilman of the second Sorte' whom we accept as the probable ancestor of a whole line of 'Richards' which we were able to follow right through to 1851. But the first of this line certainly known was Richard Lee whose marriage in 1665 was entered in the Chobham Register Book.

E –   **Richard I** (162X-17XX) Married Ann *Fields* (Attfield?) in 1665 and had three children: *Henry* b. 1665, Mary b. 1667, who died nine days after her baptism, and *Richard* b. 1670. The mother, Ann, died in 1672. His eldest son was:

F –   **Henry VII** (1665-16XX) No details, as also with his next brother:

Richard II (1670-17XX) We assume that his son (X) was:

G –   **Richard III** (1701-1773) Farmer. *CW 1758-9.* His first wife was Margaret whose six children all married within the village: *Richard* b. 1733, *Henry* b. 1735, Mary b. 1740, married John *Sherwood* in 1760, Sarah b. 1743, married John *Collier* in 1767, and *William* b. 1746. Father Richard married again in 1761, to the widow Mary Hollis née Neale, whose two daughters of her first marriage were beneficiaries of Richard's will as were his married daughters. To his son Richard he gave the farm where 'he now lives' and to his son William the freehold house 'Now occupied by Mrs. Attfield'. His eldest son was:

H –   **Richard IV** (1733-1806) Yeoman. *CW 1773. OP 1767.* Married Elizabeth *Grove* in 1761 who bore him three children: *Richard* b. 1762, Elizabeth b. 1765 and *William* b. 1768. After the death of his wife in 1770, married in 1772 Elizabeth *Hall* who bore him seven children: *Benjamin* b. 1772, *Richard* b. 1773, *James* b. 1775, Sarah b. 1776, John b. 1778, Anne b. 1779, who married William *Soan* in 1800, and Mary b. 1780, who married Henry *Grove* in 1802. These seven children were born within the space of eight years, the last when the mother was aged 37(!). Father Richard followed his cousin William VII in charge of Biddle Farm. His brother was:

Henry VIII (1735-17XX) No further details. His youngest brother was:

William IX (1746-18XX) Married in 1772 the daughter of his step-mother's first marriage: Mary *Hollis* who bore him five children: Mary b. 1772, William b. 1774, Henry b. 1776, Nanny b. 1778 and *John* b. 1780.

I –   **Richard V** (1762-1841) Farmer. *OP 1804, 1812.* Married Mary *Daborn* in Horsell church in 1788 and had five children: Richard b. 1790, Elizabeth b. 1792, John b. 1793, Sophie b.1796, married James *Tickner* 1817, James b. 1798, died under two years old. Father Richard followed his father in charge of Biddle Farm. His brother was:

William X (1768-1822) His wife was Mary but no other details are available.

The last two mentioned members were the sons of Richard IV's first marriage but now we show the sons of his second marriage.

Benjamin I (1772-18XX) Married in 1795 Ann *Young* a widow but no children are known. His brother was:

Richard VI (1773-1849) Yeoman. *OP 1834.* In 1847 calls himself 'nurseryman' the first instance of such a description in Chobham, where he had followed his elder brother on the Biddle Farm. Married Jane *Collier* in 1804 and they had seven children: Mary b. 1804, married George *Smith*, *Richard* b. 1805, George b. 1807, died eight months old, James b. 1809, Jane b. 1811, Elizabeth b. 1813 and Ann b. 1814, married Joel *Hone* in 1847. His brother was:

James I (1775-1834) Lived with Elizabeth *Sturt* and they had two children (baptised as illegitimate): James b. 1800 and Ann b. 1801, died seven months old.

John II (1780-18XX) Youngest son of William IX. His wife was Jane and they were shown in the 1851 Census – no children.

J –   **Richard VII** (1790-18XX) Bricklayer. His wife was Sarah and they had four children: James b. 1821, Emma b. 1822 in Chertsey, married George *Munday* in 1848, Eliza b. 1824 in Chertsey, married John *Crane* in 1850, and Charles b. 1828. Their first-born was Richard b. 1819 in Chobham (as were James and Charles).

Now follows the son of Richard VI:

Richard VIII (1805-18XX) Farmer and nurseryman at Biddle Farm. Married in 1838 Mary Ann *Trim*; they had four children: Richard b. 1840, Jane b. 1842, Robert Henry b. 1845 and Frederick, who was shown as aged four in the Census of 1851, but does not appear to have been baptised.

The last Richard represents the tenth generation of the Lee family but Chobham was the home of a few more 'Lee-men' who follow:

James Born in Windlesham, labourer, married Sarah (born in Middx.). They had six children, all baptised in Chobham: both parents were aged 36 in 1851.

James Born in Horsell, labourer, first marriage to Mary Chapman in 1818, second marriage in 1827 to Amelia Gosden a widow, with whom he had five children.

John Married 1781 Sarah *Berry* and had three children – were removed from Rotherwick in 1785 to Chobham where the eldest boy, John died at age five.

George Born in Old Basing, Hampshire, about 1780; in the Censuses of 1841 and 1851 shown as 'Surveyor of Highways', an appointment made by the vestry in 1838. His seven children were all baptised in Chobham. Daniel b. 1805, Solomon b. 1806, John b. 1809, George b. 1812, Jane b. 1814, John b. 1816 (the older John had died at 2 weeks old) and Henry b. 1819. His son George married Ann *Ottaway* in 1845 and they had two children: Charlotte b. 1846 and Ann b. 1849.

Two more early register entries could not be placed within the known tree: John, died 1654, whose widow Joan died in 1683; and another John, who died in 1663. His wife Margott died before him in 1662 and of their three children only Thomas, baptised 1654, survived to adulthood.

Woods

This family created quite a lot of problems apart from the fact that we found three wills dating from the last years of the 16th century – the number of sons in later years, for example, and the use of the same Christian names such as Thomas and William for more than one member within the same generation.

A –   **William I** (152X-158X) We met William only through the will of his widow Elizabeth dated 1594, in which she mentions three generations of the Biddle family, a daughter Elizabeth married to Henry *Attfield* and '*Thomas*, bastard son of the said William Woods' (her late husband). But she does not mention their son *William* who died soon after his mother.

John I (152X-157X) Provided a cart for Chobham Park works in 1545 and adventured 3s. in the Queen's Lottery in 1567.

B –   **William II** (155X-1594) Yeoman. Eldest (X) legitimate son of William I. In his will dated 1594 (the same year as his mother's) he mentions Thomas Woods, without specifying their relationship, in addition to 'his brother *Andrew* and other brothers and sisters'. His wife Isabel was appointed executrix, and the vicar, J. Haywood, was a witness. Adventured 2s. 6d. in the Queen's Lottery in 1567 and in the Lay Subsidy lists of 1571, and those of 1589 to 1593, assessed at £6 for goods, but in the list of 1595 his widow had taken over. His four brothers were:

Andrew I (154X-15XX) Mentioned in a later Muster (temp Eliz.) as a 'Bilman select'. No known children.

Robert I (155X-1596) Tailor. In his will, dated 1596, he mentions *Edward*, son of his brother *John* and another brother, *Henry*. No known children.

John II (155X-16XX) In the Muster List of 1583 and the later one (temp. Eliz.) shown as a 'Bilman of the best sorte'. He could be (X) the constable John Woods in the upheaval shown below on pp. 157-8.

Henry I (156X-16XX) In the muster of 1583 a 'Pikeman select' and in the Lay Subsidy lists of 1589 to 1593 assessed at £6 for goods, but in 1595 his valuation was down to £1 for land.

Thomas I (154X-16XX) As shown under his father, William I. We accept him as William's eldest son.

C –   **William III** (158X-1655) Son (X) of William II. His son *Thomas* was the first of a long line of 'Thomas Woods' whom we could trace on the basis of an abstract of title relating to the last of his descendants (Thomas XI – *see below*).

Thomas II (157X-16XX) Perhaps (X) son of Thomas I. No details.

John III (157X-16XX) Elder son of John II. His brother was

Edward I (158X-16XX) A 'pikeman select' in the Muster List of 1583. No known children.

Henry II (159X-16XX) His son was (X) *Henry*.

D –   **Thomas III** (163X-1685) Great grandson of William I. Married Elizabeth *Ellyott* in 1662 and their eight children were: Amy b. 1663, *Thomas* b. 1665, *William* b. 1668, Elizabeth b. 1670, *John* b. 1672, Susanna b. 1673, died aged 10, and Owen b. 1678. Son William was apprenticed to a farrier in 1683 and Owen to a carpenter in 1695 – both masters of London. In 1664 the family lived in a house with three hearths.

Thomas IV (163X-1723) Husbandman. (X) son of William III. Married Damaris *Woods* in 1658 who died seven months after her son *Thomas* was baptised in 1660. Father Thomas married again; his new wife was Wiborough who bore him two children: Wiborough b. 1662 and *Roger* b. 1663. Mother Wiborough died in 1694. Gave 3s. in 1661 as his Free Present to the king.

John IV (163X-1667) His wife's name unknown. His three sons were: John b. 1658, William b. 1662 and Henry b. 1667.

Henry III (163X-1663) Son (X) of Henry II. Married in 1655, his wife's name is not known but they had six children: Sarah b. 1655, Mary b. 1656, William, whose burial was entered in 1657, *Henry* b. 1657, John b. 1660 and Frances b. 1663. Father Henry died two months before his last child's baptism.

We could not trace the fathers of the next three members of the family:

Roger I (163X-1711) Married Elizabeth *Stonehill* in 1666 who died two weeks after their marriage. Roger married again, his new wife was Hannah who bore him five children: Hannah b. 1670, Roger b. 1672, died eight months old, Elizabeth b. 1674, another daughter (name illegible) b. 1680 and *Thomas* b. 1684. Mother

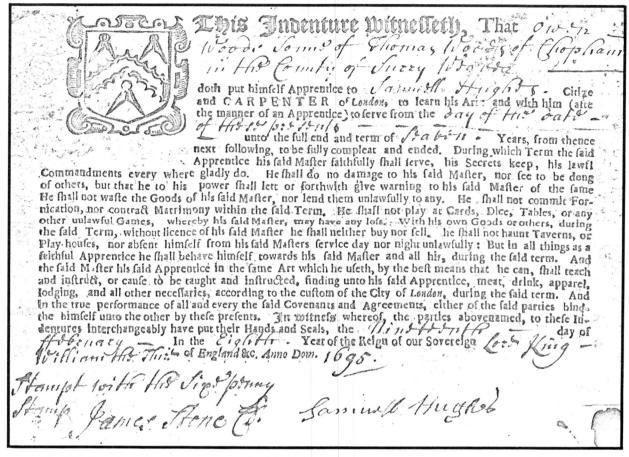

26. Chobham's earliest extant Apprenticeship Contract, 1695. Owen Woods, son of Thomas Woods, was apprenticed to a London carpenter. The Woods were rich farmers in Chobham.

Hannah died 1685 and in his third marriage two more children were born: Thomas b. 1692 and Henry b. 1694.

Luke I (162X-1714) His wife was Elizabeth and their four children were: *Luke* b. 1658, *Richard* b. 1660, Elizabeth b. 1662 and Margaret b. 1667. In 1664 their house was rated at five hearths but they shared it with Sampson Biddle's family. Mother Elizabeth died one month before her husband.

Christopher I (162X-1681) Husbandman. Constable in 1664 together with Thomas Spong. His wife was Joan and their five children were: Ann b. 1654, Sarah b. 1658, *Thomas* b. 1661, Elizabeth b. 1663 and *William* b. 1666. In 1664 their house had three hearths.

E –   **Thomas V** (1665-17XX) Eldest son of Thomas III. His wife was Frances and their only child was *Thomas* b. 1701. In 1718 father Thomas purchased 'certain other tythes or tenths' from Henry Rogers. Mentioned in the Association Oaths Roll of 1695. His two brothers were:

William IV (1668-173X) Labourer. Married Ann *Wells* in 1702 and their three children were: *John* b. 1704, Ann b. 1705, died 11 years old, George b. 1708. Mother Ann died in 1721. Shown in the Association Oaths Roll of 1695.

John V (1672-1717) His wife was Elizabeth and their seven children were: *John* b. 1697, Luke b. 1699, Elizabeth b. 1702, *George* b. 1704, Mary b. 1706, died two weeks old, John b. 1708 and Margot b. 1711.

Thomas VI (1660-1714) Weaver. Elder son of Thomas IV. Married Mary *Taylor* in 1697. No children known but his widow died in 1719. Shown, in the muster of 1675, as 'soldier' where his father was a 'person to find arms'.

Benjamin I (168X-17XX) We could not trace his father within our tree. Married Mary *Grove* in 1704 and their first child was born in Windlesham but died in Chobham within one year. Their other five children were: Mary b. 1706, Benjamin b. 1708, died 14 months old, Ann b. 1710, *Benjamin* b. 1714 and *Thomas* b. 1716.

Roger II (1663-175X) Farmer. Second son of Thomas IV. His wife was Margot and their five children were: Mary b. 1704, died aged nine years, Roger b. 1705, died one week after his baptism, Margot b. 1707, married William *Glover* 1733, and *Roger* b. 1709. Mother Margot died 1710 and father Roger married again, in 1712 at Farnborough, Elizabeth *Govell*; their four children were: Thomas b. 1714, Mary b. 1718, Jane b. 1719, died two years old, and Elizabeth whose burial was entered in 1719 (perhaps not baptised). Mother Elizabeth died 1723.

Thomas VII (1661-17XX) Eldest son of Christopher I. Shown in the Association Oaths Roll of 1695. His brother was:

William V (1666-17XX) His wife was Katherine and they had four children: William b. 1692, 'a child dyed before baptism' buried 1696, Ann b. 1697 and Thomas b. 1699.

Henry IV (1657-17XX) Labourer. Eldest surviving son of Henry III. Married Susanna *Purdam* in 1689 and their five children were: Henry b. 1691, died two years old, Mary b. 1692, *Henry* b. 1695, Sarah b. 1698 and Isabell b. 1701. Father Henry was shown in the Association Oaths Roll of 1695.

Luke II (1658-17XX) Eldest son of Luke I. Shown in the Association Oaths Roll of 1695. His brother was:

Richard I (1660-1742) Married Jane *Hiller* in 1688 and their two daughters were: Jane b. 1689, married John *Heather* 1714, and Elizabeth b. 1694, died a spinster 1778. Mentioned in the Association Oaths Roll of 1695.

F – **George I** (1704-176X) *OP 1748. CW 1756.* Third son of John V. Married Elizabeth *Fladgate* in Bisley church in 1735 and their seven children were: George b. 1736, a son (name illegible) b. 1737, *Richard* b. 1740, William b. 1743, John b. 1744, Elizabeth b. 1746 and Hannah b. 1747. His elder brother was:

John VI (1697-1783) Husbandman. His wife was Elizabeth and their two children were: Mary b. 1731 and Hannah b. 1735, married Robert *Russell* 1757. In his will John also mentioned Henry the son of his daughter, Hannah, who at the time of the will (1781) was shown as a widow.

Thomas VIII (1701-17XX) Only son of Thomas V. His wife was Mary and their five children were: Mary b. 1724, married William *Gray* 1752, *Thomas* b. 1726, John b. 1728, *Henry* b. 1731, Joseph b. 1734, died a pauper and bachelor 1793.

John VII (1704-17XX) Eldest son of William IV. Married Sarah *White*, a widow, in 1742; Sarah came from Sunninghill. No children known.

Roger III (1709-1744) Called 'junior' at his burial as his father, Roger II, was still alive aged over 80. No further details.

Benjamin II (1714-17XX) Eldest surviving son of Benjamin I. Married Sarah *Rumsey* in 1732. No children known. His brother was:

Thomas IX (1716-17XX) Married Mary *Miles* in 1741 and their two children were: Thomas b. 1742 (shown as 'born in Bisley') and Mary b. 1745.

Henry V (1695-17XX) Eldest surviving son of Henry IV. His wife was Mary and they had nine children: Mary b. 1724, Henry b. 1726, Thomas b. 1729, *John* b. 1730, Sally b. 1732, Edward b. 1733, Hannah b. 1735, William b. 1736 and a daughter (name illegible) b. 1738. Daughter Mary married Daniel *Wheatley*, 1754.

James I (169X-17XX) Cordwainer. *OP 1764. CW 1769.* We could not trace his father in our tree. Married Elizabeth *Davies* in 1726 and they had two children: James b. 1727 and *George* b. 1730.

G –   **Richard I** (1740-1825) Son of George I. No further details.

Thomas X (1726-1792) Eldest son of Thomas VIII. *CW 1764/5.* His wife was Ann and their only child (as noted in his will) was *Thomas* b. 1754. His brother was:

Henry VI (1731-1811) *OP 1773. CW 1782.* Married Ann *White* in 1763 and their two children were: *William* b. 1764 and Thomas b. 1769.

Benjamin III (1733-18XX) Labourer. He could have been (X) a son of Benjamin II. No details.

John VIII (1730-1790) *OP 1763. CW 1767.* Son of Henry V. Married Ann *Ridger* in 1763 and their seven children were: Elizabeth b. 1764, died aged 17, John b. 1766, Ann b. 1770, George b. 1772, died aged three, Mary b. 1778, Sal b. 1780 and William b. 1782, died three months old.

27. Fowlers Well Cottage. Note the roof at the back which extends right down to the ground.

George II (1730-17XX) Second son of James I. Married Mary *Brown* in 1749 and their seven children were: Ann b. 1749 (January), William b. 1749 (December), Henry b. 1750, Sarah b. 1752, *Thomas* b. 1754, Mary b. 1756 and Hannah b. 1759.

H – **Thomas XI** (1754-1824) *OP 1793.* Married Jane *Martin* from Wokingham in 1792 and their four daughters were: Ann-Elizabeth b. 1793, Elizabeth-Ann b. 1794, Mary-Ann b. 1797 and Jane-Ann b. 1799. Elizabeth Ann married Richard *Rowland* 1813 and Mary-Ann married Daniel *Heather* 1829.

Thomas was the last of a line of Thomas Woods who, according to an abstract of title relating to the Fowlers Wells Farm and its land, added severally to their property beginning in 1699 with Thomas IV, and all were referred to as 'ancestors of the said Thomas Woods' – meaning our Thomas XI. (*see above* p. 39)

William VI (1764-1827) His wife was Elizabeth and the couple were shown as having lived in Windlesham although buried in Chobham. They had five children: Mary-Ann b. 1792, died a spinster four months before her mother in 1837, Sarah b. 1797, Ann b. 1799, *James* b. 1802 and Elizabeth b. 1805.

I –   **James II** (1802-18XX) Gardener. Married Harriett *Chandler* from Clandon in West Clandon church in 1825 and they had five children: Ann born in Windlesham, married John *Tickner* 1844, James born in Chobham (but apparently not baptised) 1839, Harriett b. 1841 (in Chobham) and Sarah also born in Windlesham 1844.

Stephen I (1790-18XX) Labourer. Father unknown. Married Mary *Slyfield* in 1819 and their two children were: Eliza b. 1822 and Sarah b. 1823 died 10 months old.

Edmead alias Edmonds

A –   **Richard I** (143X-149X) He was mentioned as witness in the will of 'William Lane, the elder, husbandman of Chobham' dated 23 March 1487 together with 'Sir Richard Hassall' the vicar at that time. We assume that his son (X) was:

B –   **Richard II** (148X-155X) This was a guess on the basis that we found in the Lay Subsidy Rolls of 1571 the entry: 'widow Edmead – £2 for land' taking Richard to have been her husband. Again we assume that her son (X) was:

C –   **Richard III** (153X-159X) In the list of 1571 which showed his mother he was assessed £1 for land but in the lists of 1589 to 1595 his assessment had risen to £4 for goods (perhaps this included his mother's estate) and in the Muster List of 1583 he was made a 'Bilman of the beste sorte', as was his brother who was:

William I (154X-159X) No further details known.

John I (155X-163X) In the will of Thomas Woods dated 1614 he was a witness. In the Lay Subsidy list of 1628 assessed at £1 for land.

The second son (X) of Richard III was:

James I (155X-162X) Husbandman. In his will, dated 1596, he appointed his wife Agnes as executrix and named a brother Thomas (of Horsell) and two other members of the family: Henry of Chobham and Robert of Horsell.

D –   **Richard IV** (162X-1687) His wife Jane was buried only five days after her husband, after giving birth to seven children: Edward died 1655, Joan b. 1656, died unmarried at 25, *Richard* b. 1658, *Henry* b. 1660, Elizabeth b. 1663, Hannah b. 1666 and Jane whose burial was entered in 1673. Richard (the father) acted also as witness to a declaration of Richard Davy dated 1659. Lived in a house of three hearths in 1664.

John II (158X-166X) In the Lay Subsidy List of 1640 assessed at 8s. We assume that he was the son (X) of John I.

E –   **Richard V** (1658-172X) Married Susanna *Birchett* in 1685, their three children were Hannah b. 1686, died at age seven, Susanna b. 1689 and *Richard* b. 1694. His brother was:

Henry I (1660-1696) Wife's name not known but their son was *Henry* b. 1685.

John III (165X-1716) *CW 1711.* His wife was Mary and they had two children: William b. 1700 (X) and Mary b. 1707. Son William married Jane *Beauchamp* in 1725. Father John was mentioned in the Association Oaths Roll 1695, as was also his cousin (X) Richard V.

F –   **Richard VI** (1694-17XX) His first wife was Elizabeth and their daugher was Mary b. 1718, who married John *Felts* in 1740. His second wife was Ann who gave him six children: Sarah b. 1722, Jane b. 1729, Ann b. 1731, married John *Bartholomew* in 1755, Elizabeth b. 1734, married James *Tedder* in 1758, *Richard* b. 1737 and *George* b. 1740. The son of Henry I was:

     Henry II (1685-174X) His wife was Mary with two children: *John* b. 1725 and Mary b. 1727 who married John *Friend* in 1759.

G –   **Richard VII** (1737-   ) No details known. His younger brother was:

     George I (1740-1803) Married Ann *Savage* in 1762. They had seven children: Mary b. 1765, Richard b. 1767, Ann b. 1769, *William* b. 1771, Jane b. 1773, George b. 1775 and Robert b. 1778, died one month after his baptism.

The son of Henry II was:

     John IV (1725-178X) Married Mary *Holt* in 1751 and they had four children: John b. 1751, Ann b. 1753, Henry b. 1754 and William b. 1762.

H –   **Richard VIII** (1694-1771) Yeoman. *CW 1744-6. OP 1733, 1756.* In his will dated 1766 he was called 'of Newhouse Farm'. His wife was Mary and they had three children: *Henry* b. 1740, Mary b. 1743 who married twice, first in 1765 to James *Elmes*, and in 1783 to John *Street*, Frances b. 1746, married Thomas *Howard* in 1766. Richard made his will when nearly 80 years old and lived for a further six years.

I –   **Henry III** (1740-1780) Yeoman (Heneage Farm). *CW 1776, OP 1773.* Married Elizabeth *Stevens* in 1772 and their only child was *Henry* b. 1773. After his early death at age 40 his widow remarried twice.

The only son of George I whom we could trace was:

     William II (1771-18XX) Married Sarah *Harding* in 1796 who bore him two sons: Henry b. 1797 and George b. 1799.

J –   **Henry IV** (1773-1849) Farmer (Brimshot Farm). *OP 1813. CW 1819, 1825-44.* As the vicar's choice as churchwarden, he filled that post a record 20 years in succession. Married Mary *Fladgate* in 1803 who died in 1829 without children but Henry married again, to a widow from London, Sarah, who survived him and was shown in the 1851 Census as 'annuitant'.

To these ten generations we must add some further members whom we could not fit into the tree: John Edmead whose wife, Margaret died after the birth of her two children: Margaret b. 1689, who died aged 16; and John b. 1693. John (the father) married again; his wife, Mary, gave birth to a girl Mary in 1707, but she died at three weeks old. John senior died in 1716. In checking the list of labourers employed in the Chobham Park work in 1545-6 we also found three members of the family whom we could not place within our family tree: William, Thomas and Gylbert.

The next family to be presented are the 'Phillipps', one of whose members was elected as churchwarden in four consecutive years, a sign of the great esteem which the family commanded in those early days. However, the family disappeared before the final years of the 18th century as we shall see. The Census of 1801 does not show a member of this family.

Phillipps alias Philp

A –   **William I** (150X-157X) Mentioned in the Chobham Park worklists of 1545-6. His son (X) was:

B –   **John I** (153X-15XX) Adventured 2s. 6d. in the Queen's Lottery of 1567 and in the Lay Subsidy list of 1571 assessed at £4 for goods. His son (X) was:

C –   **William II** (156X-163X) In the Muster List of 1583 a 'Bilman of the second sorte'. Purchaser of a 'close called Inham' in 1624. His son (X) was *John*.

The Muster List of 1583 mentioned two further members of the family whom we assume were brothers of William II:

Henry I (157X-162X) Again a 'Bilman of the second sorte' in 1583; also summoned to the muster of 1596. In the Lay Subsidy rolls of 1589 to 1595 assessed at £4 for goods and witnessed the will of 'John Skeets, husbandman of Chobham' in 1601.

Thomas I (156X-16XX) Shown in 1583 as a 'bilman of the second sorte'. Father of *John* and *Thomas*.

D – **John II** (159X-1669) Son (X) of William II. Husbandman. His wife was Amy, their son was *William*.

John III (160X-1669) Son of Henry I. Wife's name unknown; their three children were: *Richard* and Mary, both baptised before the parish register started but Mary's burial was shown in 1654; Joan b. 1655. Another son (X) was Henry.

John IV (158X-16XX) Beneficiary of the will of 'John Newman of Chabham, husbandman', dated 1589, and called son of Thomas Phillipp.

Thomas II (161X-167X) Beneficiary of the will of Walter Phillipps, his 'kinsman' in 1653. Son of Thomas I.

E – **Walter I** (160X-1653) Although we could not fit Walter into the tree, the fact that his will, dated 3 June 1653, has been preserved, gave him this place here. In his will he mentions a number of kinsmen: Gabriel, William, Richard and Thomas. (Thomas II was his choice.)

William III (162X-1689) Son of John II. His wife was Joan, their six children were: Anne b. 1654, *William* b. 1656, died a bachelor in 1714, Elizabeth b. 1658, buried four months old, *John* b. 1661, Ann b. 1665 and *Richard* b. 1674. Purchaser, in 1682, of two closes of 34 acres in Chobham. Named by Walter I.

Richard I (163X-1700) Mentioned by Walter I. Married Ann *Blythe* in 1657 (the marriage was entered in both Chobham and Pirbright registers – Ann's birthplace was Pirbright). Two daughters: Ann b. 1657 and Amy buried 1660; the mother died eight months after her daughter but Richard married again, his new wife was another Ann and they had two children. *John* b. 1663 and Ann b. 1665. Richard's second wife survived him and died in 1708. His brother (X) was:

Henry II (164X-1685) His wife (name unknown) survived her husband by four years having given birth to six children: Suzan b. 1660, *John* b. 1663, Mary b. 1669, died four days after her baptism, Anne b. 1666, Jane b. 1673 and Mary b. 1678. In the Hearth Tax list of 1664 Henry was called a labourer and was exempted from paying tax.

Gabriel I (163X-1719) Son (X) of Thomas II. Mentioned by Walter I. Married Elizabeth *Smyther* in 1660 and their three children were: Elizabeth b. 1661 who married Daniel *Goring* in 1686, *Gabriel* b. 1663 and Jane b. 1667. Gabriel sen. died 1719.

F – **William IV** (1656-1714) Died a bachelor but mentioned in an indenture dated 1694 in which he purchased a close (part of Chobham Park). Also mentioned in the Association Oaths Roll of 1695. His next brother was:

John V Yeoman. (1661-172X) *CW 1705-8.* His wife was Joan and they had three girls: Joan buried 1702, Elizabeth b. 1703, married William *Critchfield* 1728, and Mary b. 1707. His youngest brother was:

Richard II (1674-1746) Mentioned in the Association Oaths Roll 1695 as 'of Chobham'. Died in Winchester but buried in Chobham. The inscription on his gravestone reads:

Richard Phillipps of this parish and who by integrity and diligence not only raised a handsome fortune but what was of more Value acquired good name and for justice and friendly disposition was universally esteemed and respected in this parish and in Winchester, Hampshire he was honoured with several places of trust all of which he faithfully discharged to ye day of his death. Died 16 April 1746 aged 69.

John VI (1663-1725) Cordwainer. Apprenticed 12 April 1675 to Abraham Harvest, cordwainer in Chobham until age twenty. Shown in Association Oaths Roll 1695. Wife was Elizabeth, the register records the baptisms of 10 children: John b. 1690, Elizabeth b. 1691, *John* b. 1692, *William* b. 1694, Ann b. 1696, William b. 1699, Joan b. 1701, another Joan b. 1702, John b. 1705 and Sarah buried 1702. We found an entry: 19 February 1702 John Philps apprenticed to Henry Bedford, taylor.

John VII (1663-17XX) No further details – son of Henry II.

Gabriel II (1663-1708) His wife was Elizabeth, who died 1695. No children. Mentioned in the Association Oaths Roll, 1695.

G – **William V** (1694-1745) Died intestate, his widow appointed administrator. Wife was Sarah, their five children were: William (VI) b. 1722 (called 'shipwright, Deptford, Kent' in the court case), Sarah b. 1723, John b. 1724, died six weeks old, John b. 1726 and Richard b. 1732.

John VIII (1692-17XX) Wife Hannah, four children: Ann b. 1727 died six weeks old, John b. 1729, Hannah b. 1731 and Elizabeth b. 1733. We do not know whether John practised the tailor's trade which he had learned.

Thomas III (169X-1783) We cannot firmly place him in our tree but suggest that he could have been a son (X) of Gabriel II, called after his great grandfather, Thomas II. His wife was Susanna. They had two children: Charles b. 1761 and Henry b. 1764.

H – **Charles I** (1761-1798) His wife was Martha, who had three children: Charles b. 1788, Susanna b. 1793 and Mary b. 1797. Charles the father was shown in the Land Tax lists as tenant of Sir William Abdy's Gracious Pond Farm, 1787-98.

There was one further member of the family whom we could not place at all with any safety within the tree: Roger Philip, buried 1655.

We have tried with the utmost care to fit in all the members of this family but the number of Johns baptised in 1661 and 1663 made a sure distinction very difficult indeed. The details of a lease dated 1741 and 1742 proved most helpful in stating that William Phillip the elder, of Chobham, was the eldest son of John Phillip of Chobham, and William Phillip the younger, the son of the said William Phillip. The lease concerned was 'Mincing Lane Close'. We could thus establish the identities of John VI and his son William V and grandson William VI.

Burchett alias Birchett

It has proved impossible to find the link between the members of this family in Henry VIII's time and their descendants, so that we have had to 'jump' one generation.

A – **Robert** (152X-158X) Three times mentioned in the Chobham Park work in 1545-6, both providing carts and as a labourer.

Nyclas (153X-158X) Twice mentioned in the work around Chobham Park as was also:

William I (152X-158X) as providing a cart and acting as labourer.

B – **Richard I** (154X-159X) Adventured 2s. 6d. in the Queen's Lottery in 1567 and mentioned in the Muster List of 1583 as a 'bilman of the second sorte'.

John I (155X-160X) Also a 'bilman of the second sorte' in 1583.

William II (156X-161X) Equally a 'bilman of the second Sorte' in 1583.

28. Burchetts Farm – this site has been farmed since the 14th century and the Burchett family is still resident in the village today.

Thomas I (155X-158X) Assessed at £1 for lands in the Lay Subsidy list of 1571. In the same list was also:

Ambrose (152X-156X) The entry was 'heirs of Ambrose Burchett'.

We are jumping the next generation as we have no details.

D –   **Henry I** (162X-1661) His wife was Mary who survived her husband by 38 years after having had three children: Richard b. 1654 died five years old; Mary b. 1658 died 16 months old, and *George* b. 1660. In 1641 assessed at 8s. for goods.

Richard II (16XX-1678) Wife Susannah with two children: Richard b. 1690 and Joan b. 1696. Mother Susannah died 1708. In the Lay Subsidy lists of 1620 to 1628 assessed at £3 for goods. In the list of presents to Charles I in 1626 listed £3 for goods.

George I (163X-1682) His wife was Elizabeth who survived her husband and was shown in 1664 as living in a house with three hearths. Their six children were: *Daniel* b. 1654, Luke b. 1656, Susanna b. 1661, married Richard *Edmead* in 1685, James b. 1665, *Allen* b. 1668, Ann b. 1676, married Thomas *Fortine* 1711. In 1675 a 'person to find arms'.

William III (161X-1692) Husbandman. His wife was Agnes and their only son Thomas died in 1654. In the Lay Subsidy list of 1640 assessed at 8s., gave 4s. as his Present to Charles II, when he was shown as 'yeoman'. In 1664 his house was assessed at four hearths. In the Muster Lists of 1675 a 'person to find arms'.

Thomas II (163X-170X) Wife was Mary and they had nine children: Thomas b. 1654, Owen b. 1657, died 31 years old, John b. 1660, died one day after his baptism, Mary b. 1661, William b. 1663, Hannah b. 1666, Charles b. 1673, Jane b. 1676 married Robert *Gavell* 1712, and Sarah b. 1781.

E – **George II** (1660-1715) Bricklayer. Son of Henry I; married Isabell *Wells* in 1697 and had two children: Mary b. 1698, died at age seven, *James* b. 1703, Isabell died 1727.

Henry II (166X-1718) Wife was Elizabeth with two children: *Henry* b. 1695 and Richard b. 1697, died three months old.

George III (166X-1727) *CW 1676-8.* Married 1685 Mary *Darney* and they had three children: *Edward* b. 1688, *John* b. 1692 and Henry b. 1693. Mother Mary died 1694 and George married again in 1701 Katherine *Berry*; their daughter was Mary b. 1702 and the register shows also a 'stillborn child' in 1706.

Daniel I (1654-1729) Son of George I; wife was Mary and they had five children: *Daniel* b. 1693, Mary b. 1695, Ann b. 1698, Richard b. 1702 and Hannah b. 1711. Daniel (the father) mentioned in the Association Oaths Roll of 1695.

Allan I (1668-1714) Son of George I. Also mentioned in the Association Oaths Rolls of 1695. No further details.

Henry III (168X-1721) Married Jane *Hunt* in 1706, no children. Jane died 1716 and Henry remarried, to Sarah, who gave him three children: *John* b. 1717, Elizabeth b. 1719 and Henry b. 1720. Father Henry was in the Association Oaths Roll of 1695.

F – **James I** (1703-17XX) Son of George II; married Ann and had two children: Mary b. 1733 and James b. 1735.

Henry IV (1695-175X) Son of Henry II; married Ann and had two children: Hannah b. 1734 and *Henry* b. 1736.

Edward I (1688-174X) Son of George III. No further details. His brother was:

John II (1692-174X) Married Anne *Field* in 1723 and had two sons: *John* b. 1726 and *Edward* b. 1729.

Daniel II (1693-1780) Eldest son of Daniel I. The burial register reads '*Mr* Daniel Burchett'. No further details.

John III (1717-1789) Son of Henry III, married Mary *Daw* in 1748 and they had 11 children: Mary b. 1749, Elizabeth b. 1750, John b. 1753, Henry b. 1755, James b. 1756, Henry b. 1758, Ann b. 1761, Daniel b. 1763, Hannah b. 1765, Sarah b. 1768 and Elizabeth b. 1770. (Nothing was known about the fate of all these children!)

G – **Henry V** (1736-1814) Son of Henry IV. Married Sarah *Sherward* (? Sherwood) in 1762 and they had seven children: Sarah b. 1762, married John *Burroughs*, 1782, Elizabeth b. 1763, *Henry* b. 1764, James b. 1766, John b. 1767, William b. 1768 and Ruth b. 1771. (Note: seven children in nine years.)

John IV (1726-1795) Son of John II. Married Agnes *Slack* 1757, was shown as bricklayer. They had four children: *John* b. 1758, *Joseph* b. 1760, Charlotte b. 1763, died a spinster 1784, Mary b. 1765, who was shown in the 1851 Census aged 84 as 'annuitant'.

Edward II (1729-1815) *OP 1796. CW 1797-9.* Son of John II. Married Ann (Nanny) *Bailey* and they had six children: Edward b. 1755, died a bachelor aged 77 in 1832, Ann b. 1757, *Morris* b. 1760, George b. 1764, Allen b. 1766 and Ann b. 1767, married William *Daborne* 1788. Son Allen died a bachelor in 1833.

H – **Henry VI** (1764-1798) Son of Henry V. Married Ann *Rowland* in 1787 and they had three children: Henry b. 1789, who died aged 21 in 1811, Ann b. 1794, married William *Evans* 1816, and *John* b. 1797.

Joseph I (1760-1831) Bricklayer, like his father John IV. Died a bachelor aged 71 in 1831. His elder brother was:

John V (1758-1802) Son of John IV. Wife was Hannah who had three children: Sarah b. 1798, James b. 1801 and John b. 1802.

Morris I (1760-1842) Yeoman (Brooklands and Copyhold Farms). *OP 1806. CW 1814, 1816.* Son of Edward II. Married Nanny *Dawborne* in 1805, the sister of his brother-in-law! His uncle Morris Bailey (brother of his mother Ann) left him £100 in his will dated 1797. He owed the high value of his estate (*see* p. 69) to the fact that he was the only son of the marriage of Edward Burchett and Ann Bailey and survived his mother and so became the heir of the two families' landed property.

I –   **John VI** (1797-18XX) Bricklayer's labourer. Son of Henry VI. Married Elizabeth *Perrin* 1821 and they had four children: *Henry* b. 1823, Elizabeth b. 1826, John b. 1828, died under the age of five, and George b. 1830, died one month old. His mother died seven weeks after his baptism. Father John married in the same year, 1830, Ann *Hudson* with one child: Ann b. 1832.

J –   **Henry VII** (1823-18XX) Master bricklayer. Son of John VI. Married Caroline *Gosden* 1839 and they had seven children: John b. 1841, who died two days after his baptism, Elizabeth b. 1842, died three days after her baptism, Henry George b. 1843, Frederick John b. 1845, died age three and a half, Elizabeth Sarah b. 1847, died three weeks old, John b. 1848 and William b. 1849.

Three entries of marriages of this family were entered in the parish register of Bisley: John B. married Alse Hogget 1753, Robert B. married Luce Coomes 1629, and Henry B. married Elizabeth Wheatley 1648.

Among the families whose members occupied leading posts in the village was the family of Rogers.

Rogers

A –   **Harry I** (152X-159X) Shown in the Chobham Park lists four times as providing a cart and twice as labourer. In 1555 he surrendered to the Queen the lease of 'Stannors and Fordes' which he had inherited from his father John, husbandman, granted in 1532 by indenture by King Henry VIII. His sons (X) were:

B –   **Henry II** (155X-158X) Assessed at £10 for goods in the Lay Subsidy Roll of 1571 and shown as 'archer' in a Muster List 'tempore Elizabeth'. In the Lay Subsidy list of 1589 his *widow* Agnes was assessed without details. His brother (X) was:

John I (156X-160X) In the Muster List of 1583 a 'bilman of the best Sorte'. In the Lay Subsidy lists from 1589 to 1595 assessed at £7 for goods.

C –   **John II** (158X-1659) His wife was Mary and they had one daughter: Ann whose burial was entered for 1692 – six years after the death of her mother in 1686.

Robert I (160X-167X) His wife was Mary, who died in 1658, but their daughter (X) Elizabeth married Thomas *Towers* in 1683.

D –   **Henry III** (165X-1720) Married Joan *Underwood* in Bisley 1692 and they had two children: *John* b. 1695 and Henry b. 1698. Shown in the Association Oaths Roll of 1695. In 1718 sold 'certain tythes or tenths' to Thomas Woods.

John III (165X-170X) In the Muster List of 1684 a 'person to find arms'. No further details.

Roger I (166X-171X) Labourer. His wife was Margaret and of their five children, four died within two days, only the oldest boy Henry b. 1702 survived.

E –   **John IV** (1695-1775) Yeoman. *OP 1768. CW 1724, 1741.* Son of Henry III. Married Ann *Hone* from Bisley at Farnborough in 1719. They had four children: Catherine b. 1720, married William *Lee* in 1742, Anne b. 1721, died one month old, Mary b. 1723, married William *Daborne* in Byfleet 1749, and *John* b. 1724. Mother Ann died two months after the birth of son John and father John married again, another Ann who bore two children: *Henry* b. 1738 and Ephraim b. 1744, who died a bachelor aged 30. In his will, dated 1763, John divided his properties among his three sons: from the Land Tax records we know that these were the Beldam Bridge Farm which went to John, another farm, called in the will 'Lee Farm' (called 'Rogers Farm' since then), which went to Henry, and the Burnstubbs Farm, which he gave to Ephraim. £200 was bequeathed to his daughter Mary and £20 p.a. to his widow for life, to be paid by the three sons, each contributing a third.

We have no details about John IV's brother Henry.

F –   **John V** (1724-1794) *OP 1776, 1787. CW 1780.* Son of John IV. Married Ann *Alexander* in 1778 and they had four children: *James* b. 1778, *William* b. 1781, Ann b. 1788, who married Jeremiah *Howard* in Windlesham in 1810, and Elizabeth b. 1792, married Thomas *Humphrey* in 1800.

      Henry IV (1738-1793) Gent. Married Elizabeth *Martin* in 1775 and they had four children: John died an infant 1780, another John died, again an infant, 1783, Elizabeth b. 1792, died five months old, and Richard, who was buried in 1794.

G –   **James I** (1778-1853) Farmer. *OP 1801, 1813, 1826 and 1829. CW 1802, 1815-21 and 1845-9.* Married Jane *Fladgate* in 1800. Called as witness for three wills in 1818, 1835 and 1836. In the Census of 1851 James was shown as 'Retired Farmer' and living in Millbrook Cottage (just on the border with Horsell). After the death of his wife, Jane, in 1849, his niece, Mary Fladgate acted as his housekeeper, as she is shown in the 1851 Census living in his house together with a female houseservant and a charwoman.

      William I (1781-1814) His wife was Elizabeth and they had one child: Mary Ann b. 1814, died two years old.

With the preceding nine families, we thought to have exhausted those that had been mentioned on the Chobham Park work lists and most had afterwards carried on right through to 1851 to fill the posts of village officials. There are, however, two more families to be considered which from time to time disappeared from the officials' lists; both present many problems when we attempt to pay full justice to their history.

Dabourn alias Dawbourne

A –   **Thomas I** (152X-157X) Wife was Raunce with one son Thomas. Provided one cart for the Chobham Park works in 1545-6.

B –   **Thomas II** (154X-1595) Labourer. In his will of 1595 he bequeathed six acres of land to his three children having made his wife, Alice, executrix. The three children were: Thomas, Elizabeth, married to John *Beacham*, and Agnes married to Henry *Sponge*. In the Muster List of 1583 a 'pikeman selected'.

C –   **Thomas III** (156X-163X) In the Lay Subsidy lists of 1589 to 1595 assessed at £1 for land. The Bishop's Transcript of 1587 shows the burial of the unnamed wife of Thomas and the baptism of his daughter Katherine.

We have no details of the next two generations as the name of Dabourn was absent from most of our secondary sources (even from the 1664 Hearth Tax returns).

F –   **George I** (168X-1728) His wife Mary survived him by no less than 55 years, dying in 1783. His two sons (X) were *John* b. 1712 and *Henry* b. 1716.

William I (1700-1787) Cordwainer. Married Ann *Bedford* from Woking in 1734 and they had seven children: *William* b. 1735, Henry b. 1737, *Richard* b. 1740, George b. 1742, *John* b. 1744, Ann b. 1750, married James *Chitty* 1790, and James b. 1747. William's wife predeceased him, dying in 1780. In his will he mentioned his daughter-in-law Elizabeth and four of his sons, making William, the eldest, his executor. (According to his will his daughter Ann had apparently married James *Fletcher* as her first husband.)

G – **John I** (1712-1790) Son of George I. His wife is Mary and they had 11 children: *John* b. 1740, William b. 1741, George b. 1742, Henry b. 1744, Henry b. 1745, died 1805, Ann b. 1746, Bett b. 1748, Jane b. 1750, Mary b. 1756, married Richard *Lee* 1788, Sarah b. 1760, died a spinster 1782, and Maria b. 1762. His brother was:

Henry I (1716-17XX) Married Ann *Howard* in 1748. No children.

William II (172X-1778) Yeoman. Married Mary *Rogers* in Byfleet, 1749; they had three children: Nanny b. 1757, married Morris *Burchett* 1805, *William* b. 1750 and John b. 1754, died a bachelor 1810.

William III (1735-1797) Cordwainer. *CW 1771, 1784. OP 1783.* Son of William I. Married Elizabeth *Russell* 1769. They had four children: William b. 1770, *James* b. 1774, *George* b. 1777, Elizabeth b. 1780, died 11 months old.

Richard I (1740-1789) Third son of William I. Married Sarah *Loveland* 1770; they had two children: Elizabeth b. 1771 and Henry b. 1776.

John II (1744-1806) Yet another son of William I. Married Elizabeth *Scott* 1765. Children not known.

H – **John III** (1740-1828) *OP 1826.* Eldest son of John I. Married Mary *Jewer* 1764; they had six children: *John* b. 1765, James b. 1767, Mary b. 1770, married W. Baxter, after his death married in 1810 John *Jewer*, and died in 1848, aged 78, William b. 1772, died a bachelor 1829, Elizabeth b. 1774, married William *Dunster* 1797, and Henry b. 1779.

William IV (1750-1827) Yeoman. *OP 1812.* Eldest son of William II. Married Ann *Burchett* 1788; they had eight children: *William* b. 1789, *John* b. 1791, Nanny b. 1793, married William *Woodhatch* 1815, Mary b. 1795 married William *Hone* 1831, *James* b. 1797, Morris b. 1800, died a bachelor 1828, Elizabeth b. 1802 and Sarah b. 1806, died aged three 1809.

James I (1774-1830) Wheelwright. Second son of William III. Married Ann *Spooner* 1797; they had four children: Sarah b. 1797, married William *Harding* 1830, William b. 1799, *James* b. 1801 and Elizabeth b. 1803, married William *Chitty* (although they lived together they kept their surnames and we could not find their marriage entry). Daughter Sarah remarried after her husband, William's, death, James *Slyfield* in 1852. James, the father, married again after the death of Ann his wife in 1806; his new wife's name was Sophia and they had nine children: Amelia b. 1807, died 14 months old, Solomon b. 1810, Mary b. 1814, Eliza b. 1816 (her two illegitimate children were brought up within her parents' home), George b. 1819, Frances b. 1821, John b. 1824, Allen b. 1826 and Hannah b. 1828. (Allen died within one week after baptism). His brother was:

George II (1777-1807) Shoemaker. His burial entry says: 'Died suddenly'. His wife was Elizabeth; they had three children: James b. 1799, Hannah b. 1801, married George *Ridger* but died 1842 aged 40, and William b. 1803, who was a delicate child and was 'half-baptised' a month before baptism in church.

I – **John IV** (1765-1836) Farmer (Saddlers Farm). Son of John III. His wife was Mary and they had eight children: Allen b. 1800, Charlotte b. 1802, Harriet b. 1805, Eliza b.

1807, married Henry *Hogsden* 1840, Amelia b. 1809 married her cousin (X) James *Daborn* 1828, Lucy b. 1811, *John* b. 1816 and Louise b. 1818, married William *Moulding* 1845. After the death of her husband Mary went to live with her son John.

William V (1789-1867) Farmer (Watts Farm). *OP 1819, 1833. CW 1837/8.* Son of William IV. Married Sarah *Chennel* 1813. Their one daughter, Ann b. 1815, died aged seventeen.

John V (1791-18XX) Farmer. (Park Farm). *OP 1825, 1838. CW 1845-51.* Second son of William IV. His wife was Ann and they had eight children: Frances b. 1828, William b. 1830, died 14 months old, Ann b. 1832, Elizabeth b. 1833, George b. 1835, Frederick b. 1837, Caroline b. 1840 and Sarah b. 1842. His brother was:

29.   Beech Cottage at the corner of the High Street and Station Road, *c.*1905. Members of one branch of the Daborn family stand outside.

James II (1797-18XX) Farmer (Copyhold Farm). *OP 1832.* His wife was Jane and they had nine children: *Henry* b. 1822, Richard b. 1825, *James* b. 1827, John b. 1829, Frances b. 1831, Mary Ann b. 1834, Jane b. 1837, Ann b. 1839 and Rebecca b. 1840. Mother Jane died aged only 36 and father James married a widow Elizabeth *Wallis* née *Soan* in 1845, seven years younger than he.

James III (1801-18XX) Farmer (Sandpit Hall Farm). Son of James I. Married his cousin

(X) Amelia in 1828 in West Molesey church and they had seven children: Morris b. 1829, Henry b. 1831, William b. 1833, Ann b. 1836, James b. 1839, Frederick b. 1843 and Amelia b. 1846. Executor of the will of John Souter in 1834 and of his cousin (X) John IV's will of 1827.

J – **John VI** (1816-18XX) Farmer (Brooklands Farm). *OP 1849*. Son of John IV. Married Caroline *Baigent* 1839 with two children: Lucy b. 1845 and Eliza b. 1847. His elder brother was:

Allen I (1800-18XX) Married Mary Ann *Turner* 1830. No children.

Henry II (1822-18XX) Labourer. Eldest son of James II. His wife was Jane *Mepham* 1844 and they had two children: William born 1845 and Emma born 1847. (They were apparently not baptised, only registered.)

We now come to the last of the very old Chobham families, i.e. families whose members are mentioned in the works' lists of 1545-6 and are later known to have been elected several times to the post of churchwarden or overseer.

Spong alias Sponge

A – **John I** (152X-159X) Provided a cart four times, shown as labouring and delivering 'oaken timber' to the works in 1545-6. In the Muster List of 1583 a 'bilman of the second sorte'.

Thomas I (153X-160X) Married Elizabeth *Cobbett* and they had three children: *Henry*, Amye, and Elizabeth, who married William *Gray* in 1703. (Thomas was overseer and his family were beneficaries in the will of Robert Cobbett, dated 1608.)

B – **Henry I** (155X-162X) Perhaps the son (X) of Thomas I. Adventured 5s. in the Queen's Lottery in 1567 and was also shown as a 'bilman of the second sorte' in the Muster of 1583. Three times acted as witness of other farmers' wills: in 1595 for Thomas Daborn, in 1597 for Richard Edmead and in 1605 for Thomas Lane, all farmers of Chobham. In the Lay Subsidy Rolls from 1593 to 1595 assessed at £2 for land.

Thomas II (154X-159X) Assessed at £3 for goods in the Lay Subsidy list of 1571.

C – **William I** (158X-163X) The eldest son of Henry I. (The details of Henry I's family are contained in the will of William Beauchamp dated 1610.) William had three younger brothers:

Henry II (159X-1660) In the Free Present to Charles I in 1626 assessed at £4 for goods, as he was also in 1628. Acted as overseer of the will of Henry Lee of 1605 and as witness in 1641 for John Wye. His brother was:

Roger I (159X-1681) His wife was Mary; their son, John was shown in the register as having been buried in 1659, and a daughter, Mary married Henry *Field* in 1663. In the Free Present to Charles II in 1661 gave 2s. and was shown as labourer. In 1664 his house had four hearths. His brother was:

Thomas III (161X-1675) His wife was Mary and their three children were: *Thomas* born 164X, Sarah born 165X, married Richard *Pullen* 1677, and Mary born 165X, married John *Field* 1682. Acted as *constable* in the Hearth Tax returns of 1664 where he was also shown in a house with three hearths.

Isaac I (15XX-1660) No definite details but Simon might be his son. Simon died in 1716.

Henry III (15XX-1660) His wife was Elizabeth who survived her husband by four years. No children known. Assessed in 1628 (Lay Subsidy Roll) at £4 for goods.

D – **William II** (162X-1706) Married Elizabeth *Pinson* in Bisley 1647 and they had eight children: Jane buried 1654, Agnes buried 1656 (both apparently baptised before the new register book was used), Damaris b. 1657, *John* b. 1661, William b. 1662, died seven months old, *Thomas* b. 1663, *Owen* b. 1665 and Mary b. 1667, married William *Spot* 1705. Mother Elizabeth died in 1667, five months after Mary's baptism. Father William married again, his new wife was Ann who gave him 10 children, Joseph b. 1669, died a bachelor 1725, *Benjamin* b. 1672, Walter b. 1674, William b. 1676, died at age five, Ann b. 1677, Sarah b. 1681, *William* b. 1682, Mary b.1683, *James* b. 1684 and Dorothy b. 1690, died 10 days old. In the free present to Charles II, William gave 2s. 6d. and in 1664 his house was assessed on three hearths.

John II (163X-1695) His wife was Joan and they had five children: John b. 1677, died within two months, Henry b. 1681, lived to 15 years, James b. 1689, died one month old, Mary b. 1690, died at 14 years, and Alice b. 1694, married John *Roberts* 1724.

John III (162X-1662) His wife was Alice who survived her husband by 15 years and was shown in the Hearth Tax list in 1664 as 'widdow' residing in a house of three hearths. In 1661 Alice gave 5s. as her Free Present to Charles II.

Thomas IV (164X-1722) His wife, Ann, died in 1683 soon after their marriage. He was son of Thomas III and shown in the Association Oaths Roll of 1695.

Thomas V (163X-1706) Married Elizabeth *Woods* in 1662 and they had six children: *William* b. 1665 and John b. 1667, Thomas b. 1672, died three years old, John b. 1675, Jane b. 1678 and Ann b. 1682, died three months old.

William III (162X-168X) His wife was Sarah and they had one son, *Henry* b. 1645. In the Free Present to Charles II in 1661 shown as labourer and gave 2s. Lived in 1664 in a house with one hearth.

E –   **John IV** (1661-1715) Eldest son of William II. His wife was Ann and their only child was *John* b. 1713. His five younger brothers follow:

Thomas VI (1663-1718) Farmer. His wife was Elizabeth and their son was *Thomas* b. 1680. Mentioned in the Association Oaths Roll of 1695.

Owen I (1665-1721) His wife, Susannah, died early in 1702 after the births of three children: Mary b. 1691, Susannah b. 1693 and *Owen* b. 1696. Father Owen married again barely five weeks after his wife's death. His second wife was Mary *Miller* and they had eight children: Joseph b. 1703, Alice b. 1705, Elizabeth b. 1717, Bartholomew b. 1709, died one week after his baptism, Robert b. 1710, Ann b. 1713, Stephen b. 1717 and Bartholomew b. 1719, died two months after his baptism. Owen's name is mentioned in the Association Oaths Roll of 1695.

Benjamin I (1672-17XX) His wife's name was not known but they had one son, *Benjamin* b. 1710.

William IV (1682-1729) *CW 1721.* If the register entries have been correctly copied, here is their content: married Dorothy, who died 9 April 1729 after the birth of a boy William who died a month before his mother. William married again the month after burying his wife and his second wife, Anne, died in the month of their marriage. William died himself six months after his second wife. He was mentioned in the Association Oaths Roll of 1695.

James I (1684-17XX) This was the youngest son of William II and we have no other details about him.

William V (1665-1718) Son of Thomas V, married Joan *Savidge* 1693 and they had two children: *William* b. 1694 and Ann b. 1697, married Joseph *Stevenson.* Mentioned in the Association Oaths Roll of 1695.

Henry IV (1645-1703) Yeoman. *CW 1684-5.* Son of William III. His wife was Elizabeth and they had eight children: Hannah b. 1668, Jane b. 1670, died three weeks old, Jane

b. 1671, Henry b. 1672, died 23 days old, Alice b. 1673, Jane b. 1674, Henry b. 1676, died age two, and *John* b. 1678. Mother Elizabeth died 1680 and Father Henry married again, his new wife was Ann who gave him six children: *Henry* b. 1683, James b. 1690, died a bachelor at age 26. Christiane b. 1694, Ann b. 1696, Elizabeth b. 1699 and William b. 1702. Father Henry was shown in the Muster List of 1684 as 'person to find arms' and also mentioned in the Association Oaths Roll of 1695.

F – **John V** (1713-1783) *OP 1736*. Son of John IV. His wife was Elizabeth and they had two sons: *John* b. 1752 and *Henry* b. 1755.

Thomas VII (1680-1726) His wife was Mary and their daughter was Jane b. 1717, married Charles *Collyer* 1741. Mentioned in the Association Oaths Roll of 1695.

Owen II (1696-1721) His wife was Elizabeth and their son was James b. 1722.

Benjamin II (1710-1783) His wife was Mary and they had 10 children: *John* b. 1741, Mary b. 1742, *William* b. 1744, Ann b. 1745, married James *Duffin* 1778, *James* b. 1747, *John* b. 1749, Thomas b. 1750, Joseph b.1750, *Thomas* b. 1756 and Benjamin b. 1756. (The last four children were two pairs of twins.)

F – **William VI** (1694-1766) Yeoman. Son of William V. Did not marry. In his will of 1760 he mentions 'my niece Ann Stevenson, spinster and living with me' (perhaps as housekeeper).

Edward I (1690-1772) Farmer. Mentioned as joint executor in the will of William Russell, dated 1744. His wife was Ann and they had six children: Jane b. 1722, Elizabeth b. 1723, Mary b. 1725, Henry b. 1728, John b. 1732 and *William* b. 1734.

John VI (1678-1719) Eldest surviving son of Henry IV. His wife was Mary and they had two children: Sarah b. 1704 and Mary b. 1706. Mary the mother died in 1710 and John married again. His new wife was Margaret who gave him three children: John b. 1712, died age seven, Henry b. 1713, died two weeks after his baptism, and another John b. 1719 (after his father's death) and died aged five weeks.

Henry V (1683-1709) Yeoman. Married Ann *Clifford* in 1707. No children. The second surviving son of Henry IV.

G – **John VII** (1752-1826) Husbandman. Son of John V. Married Elizabeth *Slyfield* 1771; they had two children: Ann b. 1773, married Daniel *Waters*, and *John* b. 1775. His brother was:

Henry VI (1755-1820) Married Mary *Absolom* in 1776 and they had six children: Henry b. 1777 died two years old, *William* b. 1779, Mary b. 1781, Henry b. 1786, Elizabeth b. 1786 and John b. 1790 died six weeks old.

John VIII (1741-179X) Eldest son of Benjamin II. Married Sarah *Grove* in 1765. On her death, Sarah's entry was 'buried 3.7.1823 age 70' making her aged 12 at their marriage, which was highly unlikely. (Perhaps this was another case of wrong copying and the death entry should have been: 'died aged 30, 3.7.1773'. John was shown to have married again in 1783; his new wife was Mary and she gave him one son: William b. 1785. His four younger brothers follow:

William VII (1744-1817) Labourer. A witness to the will of Richard Lee dated 1773. Married Ann *Towers* from Bisley in 1773. In his will, dated 1816, he mentions brothers James and John, John's son John, a nephew William and also 'Mary daughter of Phillis Spong wife of brother James'. (These details enabled us to check our report.)

James II (1747-1823) *OP 1797*. Farmer. His wife was Massey who gave him a son *James* b.

1773 (X). Massey, however, died in 1810 and James married again, a widow, Phillis, and they had one daughter, Mary.

John IX (1749-1823) Labourer. His wife was Ann and they had three children: John b. 1782, Hannah b. 1784 and Amelia b. 1787. In 1785 John with wife Ann and two children, John and Hannah were removed from Walton back to Chobham.

Thomas VIII (1756-1828) The last of the surviving sons of Benjamin II. Married Jane *Fisk* in 1775 and they had one daughter, Sarah b. 1775, who was baptised six weeks after her parents' marriage and died at nine months old.

William VIII (1734-18XX) Youngest son of Edward I. Married Jane *Collins* 1768 and then Sarah *Campion* in 1778. He had one daughter, Jane, who married David *Whitbourne* in 1791 – this must have been wife Jane's daughter, of course!

H –   **John X** (1775-1846) Son (X) of John VII. Married Charlotte *Mepham* in 1824. Their two children were not baptised in Chobham; they were: John, born 1824 and Charlotte born 1827, who married James *Roberts* in 1846.

William IX (1779-18XX) Gardener. Son of Henry VI. Wife's name not known, had three children: *William* b. 1806, Rebecca b. 1813 and *James* b. 1815.

James III (1773-1851) Agricultural labourer. (Lived at Ribsdown in 1841.) Son of James II. Married Mary *Howard* 1794 and they had three children: Sarah b. 1794, *James* b. 1796 and William b. 1798, died eight years old.

I –   **William X** (1806-18XX) Nursery labourer. Son of William IX. Married Phoebe *Chitty* 1827 in Bisley Church. No children.

James IV (1796-18XX) Married Maria *Gale* and they had 14 children: Jane b. 1819, Isaac b. 1821, Henry b. 1822 died four months old, William b. 1823, Eliza b. 1826, married James *Baigent*, Charles b. 1828, Rachel b. 1830, Esther b. 1831, George b. 1833, Sarah and Harriet, twins b. 1835, Mary Ann b. 1837, Caroline b. 1840 and Charlotte b. 1828 (X).

I –   **James V** (1815-18XX) Second son of William IX. His wife was Harriett from Chertsey and their six children were: Rosetta (Renate) b. 1842, Henry b. 1843, Maria b. 1844, Mary b. 1847, died one year old, James b. 1848 and John b. 1850.

Two more members of the family whom we cannot fit into our tree are:

George I (1815-18XX) Married Sarah from Windlesham and their eight children were: Mary-Ann born in Windlesham 1834, Eliza-Sarah b. 1836, Charlotte b. 1839, Lavinia b. 1843, George b. 1845, Emma b. 1847 and Susan b. 1847. A daughter, Sarah, born 1840, died without being baptised.

Isaac I (1813-18XX) Married Mary-Ann *Mepham* in 1838 and their eight children were: Isaac born in Windlesham 1837, Caroline b. 1840, James b. 1842, John b. 1843, died seven years old, Charles b. 1845, Mary-Ann b. 1847, Emma b. 1849 and Henry-John b. 1851. It was not surprising that we could not fit Isaac within our tree as, in the 1861 Census, he was shown as born in Chertsey. Strangely enough, his first-born child, Isaac, was, in that Census, given the surname Mepham. (He was born before his parents' wedding.)

With the last family we have reached the end of those families whose members had been mentioned in the Chobham Park works and most had survived right through to 1851. Now we come to families who were mentioned in 1545-6, then again in the Muster of 1583 and the Hearth Tax list of 1664. We have taken the two last mentioned lists as the basis of our judgement whether to include a family here as they can be assumed to have included every family in the village, not only the richer ones who are shown in the various financial documents, especially those of Queen Elizabeth's time. But these following families somehow disappeared from Chobham and a few are not even found in the early registers after 1654.

Wye alias Wey

A – **Henry I** (152X-159X) Mentioned in the Chobham Park lists once as a labourer and then as providing a cart. We have found no less than five members of the family who could represent the next generation though we have not found any reason to call any of them Henry I's son.

B – **Henry II** (155X-161X) Assessed in the Lay Subsidy of 1571 at £1 for land, as he was also shown in the later lists of 1589 to 1595.

Thomas I (156X-161X) Assessed in 1571 at £7 for land and in the Muster List of 1583 was shown as 'archer of the second sorte'. Acted as witness in the will of Thomas Daborn in 1595 and again in 1605 for Thomas Lane. His assessment for the Lay Subsidies of 1589 to 1595 had gone up to £8.

John I (153X-159X) Adventured 3s. in the Queen's Lottery of 1567.

Edward I (156X-160X) In the Muster of 1583 a 'Bilman of the best sorte'. His widow Ann was shown in the Lay Subsidy list of 1620 assessed at £1 for lands, followed by their son *Edward*.

William I (154X-159X) 'Archer select' in the Muster List of 1583, his son was *Richard* baptised in 1587.

C – **Henry III** (161X-1685) Perhaps the son (X) of Henry II. In the free present to Charles II in 1661 he was shown as husbandman and gave 2s. 6d. In the Hearth Tax list of 1664 lived in a house with one hearth. His wife was Ann, who died before her husband in 1673.

Thomas II (158X-162X) Shown as 'junior' in the Muster of 1592, as a 'pykeman'. Acted as witness of the will of Samuel Huett in 1614. (Perhaps the son of Thomas I senior?)

Edward II (163X-171X) Took over his father's farm after the death of his mother. Mentioned in the Association Oaths list of 1695. His wife's name was not known but 10 children have been found in the register book: Elizabeth buried 1663, another Elizabeth buried 1665, *John* b. 1665, Alice b. 1667, died 13 years old, James b. 1669, died the day after his baptism, the twins *Edward* and Mary b. 1670, Ann buried 1681, Elizabeth buried 1678, and Mary buried 1687. Edward's wife, described in the register without Christian name, was buried in 1679.

Richard I (1587-16XX) His birth, as son of William (I?), was found in the Bishop's Transcript of that date. Nothing further known.

John II (157X-1647) In his will of 1641 he mentions his wife Alice and no less than seven children; daughters Alice and Susan, to each of whom he leaves 12d., and Jane and Elizabeth, the first to receive £80 three months after her marriage and Elizabeth to have the same amount when she was twenty-one. His sons were treated quite distinctly: John was to be executor and to receive anything left after what had been bequeathed to others, son George to have all freeholds in Chobham and Bisley, but son Edward got only 1s. To his wife he gave four cows, two beds and bedsteads with their contents, and a pot and two kettles. The poor of the village were not forgotten, they had 20s. to be distributed 'at funeral'.

John III (162X-1659) His wife was Ellen and they had two children: Henry b. 1656, died three years old, and Mary, whose baptism was not in the register but was buried in 1668. John's wife survived him by 14 years and died in 1673.

D – **John IV** (165X-1723) In the Muster List of 1684 shown as 'soldier' whose arms were to be supplied by William Duff and another John Wye. His wife was Grace and their two children were: John b. 1676, died 11 years old, and Grace b. 1681. The burial register shows father John as 'senior'. His wife died four years before her husband.

Edward III (1670-1695) Second surviving son of Edward II. His wife was Mary who survived him by eight years. His elder brother was:

D –   **John V** (1665-173X) Yeoman. *CW 1691*. Son of Edward II. His wife was Elizabeth who bore nine children: Elizabeth b. 1695, Joan b. 1697, married Henry *Roath* in 1722, Grace b. 1699, married John *Norwood* 1723, John b. 1701 (at his baptism, his father was called 'junior'), Alice b. 1703, died five months old, Alice b. 1706, Ann b. 1708, married Philip *Beauchamp* in 1728 when she was barely 18 and her groom only 17½, much to the disapproval of Philip's father who nearly disinherited the boy (*see above* p. 70), Thomas b. 1711 and Mary b. 1714. Mother Elizabeth died one year before her husband. Shown in the Association Oaths list of 1695.

We have no further details about the next generation of this family other than their dates of baptism shown in their fathers' paragraphs.

Our next family presents a grave problem because the absence of an early will (as proved so helpful in previously settled trees) makes it impossible to establish the link between its members in the 16th century and those found in the parish register after 1654.

Emmett alias Emmott and Emot

A –   **John I** (152X-158X) Mentioned in the works' list at Chobham Park in 1545-6, where he supplied some timber for the houses.

Richard I (153X-159X) Adventured 2s. 6d. in the Queen's Lottery in 1567 and we assume that the following two entries refer to Richard's sons. (X)

B –   **William I** (156X-158X) In the Muster List of 1583 a 'bilman of the second sorte'.

Richard II (157X-164X) In the Lay Subsidy lists of the series 1589 to 1595, he only appears in 1593 when we assume he had taken over from his father; his assessment was £2.

In the will of George Stelman dated 1665, among a large number of other bequests, members of the Emmett family are shown amongst whom we find the name of

Stephen I (159X-165X) In the will he was mentioned as deceased but his three children, otherwise unnamed, were beneficiaries.

C –   **Richard III** (160X-1677) *CW 1669*. His wife was Ann, who bore seven children: Grace b. 1654, Jane b. 1659, died five years old, *Richard* b. 1669, Robert b. 1672, died four weeks old, *Robert* and Mary (twins) b. 1673, but Mary died at 13 years old, and another Richard b. 1676 died a bachelor in 1723. In the Lay Subsidy lists between 1620 and 1641 he was assessed at £6 for goods and he was also shown in 1626 in the list of Presents to Charles I. His house was assessed at four hearths in 1664 and he gave 20s. in 1661 as his Free Present to Charles II. In the Muster list of 1675 a 'Person to find arms'.

Thomas I (163X-1701) Married Elizabeth *Field* in 1658 and two children are recorded in the register: Elizabeth b. 1663, died a spinster 1696, and Thomas, of whom we could only find the burial in 1722. Mother Elizabeth survived her husband by six years. His house was assessed at four hearths in 1664 but in 1661 he had given only 2s. 6d. as his Present to Charles II. Shown in the Association Oaths Roll of 1695.

Edward I (163X-1694) Married Katherine *Jewer* in 1664 but his wife died within 13 years without children. In the register we found her death on 29 December 1687 and another entry dated 23 January 1688 of a marriage of Edward Emmett and Alice *Woodier*. We feel it to be highly unlikely that Edward would have remarried barely four weeks after his wife's death. Whilst we have no proof for the suggestion, the second marriage might have been that of the first Edward's son, Edward. Edward and Thomas I are shown in the above-mentioned will of George Stelman as was another brother, Morris, about whom we have not found any evidence.

D – **Richard IV** (1669-1711) Yeoman. *CW 1688*. His wife was Alice and their three children all died young: Richard b. 1705, died aged three, Thomas b. 1707, died four days old, and Ann b. 1710, died two years old. Shown in the Association Oaths Roll 1695. His younger brother was:

Robert I (1673-1734) His wife was Elizabeth and they had six children: Elizabeth b. 1721, *Richard* b. 1723, Thomas b. 1724, died seven days old, Mary b. 1725, died six days old, William b. 1727 and Jane b. 1728, married James *Viner* of Esher in 1749.

John I (166X-1720) His wife was Mary and their daughter was shown only as buried in 1713. John was mentioned in the Association Oaths Roll of 1695.

E – **Richard V** (1723-1796) The eldest surviving son of Robert I. His wife was Alisha (Alice), who bore him 12 children in 12 years: Richard b. 1744, Elizabeth b. 1745, married Mark *Stevenson* in 1770, Jane b. 1747, married George *Grove* in 1770, William b. 1748, Mary b. 1749, Richard b. 1750, Phobe b. 1751, Nanny b. 1752, Anne b. 1753, Mary b. 1754, another Richard b. 1755 and a third Richard b. 1756.

For the next family we were lucky to find very early documentation:

Hiller

A – **Richard I** (143X-1485) Yeoman. His will of 1485 has been preserved in the Spage Register; he made various gifts to St Lawrence church and to St Swithun, Winchester, apart from gifts to his son *Alexander* and to two servants, the residue went to his wife Alice and other son *Richard*.

B – **Richard II** (146X-152X) His wife must have been another Alice as she was mentioned in the Chobham Park works lists supplying some timber. His brother was:

Alexander I (147X-152X) No further details.

C – **Richard III** (149X-157X) Mentioned in a special report on works carried out during the demolition of Chertsey Abbey in 1539: 'Item paid to Rychard hyller of Chobham for a lode of Bockes Caryed from the abbey to the brygge'. Richard was also shown providing a cart in the works accounts of 1545-6 and was a witness to the will of John Bonyons in 1565.

Nicholas I (152X-159X) Mentioned in a Muster List of 1575 and in the Lay Subsidy List of 1571 he was assessed at £3 on goods, and in 1589 at 2s. 8d. His son was *William*.

John I (153X-159X) In the Lay Subsidy List of 1571 assessed at £1 for lands and shown as 'bilman of the second sorte' in 1583.

D – **Richard IV** (152X-1615) Shown in the Muster List of 1596 and as Overseer in the will of Nicholas Wodsdale in 1600.

William I (155X-160X) Takes over the land of his father, Nicholas, in 1591, when he is assessed at £1 for land.

John II (156X-162X) Like his father (X) John I, shown in the Muster List of 1583 as 'Bilman of the second sorte'. The Bishop's Transcript of 1587 says 'John son of John' b. 1587.

Nicholas II (155X-163X) In the Lay Subsidy lists of 1620 to 1628 assessed at £1 for land.

John III (1587-165X) Witness of the will of Henry Taylor the elder, clothworker, in 1639.

E – **Henry I** (164X-1689) *CW 1679*. Married Elizabeth *Towers* in 1667 and they had nine children: John, whose death was shown in 1674, Jane b. 1669, Henry b. 1670, Elizabeth b.

1674, died four months old, Elizabeth b. 1675, Ann b. 1676, Mary b. 1679, John b. 1681, William b. 1683, died 17 years old, and Sarah b. 1688. Father Henry was buried 23 January 1689 and his wife the day after – possibly there was a connection with the birth of their last child, Sarah, who had been baptised only seven weeks before her parents' burials.

John IV (161X-1673) In the Free Present to Charles II gave 1s., he was shown there as a labourer and in 1664 his house was assessed at two hearths. His wife was Ellen, who died in 1670, and their only child, Anne, was entered at her burial in 1656 (perhaps baptised before 1654).

F –   **John V** (168X-173X) His wife was Anne and their son, Thomas, was baptised 1722.

The details of this family were difficult to state exactly as their Christian names were easily exchanged.

A number of members of the family of Pigg served as parish officials:

Pigg alias Pyge

A –   **William I** (152X-158X) Mentioned in the Chobham Park Works lists as 'labouring'. The next two members could be his sons (X).

B –   **William II** (155X-1590) In the Muster List of 1583 a 'bilman of the best sorte' and assessed at 5s. in the Lay Subsidy of 1589 but not mentioned in the following lists of 1590-95.

John I (156X-160X) His marriage to Agnes *Burt* was shown in the Bishop's Transcript of 1587 and he was also mentioned in the 1583 Muster as a 'bilman select'.

Thomas I (157X-1657) His burial was entered in the parish register.

C –   **William III** (162X-1673) *CW 1669.* Son or grandson of William II (X). His wife was Joan and they had three children: Margaret buried in 1656 (baptism before 1654!), Jane b. 1658 and *William* b. 1655. Gave 10s. as his present to Charles II in 1661, his house was assessed at five hearths in 1664.

John II (162X-1673) His wife was Agnes, whom he married in 1655, but we know of no children.

Thomas II (163X-1665) The son of Thomas I; we do not know his wife's name but they had two children: Elizabeth b. 1663 and *Richard* b. 1665. In the Hearth Tax list of 1664 a labourer and exempted from payment.

Robert I (   ) We only know of him as he was mentioned in the Hearth Tax list of 1664 as 'Cordwayner' and exempted from payment.

Richard I (163X-1692) His wife was Rose and their only child, Amy, was buried in 1659. Rose died in 1678. In the Hearth Tax list of 1664 a 'labourer' and not chargeable.

D –   **William IV** (1655-1721) *CW 1689/90.* Son of William III. His wife was Frances and their two children were: *William*, whose baptism was not found in the register, and Jane b. 1689. Frances died in 1696.

Richard II (1665-169X) Son of Thomas II. The only reference to him was a note in the parish register: Jane, daughter of Richard Pigg, buried 1686.

William V (1656-1680) Son of Robert I. His widow was shown in the 1684 Muster List as 'person to find arms'. No further details.

E –   **William VI** (167X-1750) *OP 1734. CW 1722.* Son of William IV. Witness in the will of William Russell dated 1744 and again in a lease of Hookstone Farm in 1735. In the Muster List of 1684 a 'person to finde arms'. Also in the Association Oaths List of 1695. Married Mary *Edsaw* in 1718 at Windlesham and they had five children: *William* b. 1719, *John* b. 1722, Thomas b. 1724, Mary b. 1725 died a spinster in 1789 and James b. 1727 buried 10 weeks later.

F – **William VII** (1719-1778) *CW 1778*, but died suddenly in the year of duty so that his colleague, William Beauchamp, had to take over his account and report for him to the Bishop's registrar. His brother was:

John III (1722-1761) His wife was Mary and they had eight children: Mary b. 1744, Frances b. 1745, William b. 1746, James b. 1748, *George* b. 1750, Richard b. 1752, Charles b. 1755 and John b. 1760. Acted as witness in the will of John Alexander, yeoman, in 1753 and died intestate only 39 years old.

G – **George I** (1750-18XX) Son of John III. Married Jane *Lawrence* in 1809. No further details.

Stelman alias Stillman, Stylman and Styleman

A – **John I** (151X-157X) Provided a cart for the Chobham Park Works in 1545-6.

B – **Thomas I** (154X-1630) Adventured 5s. in the Queen's Lottery in 1567. In the Lay Subsidy lists of 1620 to 1628 assessed at £4 for goods, as he was also shown in the list of gifts to Charles I in 1626.

C – **George I** (159X-1666) *CW 1658/59*. His wife was Susan who died two years after her husband but we found no entries of their children in the register. In the Lay Subsidy lists of 1620 to 1641 he was assessed at £3 for goods, as he was also shown in the List of Gifts to Charles I in 1626. In 1661, he gave 15s. as his free present to Charles II and he lived in a house with four hearths in 1664. In his will, dated 1665, he left various sums, totalling £200, to members of a great number of families: Emmett, Wheatley, Taylor, Burchett, Pinson, Attfield, Spong, Biddle, Grove and to the village poor, 6s. 8d. and an equal amount to St Lawrence's church. He also mentioned his sister Elizabeth who had married William *Wheatley*, perhaps before 1630.

D – **George II** (164X-1728) *CW 1710*. We do not know his wife's name but they had two boys: *George* b. 1693 and John b. 1695.

Edward I (163X-1672) Married Jane *Hale* in 1663 and they had two children: *John* b. 1666 and Jane b. 1670. George I referred to Edward as his 'kinsman' making him a beneficiary of his will.

Steven I (164X-1693) Husbandman. *CW 1685-7*. His wife was Ann and their only son George was baptised in 1668. Mother Ann died in 1670 and Steven married another Ann who bore him five children: Ann b. 1673, Steven b. 1674, died 10 years old, Alice b. 1676, Sarah b. 1678 and *John* b. 1681. In the 1684 Muster List, Steven was shown as 'person to finde arms'.

E – **John II** (1666-1727) Son of Edward I. Married Mary *Wheatley* in Bisley in 1694 when both are said to be 'of Chobham'. They had two children: Mary b. 1694 and John b. 1698. Father John was shown in the Association Oaths Roll of 1695.

John III (1681-175X) *OP 1735*. Son of Steven I. Married Mary *Dawkins* and they had 11 children: Mary b. 1706, John b. 1710, died one month after his baptism, George b. 1711, John b. 1713, died 16 months old, Ann b. 1715, Sarah b. 1717, Henry b. 1720, Jane b. 1722, John b. 1724, died two weeks old, Alice b. 1725, died three days old, and Frances b. 1726, died a spinster in 1780.

E – **George III** (1693-17XX) *CW 1733, 1737. OP 1734*. Son of George II. Married in 1745 in Windlesham but his wife's name is not known. They had one girl, Jane, b. 1746, who was stated to have married Edward *Bailey* in 1764 (aged only 16).

Our next family was the Martins whom we met (*see above* p. 10) when we talked about Henry VIII's efforts to obtain land he wanted to complete his deer park in Chobham. Although the first-mentioned member of the family was shown as 'from Chertsey, joiner,' we accept the family as resident in Chobham on the land obtained from the King in exchange for the surrendered land.

Martin alias Marten, Marter, Marden

A –   **Thomas I** (145X-149X) Joiner from Chertsey, his wife was Johan and their son Nicholas.

B –   **Nicholas I** (148X-1540) Obtained his mother's land as the King's copyholder and was followed by his son *John*.

We were fortunate to find two early wills of this family in the Winchester Record Office.

William I (149X-1532) After gifts to St Lawrence's in Chobham and the 'mother church at Winchester' he mentioned a brother John and appointed his wife Alice an executrix.

John I (150X-156X) We only know him as mentioned in his brother's will.

Richard I (149X-1560) His widow Margaret also mentioned her two brothers, Richard and Thomas Woods, as beneficiaries in her will dated 1565. She added (rather cryptically) the children of her 'brother Nicholas Attfield' which gives her a blood-relationship to two of the old Chobham families!

C –   **John II** (153X-159X) Farmer (Halebourne Farm). Son of Nicholas I and heir to his father's land. In the Lay Subsidy of 1571 assessed at £1 for land; at the Muster of 1583 a 'bilman of the second sorte'.

George I (154X-162X) Husbandman. Adventured 2s. 6d. in the Queen's Lottery of 1567. His sons were *James* and *George*.

Thomas II (155X-162X) Called upon to act as witness in the two wills of Henry and Allen Attfield, both in 1596. In the Lay Subsidy lists of 1589 to 1595 assessed at £1 for land.

D –   **James I** (158X-164X) Son of George I. In 1626 assessed at £4 for land. In the Lay Subsidy list of 1640/1 he was shown as having taken over from his brother George. His elder brother was:

George II (157X-1629) In the Lay Subsidy lists of 1620-8 he was assessed at £2 for land.

Henry I (159X-163X) Again assessed in 1626 at £2 for land.

E –   **John III** (162X-1681) We do not know whose son he was but the parish register shows his death in 1681.

James II (162X-1669) His wife was Dorothy and they had two children: *Henry* b. 1654 and Jane b. 1664, a late baptism as mother Dorothy had died in 1658. James gave 2s. 6d. as his free present to Charles II in 1661 and his house was shown to have had one hearth in 1664.

The next two members we cannot fit in after their parents so we show them in their generation.

E –   **Richard II** (163X-16XX) The register records his daughter Susan as baptised in 1654.

Owen I (163X-16XX) His marriage in 1656 to Hannah *Fabeen* was recorded in the parish register.

F –   **John IV** (166X-171X) Father of John b. 1698 and Daniel b. 1710. (The register entry adds to his baptismal lines 'born 25.12.1709 as his grandmother informs me'.)

George III (165X-1710) Married Mary *Woodyear* in 1692 at Bisley and they had three girls: Mary b. 1696, married William *Call* from Windlesham in 1718, Anne b. 1700 and Sarah b. 1702, who died two weeks after her baptism. Named in the Association Oaths Roll of 1695.

Henry II (1654-171X) Son of James II. His wife's name is not known but their two boys were: *Henry* b. 1680 and *James* b. 169X. Henry was mentioned in the Association Oaths Roll of 1695.

Joseph I (165X-17XX) Another entry in the register which we cannot place within the tree. Married Ann *Sparding* in 1670, no children recorded.

G – **Henry III** (1680-1729) His wife was Sarah and they had two children: Sarah b. 1713 and Henry b. 1718, who died at age four.

James III (169X-17XX) Father of James IV, no further details.

George IV (168X-1765) *CW 1755, 1765. OP 1751, 1762.* Died having just finished his year as churchwarden. Acted as executor of the will of William Russell, husbandman, of 1724.

Robert I (168X-17XX) Another entry which we cannot place within the tree proper. Wife's name not shown but a daughter, Ann, was baptised 1711.

H – **James IV** (173X-1800) Freeholder. *OP 1783. CW 1787/8.* Called to act as executor in the will of William Daborn, dated 1772. His wife was Ann and they had nine children: William b. 1759, *Henry* b. 1760, John b. 1762, died aged eight, George b. 1770, Sarah b. 1772 and *Richard* b. 1774. Mother Ann's death was not registered but James married again, in 1782, Sarah *Cooke* and they had five more children: Elizabeth b. 1782, James b. 1783, *Henry* b. 1785, Mary b. 1788 and George b. 1792.

I – **Thomas III** (176X-1805) Married Elizabeth *Grove* in 1789 and they had eight children: James b. 1790, Ann b. 1792, William b. 1793, Thomas b. 1797, George b. 1799, who died nine years old, Henry b. 1801 and John b. 1803. Both parents were buried within five days of each other and the register reads: 'Smallpox'.

Henry V (1760-1842) Second son of James IV. His wife was Sarah *Loveland* and they had two children: Henry b. 1807 and Harriett b. 1805 (baptised in Horsell) who married John *Daborn* in 1844 in Horsell church.

Richard I (1774-18XX) His marriage (by licence) to yet another Sarah *Loveland* in 1800 at Bisley church presents a question: both were shown as resident in Bisley yet they had to obtain a licence to marry there. We can say with certainty, therefore, that they were both Chobham residents in reality.

Henry VI (1785-18XX) Yet another son of James IV. Married Elizabeth *Smither* in 1810 and they had two children: *James* b. 1810 and Henry b. 1811.

J – **James V** (1810-18XX) Agricultural labourer. His wife was Ann and they had nine children: James Richard b. 1832, William b. 1835, Ann Elizabeth b. 1837, Richard b. 1839, who died two weeks after his baptism, Emma b. 1840, John b. 1843, who died five days after his baptism, George b. 1844, Elizabeth b. 1848 and Peter-Eady b. 1850.

We also found another James Martin, from Bisley, but want to show him here as all his 10 children were baptised in Chobham (the family lived in Grants Green Cottage (spelt in 1841 'Grance Green').

James (1801-18XX) His wife was Maria, from Woking, whom he married in 1825 at Woking, and their 10 children were: Richard b. 1829, William b. 1831, died aged four years, James b. 1834, died six days after his baptism, Mary Ann b. 1835, Thomas b. 1838, Jemima b. 1840, Eliza b. 1840, Sarah b. 1844, died 11 months old, Esther b. 1848 and George-Henry b. 1850.

Pinson alias Pynsonne

A – **Thomas I** (152X-159X) In the Chobham Park accounts listed as a labourer. Two of his sons (X) were shown in the Muster Lists of 1575 and 1583.

30. The east side of the High Street before some of the old houses were replaced by modern shop fronts.

31. The 1853 cannon. This now stands in front of 'Cannon Cottage', near to the parish cross.

B –   **William I** (155X-161X) In the 1575 Muster an 'Archer of the best sorte' and in 1583 again an 'archer select'. His brother (X) was:

Henry I (155X-162X) An 'archer of the best sorte' in 1575.

C –   **Richard I** (158X-1656) His burial was entered in the parish register. His son (X) was:

D –   **Richard II** (161X-1675) We only know of him because his burial was entered in the parish register.

Henry I (163X-1714) Married in 1659, his wife was Susannah and they had six children: Susan b. 1663, Sarah b. 1666, Mary b. 1669, died a spinster aged 30, William b. 1674 and Joan b. 1684, buried 10 years old.

John I (162X-1722) Married Elizabeth *Field*, 1653, in Bisley and they had seven children: George b. 1657, buried nine years old, James b. 1660, Elizabeth b. 1663, John whose baptism was not entered, Margaret b. 1669 and her twin sister Susanna (John and the twins died and were buried a week after the twins' baptism), and another girl, Mary b. 1666. Mother Elizabeth's burial was given at the date of her three children's burial.

E –   **William II** (164X-1714) *CW 1691*. His wife was Ann and their daughter, Ann, b. 1670, died at age 14 as a spinster.

John II (166X-1710) Married Elizabeth *Goring* 1691 and their only child, Jane was buried 1720.

The last of the families whose members we found engaged in the works in 1545-6 and which later provided churchwardens was the Attlee family.

Attlee

William was *churchwarden* in *1675* and again in *1698*. Four members of the family were mentioned in the Chobham Park Works reports: John, Allen, Thomas and William. The parish register shows the baptism of Mary Attlee as daughter of William and we also found, in a declaration dated 1659, the name of John Attlee, where he was shown as deceased when his widow had married again, to Richard Davy, junior. There were no further traces of this family in later times.

As with the Attlee family, there were a few families who held the post of churchwarden before 1730 but about whom we could not find enough later details to enable us to present them in tree form: Bedborough (1702/3, 1709); Bradford (1688); Corffe (1683, 1695); Edsaw (1702, 1709); Hall (1660/1); Jolly (1708). The dates in brackets are the dates of election as churchwarden.

We have now exhausted the families whose members could be traced to Henry VIII's time and we found holding official posts in the village before 1730, but here is another equally-old Chobham family, one of whose members held office after that date.

Stevenson

A –   **John I** (151X-157X) John supplied a cart five times for the Chobham Park works, more than any other farmer. He also supplied 'ewe' (yew) boughs.

John Stevenson obviously must have been an important farmer in Henry VIII's time though it is surprising not to have found his family's name in the various lists we have searched between 1560 and the beginning of the 18th century. So we had to give our next member of the family the generation letter G.

G –   **Robert I** (171X-177X) His wife was Mary and three boys were baptised for them: *James* b. 1743, *Daniel* b. 1746 and *James* b. 1763.

Joseph (172X-177X) His wife was Ann Spong whom we know through her uncle's will dated

1760. William Spong, yeoman, calls her his niece and mentions Ann Stevenson, spinster, as living with him as housekeeper. We assume that young Ann was Joseph's daughter.

H – **Mark I** (174X-1802) Bricklayer. Married Elizabeth *Emmett* in 1770 and their six children were: Mary b. 1770, *James* b. 1772, Elizabeth b. 1774, *Richard* b. 1778, Mark b. 1781 and William b. 1782, died a bachelor aged twenty-two. Father Mark was the first Stevenson to be a bricklayer, a craft which many members of his family took up.

Daniel I (177X-18XX) Married Mary *Adams* in 1797; no children known.

James I (1743-1825) Tailor. Married Sarah *Beauchamp* in 1781 and their seven children were: Elizabeth b. 1782, *James* b. 1784, *William* b. 1786, Sarah b. 1787, Mary b. 1789, *George* b. 1792 and Hannah who is mentioned in her father's will but was apparently not baptised. In his will, father James appointed his 'friend' James Stevenson as trustee.

William I (17XX-1779) His wife was Jane. No children known.

Richard I (17XX-1796) His wife was Jane who died in 1801, described as 'his wife', although he was dead at that time (an error which was very rare indeed in the register). No children known.

John II (1737-1814) Shown in the 1801 census and again in 1811. No further details.

I – **James II** (1772-1845) Bricklayer in 1820, 'independent' in 1831. Married Ann *Stevens* in 1803 and their five children were: Eleanor b. 1804, Mary b. 1805, James b. 1808, died a bachelor in 1833, Eliza b. 1810 and Ann b. 1811, died a spinster 1844. His younger brother was:

Richard II (1778-18XX) Bricklayer. His wife was Frances but neither their marriage nor the children's baptisms are shown in the Chobham register. Their five children were: William b. 1813, died a bachelor 1841, Richard b. 1815, Elizabeth b. 1818, James b. 1820 and *Joseph* b. 1823.

James III (1784-1837) Labourer. *OP 1825.* Eldest son of James I. Married Ann *Giles* in 1813. (Ann, after the early death of her husband, was shown as 'charwoman' in the 1851 Census.) Their five children were: Mary b. 1815, George b. 1817, Ann b. 1822, died four months old, James b. 1824 and Charlotte b. 1830. His two younger brothers follow:

William II (1786-18XX) Bricklayer. His wife was Ann and their six children were: William b. 1814, Ann b. 1816, Mary b. 1819, died aged four, Charles b. 1821, Eliza b. 1824 and George b. 1826.

George I (1792-1831) Bricklayer. Married Elizabeth *Wattingham* in 1823, who died eight months after her husband. Their three children were: Henry b. 1824, George b. 1827, died two years old, Stephen b. 1828, died 14 months after his baptism. In his will father George appointed his wife and 'uncle James, farmer in Chobham' as executors. This 'uncle' could only be James b. 1763, the youngest son of Robert I – we have no other details about this James.

All three sons of James I were bricklayers.

Alexander

A – **Thomas I** (165X-172X) We do not know his wife's name but their six children were: *Thomas* b. 1685, Judith b. 1687, *John* b. 1690, Joan b. 1691, buried three weeks old, *Arthur* b. 1692 and Ann b. 1695, married Martin *Beauchamp* in 1729.

B – **Thomas II** (1685-1766) Carpenter. *CW 1742-3.* (Note: He was the first craftsman to be elected churchwarden.) Married Ann *Friend* in 1727 and their two children were: *Thomas* b. 1729 and Anne b. 1732 married John Rogers in 1778.

John I (1690-1757) Carpenter and builder. His wife was Mary but we do not know of any children.

Arthur I (1692-17XX) His wife's name was not known but their one son was Thomas, whose burial was shown 'under Arthur Alexander's son' in 1718.

C – **Thomas III** (1729-17XX) We know only the names of his two children: Sarah and Thomas. No further details.

The following two members belong to this generation but we do not know their fathers.

Edward I (174X-1828) Gardener (1831 Census). His wife was Elizabeth who died aged 69 in 1812. Their only known child was Elizabeth who married William *Berkshire* in Ripley in 1809 and died aged 66 in 1840.

John II (17XX-1789) His wife's name was not known but their daughter was Elizabeth who married Morris *Bailey* in 1767 and died aged 87 in 1826. In his will, father John bequeathed £100 to his daughter, who was described there as 'his only child'.

D – **Thomas IV** (17XX-18XX) Butcher (1831 Census). We assume that he was the son of Thomas III. His wife was Louisa and we know of two children: Louisa, whose burial record in 1832 gives her age as three, and George b. 1831, buried two weeks old.

We are now starting families which were first recorded in Chobham in Queen Elizabeth's time:

Luff alias Luffe

A – **Bartholomew I** (153X-159X) Adventured 2s. in the Queen's Lottery, 1567.

B – **Bartholomew II** (157X-1666) In the Lay Subsidy Rolls of 1620-1641, shown with £1 for land. The same amount was also shown as his Present to Charles I in 1626. In 1661 he was shown as innholder (*White Hart*) when he gave 5s. as his Present to Charles II, and his abode, presumably the *White Hart*, was recorded as having six hearths in 1664. His wife was Alice, who died 1665.

Joseph I (162X-1666) Perhaps Bartholomew's brother – married Susan in 1656 and they had one son, Joseph b. 1659. Susan died in 1685. He was shown as 'weaver' in 1664 and his house was exempted from payment of the Hearth Tax.

Robert I (16XX-1669) Labourer in 1661 when he gave 1s. as his Present to Charles II. Lived in a house with two hearths in 1664.

William I (164X-170X) Yeoman in 1703. *CW 1676-8 and 1680*. His wife was Alice and they had eight children: Alice b. 1669, died 14 months old, Mary b. 1671, Alice b. 1673, *William* b. 1676, *Bartholomew* b. 1679, John b. 1681, died a bachelor 1716, and the twins, Joseph and Ann b. 1684, but Joseph died one month old. (Father William issued the token, *see* p. 43.)

C – **William II** (1676-1728) Called 'the elder' and said to have been a 'Barber and Chyrurgeon'. His wife was Ann and they had three children: Ann b. 1698, who died at age five, William b. 1700, who married Mary *Stelman* (as her kinswoman, Sarah Stelman showed in her will – *see above* pp. 43, 45). His brother was:

Bartholomew III (1679-1730) His wife was Joan and they had 12 children: Bartholomew b. 1707, John b. 1709, died three years old, Mary b. 1711, John b. 1713, died five days after his baptism, Jane b. 1714, William b. 1717, Ann b. 1720, James b. 1722, died nine months old, Alice b. 1724, died nearly two years old, Richard b. 1730, who was baptised four months after his father's death.

Shrubb

A –   **John I** (154X-159X) Adventured 2s. 6d. in the Queen's Lottery of 1567 and in the Muster of 1583 a 'bilman of the second Sorte'.

Roger I (154X-1592) In the Lay Subsidy list of 1571 assessed at £3 for goods and a 'bilman of the second sorte' in 1583. In the Lay Subsidy lists of 1589 to 1590 assessed at £4 for goods. Acted as overseer of the will of John Newman, husbandman dated 1589.

B –   **John II** (157X-164X) In the Lay Subsidy lists of 1620 to 1628 assessed at £1 for land, agreed to lend Charles I £1 in 1626.

Thomas I (156X-161X) In the Lay Subsidy lists of 1593 to 1595 shown as having taken over from his father Roger I. Witnessed the will of Elizabeth Woods, widow in 1595. Named in the Muster List of 1596 and acted also as witness in the will of Henry Woods in 1603.

C –   **Thomas II** (164X-1700) His wife was Elizabeth and they have seven children: Frances b. 1684, Rebecca b. 1690, Joan b. 1692, Hannah, whose burial was entered in 1690, Thomas b. 1694, Edward b. 1697 and Ann b. 1699, died at age nine. Lived in a house of three hearths in 1664 and gave 5s. as his Free Present to Charles II in 1661.

John III (162X-1693) *CW 1656/7 and 1675.* Gave 5s. as his Present to Charles II in 1661 and his house was shown with three hearths in 1664. In the Muster List of 1684 a 'person to find arms' (with Thomas Shrubb shown as 'soldier'). Also mentioned in the Muster List of 1675.

Thomas III (162X-168X) His wife was Mary and they had six children: Mary b. 1657, Susan b. 1661, John b. 1664, died 10 days old, Hannah b. 1665, died a spinster 1674, Thomas b. 1668 and John b. 1671.

Henry I (164X-171X) His wife was Joan and they had two children: Elizabeth b. 1687 and Joan b. 1704.

The Association Oaths Roll of 1695 shows two Shrubbs: Thomas who would be Thomas II and Daniel whom we could not find anywhere else.

Norwood alias Norrard and Norrod

A –   **Arthur I** (153X-158X) Adventured 3s. in the Queen's Lottery of 1567 and witnessed the will of Andrew Woods, tailor, in 1565. In the Muster of 1583 an 'archer select'. His daughter, Elizabeth was born in 1587 as shown in the Bishop's Transcript of that year.

B –   **Robert I** (155X-1600) In the Lay Subsidy Roll of 1571 assessed at £6 for goods, as he was also valued from 1589 to 1595. Acted as witness to the will of Robert Woods, tailor, in 1596. A 'bilman of the second sorte' in the Muster List of 1583. In his will, dated 1600, he mentioned his wife Alice and four children: sons John and Arthur, and daughters Agnes, wife of William *Burchett*, and Elizabeth, wife of Andrew *Woods*.

John I (156X-161X) Acted, like his kinsman Robert I, as witness in the will of Robert Woods in 1596.

C –   **Arthur II** (158X-1630) In the Lay Subsidy lists of 1620-1628 valued at £1 for land; in 1626 he gave the value of £1 for land to be lent to Charles I.

John II (161X-1689) Tanner. *CW 1682* and his house, in 1664, had two hearths. His wife was Marty who died in 1661, having born a girl, Amy (who herself had died in 1659). John married again, and his second wife was Alice who bore four children: John

b. 1663, died a bachelor 1717, Agnes b. 1667, *Arthur* b. 1669, Mary b. 1673 and Hester b. 1675. Mother Alice died 1678. He gave 5s. as his Present to Charles II.

Robert II (159X-165X) In the Lay Subsidy lists of 1620-1641 valued at £6 for goods.

D – **Arthur III** (1669-17XX) His wife was Anne and their son was Arthur b. 1718, died five months old.

Hudson

A – **Owen I** (152X-158X) Adventured 2s. in the Queen's Lottery in 1567.

B – **Owen II** (158X-1663) His widow was shown in the Hearth Tax list of 1664 living in a house with three hearths. Owen was also a beneficiary of the will of William Beauchamp, dated 1610, as well as his children: *Owen*, Edward, Jane and Mary who each are to receive £20.

C – **Owen III** (159X-1688) His wife was Frances and they had five children: Richard b. 1654, George b. 1657, John b. 1660, Elizabeth b. 1672, married Richard *Smither* in 1698, and Jane b. 1674. As his Present to Charles I in 1626 he was assessed at £3 for goods. In the Muster List of 1684 shown as 'person to finde arms'.

D – **Owen IV** (164X-1731) *CW 1718*. Apparently the eldest child of Owen III who was baptised before the start of our new register. His wife was Elizabeth and they had three children: Mary b. 1676, died a spinster in 1762, *Owen* b. 1677 and Amy b. 1680, married Edward *Lloyd*.

E – **Owen V** (1677-17XX) He was mentioned in the Association Oaths Roll of 1695. No further details known.

Thomas I (1776-1842) Shopkeeper. Married Ann *Fladgate*, of Horsell, in 1794 and they had 10 children: Ann b. 1794, married John *Burchett* 1830, *James* b. 1796, Richard b. 1798, *Thomas* b. 1800, Robert b. 1803, died aged six, Henry b. 1805, died six months old, Mary b. 1807, died 16 years old Henry b. 1809, died an infant, Sarah b. 1810, married W. *Isaacs* in 1837, and William b. 1814.

William I (17XX-18XX) His wife was Katherine and their daughter was Henrietta b. 1725.

Thomas II (178X-1820) His wife was Ann and they had five children: William b. 1810, Thomas b. 1812, died aged five months, Ann b. 1813, Mary b. 1816 and John b. 1819.

F – **Thomas III** (1800-18XX) Grocer, coal and corn merchant. Son of Thomas I. Married Ann *Lipscomb* in 1830 and they had seven children: Thomas b. 1829, Juliana b. 1830, died a spinster 1850, Mary J. b. 1833, Emma b. 1836, died 1851 aged 14, Alice b. 1839, died two days after her baptism and Robert b. 1834, died aged four. His elder brother was:

F – **James I** (1796-1832) Grocer. Married Leah *Bolton* in Cranleigh 1826 and they had three children: William b. 1827, Mary Ann b. 1829, died nine years old and Richard b. 1831.

We found in the list of the Free Present to Charles II in 1661, an entry that John Hudson offered a sum of 10s. but we were unable to trace John to a proper place in the tree.

Spot alias Spott

A – **Henry I** (155X-162X) Shown in the Muster of 1583 as a 'Bilman of the second sorte'.

B – **Henry II** (161X-1661) Married Margarite *Field*, a Chobham girl, at Bisley in 1646 with one child: Frances b. 1656. Henry's wife died 1659 but we suspect that they also had a boy, *Henry*, who was baptised before 1654.

Richard I (162X-1668) Taylor, as described in the Hearth Tax list of 1664. One child only known as having been baptised, Thomas b. 1655, who died at age seven, and a daughter, only registered at her burial in 1705.

John I (161X-166X) *CW 1639.* Nothing further known. But this could be the John Spot whose marriage at Bisley to Joane *Edmead* is entered in 1642 in the old Bisley register.

C –   **Henry III** (164X-16XX) Son (X) of Henry II. Wife's name unknown but they had four children: *Henry* b. 1671, William b. 1673, Mary b. 1676, died three weeks old, and another son (name illegible in register) baptised 1678.

Daniel I (163X-1686) His wife was Mary and they had nine children: Daniel b. 1669, Jane b. 1671, Richard b. 1673, John b. 1675, Margret b. 1677, died a spinster 1702, *William* b. 1678, George b. 1680, died a bachelor 1712, Joseph b. 1683 and Elizabeth b. 1686, died four weeks old.

D –   **Henry IV** (1671-173X) Son of Henry III. His wife was Ann who died 1721 after the births of two girls: Ann b. 1706, died a spinster 1724, and Mary b. 1709.

William I (1678-1711) Son of Daniel I. Married Mary *Spong*, a Chobham girl, at Pirbright church, in 1705, who died in 1717 after the birth of one girl: Sarah b. 1709.

Taylor

A –   **John I** (151X-157X) Adventured 5s. in the Queen's Lottery, 1567.

B –   **Thomas I** (155X-160X) In the Lay Subidy list of 1571 assessed at £3 for goods. In the Muster of 1583 a 'bilman of the second sorte' and in another Muster List shown as 'archer select'. In the Lay Subsidy lists of 1589 to 1595 his assessment had gone up to £5 for goods.

Henry I (154X-159X) Adventured 3s. in the Queen's Lottery, 1567.

C –   **John II** (158X-165X) In the Lay Subsidy lists of 1620-1641 assessed at £4 for goods and in 1626 his name shows an amount of £4 as his gift to Charles I.

Henry II His wife was Damaris and their two children were: Susan (158X-1664) b. 1656 and Owen b. 1658. A boy Henry was shown as buried in 1662. In the Lay Subsidy lists of 1620 to 1641 assessed at £2 for land and in 1626 his name was set against an amount of £2 as his gift to Charles I.

D –   **George I** (162X-169X) Married in 1656 and they had seven children (wife's name not known): *George* b. 1655, *John* b. 1659, *Henry* b. 1662, William b. 1665, Damaris b. 1668, Thomas b. 1672, died a week after his baptism, and Deborah b. 1673. In 1661 he gave 6s. 8d. as his Free Present to Charles II and he lived in a house with two hearths in 1664.

Henry III (162X-1694) *CW 1656/7.* His wife was Elizabeth and they had four children: Mary b. 1682, Henry b. 1686, Jane b. 1690 and Anne b. 1695. In 1664 lived in a house with three hearths.

Richard I (162X-1668) His wife was Elizabeth and their only son, Richard was buried in 1687. He lived in a house with one hearth in 1664.

Gabriel I (162X-1689) Married Catherine in 1657 and the couple were mentioned, as beneficiaries, in the will of George Stelman, dated 1665. They had six children: George b. 1657, Sarah b. 1660, Hannah b. 1662, Damaris b. 1664, died a spinster aged 46, Ann b. 1667, died a spinster aged 55, Jane b. 1670 and Maurice b. 1676.

D –   **James I** (163X-1716) Married Mary *Fletcher* in 1664 and they had six children: Anne b. 1665, Mary b. 1667, married Thomas *Woods* 1697, Jane b. 1670, Mary b. 1672, James b. 1676 and another girl, Martha, entered as buried in 1717. Mother Mary died 1705 and James married Clemence who died in 1714.

Robert I (164X-1690) His wife's name was not known but they had seven children: Robert b. 1672, Hannah b. 1674, Mary b. 1675, John b. 1678, *Henry* b. 1682, *James* b. 1685 and Ann b. 1688, who died four months old.

E – **George II** (1655-1719) Eldest son of George I. Married Ann *Gunner* in 1692 and they had two children: *George* b. 1693 and Ann b. 1695. Mother Ann died 1709. His two brothers follow:

John III (1659-17XX) We know only that John had a son *John* b. 1693.

Henry IV (1662-1722) His wife was Elizabeth *Hone* and their only child was Elizabeth b. 1706.

Richard II (165X-1687) Shown in the Muster List of 1675.

Henry V (1682-1717) Son of Robert I. His wife was Mary and their six children were: Mary b. 1709, Jane b. 1710, Henry b. 1713, in which year his elder sister Jane had died just three years old, *John* b. 1715, and twins William and Jane b. 1717.

James II (1685-17XX) Another son of Robert I; his wife was Maria and their only child was Monica b. 1742.

F – **John IV** (1693-17XX) Son of John III. Married Elizabeth *Bridist* of Chertsey in 1745. No children known.

George III (1693-17XX) Son of George II. His wife was Mary and their daughter Mary was baptised 1723.

G – **James III** (171X-17XX) His wife was Sarah and they had seven children: Sarah b. 1738, Edward b. 1739, *John* b. 1742, Henry b. 1745, George b. 1747, Elizabeth b. 1748 and Frances b. 1761, married William *Brookman* 1780.

Edward I (1710-1790) His wife was Ann and their three children were: Edward b. 1739, Ann b. 1740 and another boy whose name in the register was illegible, b. 1742. Mother Ann was entered in the register as buried in 1789 from the workhouse.

John V (1715-17XX) His wife was Mary and they had two children: Elizabeth b. 1742, married Robert *Thomas* 1770, and *Francis*, whose baptism we could not find, born about 1760 (X).

H – **John VI** (1742-17XX) Son of James III. Married Ann *Turner* in 1760 and they had three children: John b. 1767, *William* b. 1770 and *John* b. 1774.

James IV (1750-1836) Married Ann *Crane* in 1774 and they had one son, *James*, b. 1776.

Francis I (176X-1805) Son of John V. Married Hannah *Smither* 1787 and they had three children: Jane b. 1787, John b. 1790 and Hannah b. 1794. Mother Hannah died 1795 and Francis married again in 1796, Elizabeth *Stevenson*, who bore him no children. Of the children of his first wife, John died aged 16 and Hannah died aged thirteen.

James V (1765-1824) Yeoman (farmed Bowling Green Farm). Married Mary *Baker* in 1784 and their only child was *James* born approximately 1785 (X).

Henry VI (1762-1850) Married Sarah *Mitchell* in Bisley in 1785 and they had 11 children: *Henry* b. 1787, *James* b. 1788, Sarah b. 1790, *Frank* b. 1793, *William* b. 1795, John b. 1797, Mary b. 1799, Thomas b. 1800, died four weeks old, Martha b. 1802, died six months old, Hannah b. 1805, died aged seven months, and *Richard* b. 1806.

I – **William I** (1770-1846) Son of John VI. Yeoman. Married Sarah *Martin* in 1791. They had eight children: Charlotte b. 1791, died four months old, Charlotte b. 1793, married Maurice *Church* 1824, Mary b. 1797, *William* b. 1800, John b. 1802, died a bachelor aged 26, James b. 1805, *Henry* b. 1808 and Ann b. 1811, married John *Harding*

1830. Father William acted as executor of the will of William Knight dated 1833. His younger brother was:

John VII (1774-1848) Shoemaker. Married Ann *Smith* 1795. They had eight children: *John* b. 1796, Mary b. 1797, James b. 1799, Susanna b. 1802, *William* b. 1805, Richard b. 1807 and Jane b. 1809. Mother Ann died 1815 and John married again in 1827, to Hannah *Giles* of Aldershot. They had five children: Arthur b. 1829, George b. 1831, died three years old, Henry b. 1833, Maurice b. 1835, died aged 16, and Thomas b. 1837, died nine months old.

James VI (1776-18XX) Son of James IV. Labourer. Married Sarah *Bignell* in Ashtead, 1793 and they had 12 children: James b. 1796, William b. 1798, Martha b. 1800, James b. 1802, died aged 12, *Henry* b. 1805, Francis b. 1807, Isaac b. 1809, *Stephen* b. 1811, *Richard* b. 1813, William b. 1815, George b. 1817 and the last child, Henry, b. 1822.

William II (1777-18XX) Labourer. Died in the Workhouse. Married Mary *Sturt* 1802, in Abinger, and they had eight children: Henry b. 1807, Lucy b. 1809, married W. *Castle* in 1828, Charlotte b. 1811, Martha b. 1813, Mary b. 1815, Hannah b. 1818, *Samuel* b. 1821 and Ann b. 1825.

James VII (1790-18XX) Son of James V. Labourer. His wife was Sarah who died 1808 without a child. James married again 1815 Mary *Newman*, and yet again in 1829 a widow Elizabeth *Gold*.

Henry VII (1787-18XX) Eldest son of Henry VI. His wife was Ann *Stevenson* 1811 and they had 10 children: Henry b. 1811, Frances b. 1813, Martha b. 1816, Sarah b. 1818, *William* b. 1820, Mary Ann b. 1822, died four months old, Stephen b. 1824, Lois b. 1826, Ann b. 1828 and Charlotte b. 1830. His four brothers follow:

James VIII (1788-18XX) Labourer. Married Sarah *Hone* 1814. They had six children: Sophia b. 1815, *James* b. 1817, William b. 1819, Mary Ann b. 1827, married Stephen *Shorter* 1847, and two more girls who were apparently not baptised: Esther born 1831 and Caroline born 1835.

Francis II (1793-18XX) Labourer. Married Elizabeth *Cotterel* in Woking, they had 11 children: William b. 1814, Sarah b. 1816, married James *Holmes* 1836, James b. 1818, Martha b. 1820, Henry b. 1822, Mary b. 1824, married Stephen *Ottaway* 1845, John b. 1826, Eliza b. 1830, Stephen b. 1833, Harriet b. 1837 and Louisa born, not baptised, 1839. (Harriet died aged seven days.)

William III (1795-18XX) Labourer. Married Susanna *Parfett* in Guildford 1816, they had nine children: Mary b. 1817, James b. 1819, Samuel b. 1820, Joseph b. 1823, William b. 1823, died aged two months, Sarah b. 1827, Richard b. 1831, died three months old, Jemima b. 1833 and Eliza b. 1836.

Richard III (1806-18XX) Coal and corn labourer. Married Elizabeth *Hayward* of Horsell 1829 and they had five children: James b. 1829, John b. 1832, Henry b. 1834, William b. 1838 and George b. 1847.

J –   **William IV** (1800-18XX) Gardener. Son of William I. Married Sarah *Field* 1834 and they had five children: William b. 1835, Eliza b. 1837, Alfred b. 1839, George-Henry b. 1841 and Mary-Jane b. 1843.

John VIII (1796-18XX) Son of John VII. Married Frances *Bush* in 1817. They had six children: Mary b. 1818, died aged 17, Martha b. 1819, Sarah b. 1822, died aged two, Margaret b. 1825, David b. 1825, died four years old and Caroline b. 1828, died two months old. His brother was:

William V (1805-18XX) Brickmaker. Married Eliza *Sleet* 1827, they had six children: Sarah

b. 1827, died one month old, Charlotte b. 1828, died seven years old, James b. 1831, William b. 1834, Martha b. 1837 and George-Henry b. 1841.

Richard IV (1813-18XX) Son of James VI. Married Catherine *Collyer* 1835. No known children. His two elder brothers follow:

Henry VIII (1805-18XX) Married Mary Ann *Collyer* 1830 and they had four children: William b. 1831, died three months old, Frances b. 1835, died three months old and Eliza b. 1840.

Stephen I (1811-18XX) Labourer. Married Rebecca *Smith* 1830. They had seven children: Mary b. 1830, married Jonathan *Duffin* 1850, Stephen b. 1831, William b. 1832, Caroline b. 1834, Emma b. 1837, James b. 1839, died four months old and Eliza b. 1840.

James IX (1815-18XX) Farmer. Married Lucy *Everard* in Brixton. They had seven children, the first two of whom were not entered as baptised (they were born 1837 and 1839 and were apparently 'just registered'). Their names were James-Daniel and John. The others were Harriet-Laura b. 1842, James b. 1844, Charlotte b. 1845, George b. 1847 and Carla-Ann b. 1849.

William VI (1820-18XX) Labourer. Son of Henry VII. Married Lois *Crane* in 1846; they had two children: Esther b. 1847 and Lois b. 1850.

James X (1817-18XX) Labourer. Son of James VIII. Married Sarah *Gosden*, née Sleet, 1842 and they had five children: James b. 1842 (father James was now shown as 'farmer'), George-Henry b. 1844, Esther b. 1848, died aged two, and Fanny b. 1850.

Samuel I (1821-18XX) Labourer. Son of William II. Married Rhoda *Harding* 1843. They had four children. Hannah b. 1844, William-Henry b. 1846, Samuel b. 1848 and Ellen b. 1850.

Henry IX (1808-1841) Youngest son of William I. Married Sarah *Chittey* in 1828 in St Lawrence's church, but their first three children were shown in the Baptist chapel register: Ann, born 1828, James born 1831 and William born 1832. Their fourth child, William, born 1838 was apparently registered in the Registrar's book; he died seven years old.

James XI (1790-18XX) Farmer (Bowling Green Farm). Married Charlotte *Newman* in 1812 and they had eight children: William b. 1813, James b. 1815, John b. 1817, Charlotte b. 1821, died one year old, Stephen b. 1824, Martha b. 1826 and Mary b. 1830. These seven children had been baptised in St Lawrence's but Charles born 1832 was shown in the Baptist chapel records and the last child, Lucy, born 1838, was entered by the official registrar.

Hone

A – **Thomas I** (154X-161X) Shown in the 1583 Muster List as 'Bilman of the second sorte'.

John I (153X-1600) His will, dated January 1600, mentions his wife Millisent as executrix and his son Robert. John was also recorded as witness of the will of John Felde of Bisley, husbandman. A Joseph Hone was a beneficiary of the same will but we could not place him within our tree.

B – **Robert I** (157X-163X) Son of John I. His son (X) was:

C – **Robert II** (161X-1661) His widow was shown as 'labourer's widow' in the Hearth Tax list of 1664, in a house of one hearth and exempted from payment. She was called Faby (Phoebe?) and their two children were: George b. 1655 and Sarah b. 1658, who died aged three.

D – **Fabian I** (163X-17XX) His wife was Susan who died soon after their marriage in 1661. Fabian was mentioned in an indenture of 1650.

John II (163X-17XX) Married Jane *Wells* 1661. No children.

E – **John III** (167X-17XX) Married Ann *Spong* 1719. No children.

Richard I (168X-1711) Married Amy *Burchett* 1710 and their son was Richard b. 1711, who died, after his father's death, in 1712.

William I (168X-174X) Married Mary *Smith* at Bisley in 1720 and their two boys were: William b. 1724 and John b. 1727. Mother Mary was buried one month after the birth of her son John.

Henry I (169X-17XX) His wife was Elizabeth and they had two boys: *Henry* b. 1724 and *James* b. 1728.

F – **Henry II** (1724-179X) Son of Henry I. Married Ann *Bartholomew* in 1758 and their six children were: Ann b. 1756, *Henry* b. 1760, *John* b. 1762, Katherine b. 1765, Elizabeth b. 1767 and James b. 1771. Father Henry acted as witness of the will of Richard Lee, retired farmer (of Biddle Farm), dated 1773, and was a beneficiary of the will of his father-in-law John Bartholomew the same year. His younger brother was:

James I (1728-178X) Married Mercy *Chitty* 1752 and their two sons were *John* b. 1756 and Ambrose b. 1761.

James II (172X-179X) Married Amy *Reed* in 1740 and their son was *James* b. 1741.

G – **Henry III** (1760-1834) Son of Henry II. His wife was Mary and they had five children: Sarah b. 1791, *John* b. 1794, *Henry* b. 1797 and Phoebe b. 1799, who died nine months old.

John IV (1762-1813) *OP 1791, 1799. CW 1794, 1800/01.* Son of James I. Married Sarah *Lidger* 1786 and they had six children: Sarah b. 1786, married William *Sanders* 1809, Mary b. 1787, married William *Budd* 1805, *William* b. 1790, *John* b. 1791, *James* b. 1793 and *Joel* b. 1795. Mother Sarah died one year after the birth of her sixth child and father John married again, at Byfleet church in 1802, Ann *Booth* and they had four children: Arthur b. 1803, died aged 10, *Stephen* b. 1805, Ann b. 1807 and George b. 1812. John was described in the will, dated 1794, of Thomas Turner, weaver, as 'friend'.

G – **James III** (1741-1820) Son of James II. His wife was Hannah and their daughter was Elizabeth b. 1793. James was witness of the will of widow Mary Fenn dated 1811.

H – **Henry IV** (1797-18XX) Son of Henry III. Farmer (Satchells Farm). Married Mary *Crane* 1819. Their nine children were: George b. 1821, Martha b. 1823, Stephen b. 1826, Hannah b. 1828, Ellen b. 1831, John-William b. 1831, Ann b. 1833, Harriett b. 1835 and William b. 1839. His elder brother was:

John V (1794-18XX) Shoemaker. Married Jane *Hampton* at Horsell church in 1817 and they had 10 children: Caroline b. 1818, died 11 years old, Henry b. 1819, Hannah b. 1821, died three months old, Eliza b. 1823, died three months old, Eliza b. 1826, James b. 1828, George b. 1830, Jane-Ann b. 1832, Ann b. 1834 and John b. 1837.

William II (1790-18XX) *OP 1824. CW 1839-42.* Farmer (Fellow Green Farm). Eldest son of John IV. Married Harriet *Yates* of Bisley at Bisley church in 1815 and they had six children: Mary-Ann born Bisley 1816, married John *Chitty* 1842, *William* b. 1821, Harriet b. 1822, Ann b. 1824, died five months old, Jane b. 1825 and Sarah b. 1826. Mother Harriet died 1829 and William married again in 1831; his new wife was Mary *Daborn* and their three children were: Richard b. 1831, Alfred b. 1833 and Emily b. 1838. Son Alfred died aged seven. His four brothers follow:

John VI (1791-1835) Married Ann *Collyer* 1817 at St Mary's, Guildford, and their two children were: John b. 1818 and William b. 1822. Mother Ann was a witness of the will of Dr. Robert Harrup, surgeon, in 1821.

James IV (1793-18XX) His wife was Elizabeth. No children.

Joel I (1795-18XX) *OP 1845.* Farmer (Burrow Hill Farm – also called Sleets Farm). Married Jane *Hill* in 1823 and their eight children were: *Joel* b. 1824, Sarah b. 1826, died three months old, William b. 1828, James b. 1830, John b. 1832, Ann b. 1834, Arthur b. 1836 and Rosina b. 1840. In the 1851 Census father Joel stated that he employed three sons as labourers on the farm.

Stephen I (1805-18XX) Shopkeeper. Married Mary *Blishen* in Brixton church in 1829 and their four children were: Stephen b. 1832, Arthur b. 1834, Frances b. 1836 and William b. 1840. Son Arthur died aged two and a half years old.

I – **William III** (1821-18XX) Farmer. Son of William II. His wife was Sarah from Windlesham and they had three children: Frederick born 1834 in Chobham, Elizabeth born in Windlesham 1848 and Herbert, again born in Chobham 1851. In the 1851 Census they state that in their house lived William's sister as a servant as well as another young girl and two labourers employed on the farm.

Joel II (1824-18XX) Grocer. Son of Joel I. His wife was Ann and they married in 1847.

Towers

A – **Humfrey I** (154X-162X) Shown as 'archer of the second sorte' in the Muster List of 159X (Temp. Eliz.) and in the Lay Subsidy Roll of 1589 assessed at 5s. 4d. His son (X) was:

B – **John I** (158X-1641) Tailor. His will dated 5 June 1641 is in the Hampshire Record Office. His son (X) was *John.* (Shown in a feoffment dated 1624.)

Daniel I (159X-1659) His wife was Rebecca who survived him by 23 years. Their son (X) was *Daniel.*

James I (160X-1659) His wife was Susannah and their daughter Susannah was born after her father's death – baptised 1661, died seven years old. Her baptismal entry reads: 'daughter of widdow Towers'.

Nicholas I (159X-1654) His wife was Judith who was shown in the Hearth Tax list of 1664 as 'widow Towers'. She survived her husband by 31 years.

Richard I (162X-1665) His wife's name was not known but their two children were: *Richard* b. 1654 and John b. 1657.

Philip I (161X-1675) His wife was Joan and their two children were: Ann b. 1655, died six months after her baptism, and another Anne b. 1657. The family was shown in 1664 in a house of three hearths. Mother Joan died 18 months after her second daughter's baptism.

C – **John II** (161X-1696) Chobham's 'Register' of 1655. Married Susanna *Bonsey* in 1669. No children known. Mentioned in an indenture dated 1689. His widow survived him by 21 years.

Daniel II (162X-1696) His wife was Alice and their four children were: Richard b. 1655, Margaret b. 1657, Ann b. 1660, died a spinster aged 17, and Elizabeth b. 1665. (An unnamed daughter was shown as buried in 1685 – Elizabeth?). Daniel was shown as 'labourer' in 1664 and exempt from paying Hearth Tax.

James II (163X-1693) Perhaps (X) son of James I. His wife was Honour and their six children were: *William* b. 1672, Joseph b. 1677, Anna b. 1682 and Bartholomew b. 1685. The register also shows the burials of two sons who had not been baptised:

Thomas, buried 1691, and John, buried 1692. Mother Honour died in 1690, father James in 1693 as did son Bartholomew. In the Free Present to Charles II, James was shown as 'yeoman' with a gift of 5s. and his house had one hearth in 1664. He was also shown in the Muster Lists of 1675 and 1684 as 'person to finde arms'.

Richard II (1654-17XX) Elder son of Richard I. Shown in the Association Oaths Roll of 1695.

Philipp II (164X-168X) Husbandman. Married Ann *Gray* in 1670 and their five children were: Ann b. 1671, Annie b. 1674, Philip b. 1677 and James b. 1684. Another son, John was entered as buried in 1680. We found the following indenture: Philip T., son of late Philip T. placed as an apprentice with Thomas Field, tailor, on 1 August 1688.

Thomas I (164X-1696) Married Elizabeth *Hudson* in 1673 and their three children were: Elizabeth b. 1674, died eight years old, *John* b. 1678 and another Elizabeth, entered as buried in 1683. Mother Elizabeth died in 1695, closely followed, 14 days later by her husband. Father Thomas was shown in the Muster List of 1684 as 'soldier'.

C – **Thomas II** (165X-17XX) As with Thomas I, we could not trace Thomas's father. Our Thomas married Elizabeth *Rogers* in 1683 and their three children were: Elizabeth b. 1684, died four months after her baptism, Thomas b. 1686 and Daniel b. 1688, died one month after his baptism.

D – **William I** (1672-1745) Eldest son of James II. His wife was Ann and their three children were: *William* b. 1714, *James* b. 1716 and Sarah b. 1720. Father William died intestate and his son James was shown as shoemaker and appointed joint administrator.

John III (1678-17XX) Only son of Thomas I. We only know that his son was buried in 1715.

E – **Daniel III** (165X-17XX) We assume (X) that he was a grandson of Daniel II and, as the eldest child, born and baptised before 1654. His wife was Sarah and their son was John b. 1703.

William II (1714-1794) Eldest son of William I. Married Mary *Collyer* in 1739 and their nine children were: Mary b. 1739, William b. 1741, *James* b. 1743, Henry b. 1746, Sarah b. 1749, *John* b. 1751, Anne b. 1757, George b. 1765 and William b. 1766. Mother Mary died in 1792 aged 73 and father William followed his wife two years later. Mother Mary was a beneficiary of her father's, Benjamin Collyer's, will, dated 1753. William's brother was:

James III (1716-1793) *OP 1771.* Shoemaker. Married Ann *Ridger*, a widow from Chertsey in 1741 and their five children were: Jane b. 1741, married Henry *Rycroft* from Rotherhithe in 1764, Ann b. 1744, died a spinster aged 77, Elizabeth b. 1748, married William *Collyer* in 1770 and William *Provost* in 1785, and Sarah b. 1753, died a spinster aged 21.

James IV (1720-1800) From Windlesham. Married Rebecca *Giles* in 1746 and their three children were: Rebecca b. 1747, *James* b. 1750 and John b. 1754.

F – **James V** (1743-18XX) Second son of William II. His wife was Mary and their daughter Mary was b. 1767. No further details. A younger brother of his was:

John IV (1751-1840) Married Hester *Cobbett* in 1775, who died 23 years after her marriage without offspring. Father John married again, his new wife was Margaret who died, again without having born a child, in 1809.

James VI (1750-18XX) Married Mary *Birdy* in 1775 and their seven children were: Mary b. 1775, Jenny b. 1776, Maria b. 1779, James b. 1781, died a bachelor aged 25,

William b. 1783, died six years old, John b. 1787 and David b. 1791, died aged three months.

We also found the following marriage which we cannot place in our tree:

Jesse Married Elizabeth *Neale* in 1788 – no further details.

In the Lay Subsidy Rolls of 1622 to 1628 we also found an entry which we could not place within the tree:

William Mentioned in 1622 and 1628 as assessed at £1 for lands. No other details.

Cobbett

A – **Thomas I** (154X-16XX) Mentioned in the 1583 Muster where he was shown as a 'Bilman select' and in the Lay Subsidy lists of 1593 to 1595 assessed at £3 for goods.

We could not trace the next two generations in Chobham but found that they had apparently moved to Bisley.

D – **Henry I** (163X-16XX) Mentioned in the 1684 Muster as 'person to find arms'. His wife's name is not known but they had six children: *Henry* b. 1661, *John* b. 1663, Elizabeth b. 1665, William b. 1667, Jonathan b. 1671 and Sarah b. 1675. Father Henry gave, as his Free Present to Charles II, 2s. 6d. in 1661.

E – **Henry II** (1661-1723) His wife was Mary and their two sons were: *Henry* b. 1708 and John b. 1712. His next brother follows.

John I (1663-17XX) We do not know his wife's name but there are two girls in the parish register: Ann b. 1690 (January) and Susanna b. 1690 (November). In the register was also a marriage of Mary Cobbet to William Patience in 1721 and we think that Mary could have been another daughter of John I.

There are no entries in the register referring to the other brothers of Henry and John but we found:

James I (168X-1717) Married Mary *Elliot* in 1715 and they had one son, James b. 1716. Here again we must add something which appears to fit into the tree: we have seen the wills of two members of the Cobbett family who seem to fit into this generation or, rather, family: *Richard* born (X) 1717 and Samuel born (X) 1718. But we are not sure whether they were, in fact, sons of James I.

F – **Henry III** (1708-17XX) Married Hannah *Gough* in 1735 and their two children were: *Henry* b. 1736 and Hannah b. 1740.

Richard I (171X-1778) *CW 1751*. Married Hannah *Woods* of Chobham in Bisley church in 1734 and in his very detailed will, dated 1767, he referred to a brother James (is this the son of James I b. 1716?) and a nephew Samuel (whom we accept to be the son of the following Samuel I – X). He also mentioned another member of the family, Edmund, and his daughter Elizabeth, without giving their relationship to himself. Yet another Cobbett was mentioned: Henry of Horsell, deceased in 1667, and his son Henry.

Samuel I (1718-1799) *OP 1772. CW 1774*. Richard I's brother whose will dated 1785 we have in full. He left most of his goods to three girls whom he called 'daughters-in-law': Mary the wife of James Fladgate, Sarah and Ann. From the context of the will it seems that they were the daughters of his wife's first marriage, who had died in 1782, three years before the date of the will. Strangely enough, father Samuel does not mention his son Samuel in his will, perhaps as his brother Richard had well provided for young Samuel.

G – **Henry IV** (1736-17XX) Married Mary *Walden* in Horsell church in 1756 and they had one son *Henry* b. 1756.

Joseph I (172X-18XX) Married, in Chobham church, Martha *Ockley* in 1752 when both are stated to be from Stoke.

H –   **Henry V** (1756-1829) Married Sarah *Slaughter* in 1777 and their two children were: *Henry* b. 1784 and Mary b. 1790, married Henry *Searle*.

William I (176X-18XX) His wife was Sarah and they had one son, *William* b. 1795, and (X) possibly a daughter Ann, who married Morris *Searle* in 1807.

Richard II (1798-18XX) Shoemaker and publican (in 1851 Census at the *Hare and Hounds Inn* in Westend). Married Mary *Attwater*, a Chobham girl, though he was stated to be from Farnham, in Frensham church in 1825. Their two children were baptised in Windlesham: Jane born 1839 and Henry born 1840. Also living in his house (the inn?), was a young man of 20, described as shoemaker and lodger. Mother Mary was shown, in 1851 Census, as 'Straw Bonnet Maker'.

I –   **Henry VI** (1784-1842) Farmer (Flexlands). Married Anne *Chennell* in 1809 and their three sons were: *Henry* born 1810, *Carmi* born 1811 and Gabriel born 1816, died a bachelor aged twenty-six.

J –   **Carmi** (1811-1869) Nurseryman (in 1841 Census). But we know that he had moved to a part of Horsell (Millbrook) by 1851 which was better suited for growing roses, his speciality. Married Eliza *Ottaway* and their five children were: Mary Ann b. 1839, Henry b. 1841, Alice born 1844, Eliza Charlotte born 1849 and James born 1846. (The last three children were born in Horsell.)

William II (1795-18XX) The facts of his marriage and the births of his children have been found in the records of the Baptist chapel in the Westend, Chobham. His wife was Ann *Marchant* and their four children were: Mary born 1822, Ann born 1824, Esther b. 1828 and James born 1832.

Grove

A –   **Thomas I** (161X-1669) At his burial called 'senior' and 'of London'. His wife was Susan and they had four children (as shown as beneficiaries in the will of George Stelman, dated 1665) Susan, *Richard*, Samson b. 1656, died a bachelor 1695, and Ann buried 1659. In the Hearth Tax list of 1664, Thomas was shown as 'smith' and exempted from payment of the tax.

Henry I (162X-1668) Labourer in 1664 and exempted from paying the Hearth Tax. His wife was Mary and they had eight children: John b. 1654, died 1662, William b. 1656, died 17 months old, Anne b. 1658, died four years old, Mary b. 1660, Elizabeth b. 1663, Margaret b. 1666 and her twin sister Elizabeth b. 1666, and a son Henry buried 1669.

John I (162X-1661) His wife's name is not known but they had four children: *William*, Anne b. 1654, John b. 1656 and Amy b. 1659

B –   **Thomas II** (164X-1699) Married Susan *Hone* in 1662 and their five children were: Thomas b. 1677, died five months old, Mary b. 1678, Jane b. 1680, Ann b. 1683, married Henry *Howard* 1705, and *Thomas* b. 1692. In the Hearth Tax list of 1664 shown as 'junior' and 'smith', like his father Thomas I, and lived in a house with two hearths.

William I (164X-1708) Eldest child of John I. His wife was Elizabeth and they had five children: Elizabeth b. 1663, Damaris b. 1665, William b. 1668, died five years old, Katherine b. 1673 and Ann b. 1676, married William *Holt* 1702. William was shown as 'weaver' in 1664 and was exempted from paying the Hearth Tax. He was also shown in the Association Oaths Roll of 1695.

Richard I (164X-1673) Son of Thomas I. His wife is not known and their only child was *Thomas*.

C –   **Thomas III** (1692-175X) Son of Thomas II. His wife was Jane and they had four children: Thomas b. 1714, *Henry* b. 1716, Richard b. 1719, died four years old, and Jane b. 1721, died one year after her baptism.

William II (167X-175X) Labourer. Married Martha *Tanner* in 1705 and they had six children: *William* b. 1706, George b. 1707, *John* b. 1710, Mary b. 1712, died 18 months old, Thomas b. 1714 and Samuel b. 1721, died 15 months old.

Thomas IV (168X-1753) His wife was Sarah, who died two weeks after the baptism of her son Richard in 1724, who also died two weeks after his baptism. Thomas married again eight months after his wife's death; his new bride was Damaris *Hone*, from Woking, and they had seven children: John b. 1725, Sarah b. 1728, James b. 1730, William b. 1733, Samuel b. 1736, Richard b. 1738 and Abraham b. 1741. (Son (X) of Richard I.)

D –   **Henry II** (1716-1757) Son of Thomas III. His wife was Mary and their son was *George* b. 1746. Mary died soon after George's baptism and Henry married again in the same year; his bride was Ann who bore him four children: Ann b. 1748, William b. 1752, Ann b. 1754 and Mary b. 1756. Henry was shown in the will of John Alexander, dated 1753, as tenant of Pennypot Farm.

John II (1710-1771) *CW 1757*. Son of William II. His wife was Elizabeth and they had eight children: Elizabeth b. 1737, married Richard *Lee* in 1761, John b. 1741, *Henry* b. 1743, George b. 1746, Maria b. 1750, Jane b. 1753, married Thomas *Lidger* 1788 and, after her husband's death, James *Smith* in 1793, Anne b. 1756 and Amy b. 1758. His elder brother was:

William III (1706-1777) Farmer. *OP 1757. CW 1762/63.* His wife was Elizabeth and their only child was *William* b. 1733.

E –   **George I** (1746-1817) Eldest son of Henry II. Married Jane *Emmett* in 1770. He was a farmer and they had six children: Elizabeth b. 1770, Henry b. 1773, William b. 1774, Jane b. 1775, Phoebe b. 1777 and Richard b. 1779.

Henry III (1743-1805) Cordwainer. *OP 1780*. Son of John II. His wife was Elizabeth and they had two children: *Henry* b. 1780 and *John* b. 1781. Mother Elizabeth died two weeks before her second son's baptism.

William IV (1733-1808) Farmer. Son of William III. His wife was Elizabeth and in his will William mentioned five sons and five grandchildren. Although his estate was valued at £2,000 (*see* p. 69) we could not find William in the 1801 Census nor in any other document. His sons were: Charles, Peter, *James*, Henry and William.

F –   **George II** (1784-184X) Labourer. Possibly (X) the youngest son of George I. He married Sarah *Shorter* in 1804 but no children are known.

Henry IV (1780-1831) Shoemaker. Eldest son of Henry III. Married Mary *Lee* in 1802 and they had 11 children: Mary b. 1803, Henry b. 1804, William b. 1806, Edward b. 1807, died aged five, Frederick b. 1809, George b. 1811, Martha b. 1812, Elizabeth b. 1813, Jane b. 1816, Ann b. 1819 and Sarah b. 1821. In his will, Henry's father-in-law, Richard Lee, left £100 to each grandson if their father died before they had reached their twenty-first year. His brother was:

John III (1781-1850) Wheelwright (owned land in New England). Married Ann *Smith* in 1805 and their eight children were: John b. 1806, Jane b. 1807, Ann b. 1809, died one year old, Henry b. 1811, the twins Mary and Martha b. 1813, Maria b. 1816 and Arthur b. 1818.

James I (1774-1845) Farmer. Son of William IV. His wife was Elizabeth. No children known.

We have also found a marriage of John Grove with Ann *Towers* in 1729 which we are unable to fit into our tree.

Slyfield alias Sleafield

A –   **John I** (162X-170X) Husbandman. His wife's name is not known but they had three children: John b. 1659, *Henry* b. 1661 and Mary b. 1664. Gave 2s. 6d. as his Free Present to Charles II in 1661 and in 1664 lived in a house with five hearths. Shown in the Association Oaths Rolls of 1695.

B –   **Henry I** (1661-1724) *CW 1698 and 1721.* His wife was Hannah and they had five children: Hannah b. 1690, died at age 19, *Henry* b. 1692, Joan b. 1695, died six weeks after her baptism, Mary (Joan's twin sister), and *John* b. 1698. Also shown in the Association Oaths Roll of 1695.

C –   **Henry II** (1692-17XX) *CW 1731. OP 1737.* Married twice. First wife was Sarah who bore one child: Hannah b. 1726. His second wife was Mary and they had three daughters: Mary b. 1727, Sarah b. 1729 and Elizabeth b. 1730. His brother was:

    John II Yeoman. (1698-1774) *OP 1739. CW 1748/9.* His wife was Elizabeth and their four children were: Elizabeth b. 1723, married Henry *Knowles* 1762, *John* b. 1724, Henry b. 1726 and Hannah b. 1734.

Note: when we have finished the details of the family tree we shall return to the will of John II.

D –   **John III** (1724-1770) Elder son of John II. Married Sarah *Foulke* from Thorpe in 1750 and their only child was *John* b. 1753, who was mentioned in his grandfather's will (*see below*). His brother was:

    Henry III (1726-1787) Yeoman. *OP 1776. CW 1777.* Married Elizabeth *Friend* in 1755 and they had six children: Henry b. 1755, Elizabeth b. 1756, Henry b. 1758, Hannah b. 1760, *Henry* b. 1766 and *George* b. 1768. Father Henry married again in 1774. His new bride was Sarah *Cooke* and they had another two children: James b. 1775 and Sarah b. 1776. Mother Sarah died 1777.

    George I (173X-1772) We could not trace his baptism in Chobham. Married Mary *Turner* in 1760. No children known.

E –   **John IV** (1753-1799) *OP 1780. CW 1781.* Married Ann *Bonsey* in Woking in 1775 and they had five children: John b. 1775, Elizabeth b. 1777, Henry b. 1780, Ann b. 1783 and James b. 1785.

    George II (1768-18XX) We know about him from his grandfather's (John II) will.

    Henry IV (1766-1835) Langshot Farm. The third son of Henry III baptised 'Henry' to survive. Married Elizabeth *Newman* in 1790 and they had five children: Henry b. 1796, Ann b. 1797, *James* b. 1801, Sarah b. 1804 and Hannah b. 1807, died aged five (the register notes 'burned to death').

F –   **James I** (1801-18XX) Agricultural labourer. Married Martha *Hampton* in 1828 and they had six children: Martha b. 1829, James b. 1830, George b. 1832, William b. 1834, Hannah b. 1836 and Mary b. 1839, died aged seven. Mother Martha died in 1843 and James married four months later a widow, Ann *Underwood* née *Roberts*.

John II made his will on the 29th May 1773 at the age of 75; at first he gave £100 to his eldest child, Elizabeth, who had married Henry Knowles of Horsell in 1762 – in a later part of the will he added some £200 to be given to Elizabeth's two children. By far the most disturbing part of the document was the treatment of his son Henry: at first John appointed three trustees to run his estate, which he calls 'Rowland Farm' and to 'suffer and permit my son Henry to farm and use the same free of rent' but under condition that Henry will be subject to 'such rules command and power of my trustees as they think best'. Further that

> if they shall see such mismanagement in him or in his goings on and particularly if he shall not maintain educate and bring up his children in a Christian-like manner to bring ejectments and my desire was that they turn him out and take and let the Farm.

Such strictures need some explanation, which we hope we have found. Son Henry had married Elizabeth in 1755 and of their first four children, two died as babies, the last of whom, Hannah, being baptised 1760. A further child was expected to be born early in 1766, but to father John's disgust and surprise he heard that a girl from Bisley, Elizabeth Snivel, had arrived in Chobham on 23 October 1765, asking for relief in Chobham and naming son Henry as father of her child. Worse still, the child was baptised on 27 January 1766 as John Slyfield. This was, as we know, the time of the non-resident vicars, so that the minister in charge did not realize the full import of the fact that he had baptised a grandson of John Slyfield senior. Worse still the boy had been baptised only three weeks before son Henry's legitimate and expected son, Henry, was baptised.

Facing his furious father, Henry admitted his fatherhood of the boy; it obviously raised in the old man's mind the problem of how to protect Henry's legitimate children from being pushed aside for the benefit of the new arrival. Father John's worries had, of course, been increased by the arrival, five weeks after the baptism of the illegitimate boy, of yet another child, a boy, to Henry's wife as expected, and made worse still by the early death of his elder son John in 1770, then by the death of Henry's wife, Elizabeth, a year later. So as to ensure the future of his family, he decided to see a solicitor to find a way out of his problem: hence the appointment of Trustees with detailed instructions on how to deal with his grandson, John (the son of his deceased elder son John) and providing especially for Henry's youngest son, George (born in 1768). To appoint Henry, after all the conditions described, as his will's executor was, perhaps, an afterthought to ensure Henry's co-operation and to force him to toe the line.

That he was successful with his scheme was shown by the contents of Henry's own will which he made only four months after his father's death. Henry III made his second wife Sarah his sole executrix with the condition that she should inherit all his estate but share it with any children, if alive, of his former wife Elizabeth, thus enacting his father's demands. Fortunately, we are able to report the outcome of this problem: the Land Tax Lists of 1780 show that (1) Henry Slyfield held a small part of his father's land until his death in 1787, after which date Sarah took over; (2) Henry Street (one of the trustees) was shown as owner of a larger acreage with Henry Slyfield as occupier, again followed by Sarah as occupier; and (3) John Slyfield (the grandson) held his land, again a smaller acreage, until he sold it in 1796 to Thomas Woods. (From which transaction we could establish that this transferred land was the Fowlers Well Farm in Chobham.)

One more word about the fate of young John (the unforunate cause of all this upheaval): he married a local girl and between 1794 and 1809 they had nine children, of whom two died only days after their baptisms – John became known in the village under the nick-name 'Crock'! John's mother married a local man in 1776.

Street

A – **Henry I** (161X-169X) Married Marcy *Haring* in 1640 and their son (X) was Henry. Father Henry was mentioned in the Association Oaths Roll of 1695.

B – **Henry II** (164X-1688) His wife was Mary and they had six children: Jane b. 1672, Ann b. 1675, *John* b. 1677, *Henry* b. 1680, Mary b. 1682 and *James* b. 1686. In 1664 shown as smith in a house with one hearth and exempted from payment.

C – **John I** (1677-174X) Eldest son of Henry II. His wife was Judith and their seven children were: Mary b. 1712, died 10 years old, *Henry* b. 1713, John b. 1716, Thomas b. 1721, died four years old, James b. 1723, Thomas b. 1725 and *Arthur* b. 1726. His two brothers follow:

Henry III (1680-1752) His wife's name is not known but they had one son, *John* b. 1711.

James I (1686-174X) Again we do not know his wife's name but we know the names of his sons from the wills of his brother Henry and aunt Mary. They were: *John*, *Henry*, James and Francis. Their baptismal dates we do not know.

D – **Henry IV** (1713-1793) Smith. Son of John I. Married Jane *Bartholomew* at Wisley in 1749 and their eight children were: Jane b. 1750, married William *Fladgate* 1775, *Henry* b.

32. The north end of the High Street.

33. The High Street with the churchyard wall on the left and the *Sun Inn* on the right.

1752, Thomas b. 1758, Mary b. 1759, died a spinster 1837, Elizabeth b. 1761, Arthur b. 1754 and James b. 1765. Called 'Yeoman-blacksmith'!

Arthur I (1726-177X) Second surviving son of John I. His son was *Arthur* b. 1754.

John II (1711-1786) Carpenter. *OP 1759. CW 1756/7, 1771.* Son of Henry III. His wife was Catherine and their two children were: Mary b. 1739 and John b. 1740. An entry in the parish records shows that John and Catherine were removed from Guildford to Chobham in 1740. Catherine must have died soon afterwards and father John married again; his new wife was Ann and their five children were: *Henry* b. 1750, Ann b. 1751, *Henry* b. 1753, Mary b. 1756 and John b. 1766. Father John was nominated executor of the will of his aunt Mary. He also witnessed the will of the widow Hannah Savage, dated 1765.

John III (1711-17XX) Here we know only that his son was *John* b. 1756.

E – **Henry V** (1752-1843) *OP 1782. CW 1783.* Eldest son of Henry IV. Married Sarah *Chitty* 1777.

Arthur II (1754-1843) Only son of Arthur I. Called 'educated' in the 1831 Census and in 1835 'independent' meaning 'of independent means'!

Henry VI (1750-1824) Married Jane *Knowles* in 1774. Eldest son of second marriage of John II. Their seven children were: Henry b. 1774, died two days old, Jane b. 1775, *James* b. 1776, Henry b. 1777, *George* b. 1784, Jane b. 1785 and Sarah b. 1786. His brother was:

Henry VII (1753-179X) Married Mary *White* at Windlesham in 1775 and their three children were: Ann b. 1776, James b. 1777 and Mary b. 1780.

James II (174X-178X) His wife was Ruth. No children known. Perhaps (X) the son of James I named above.

F – **James III** (1777-18XX) Blacksmith. Son of Henry VI. Witness of the will of Dr. Robert Harrup of Chobham, surgeon, dated 1821, and was appointed executor in the will of Thomas Wilkinson, mealman, dated 1845. Married the widow Damaris Street in 1803 and they had three children: James b. 1800, died five days old, Arthur b. 1812, died 15 years old, *George* b. 1815.

John IV (1756-1839) *OP 1808 and 1821. CW 1793, 1812/3 and 1817/8.* Only son of John III. Married a widow, Mary *Elmes* née *Edmead* in 1783 and their only child was Henry b. 1784. Was appointed as Workhouse Master 1784 and 1787-89.

George I (1784-18XX) Blacksmith. Son of Henry VI. Married Elizabeth *Everest* 1816 and their only daughter was Mary b. 1817, married Richard *Rowland* 1843, but died one month after the marriage.

G – **George II** (1815-18XX) Master blacksmith. Son of James III. Lived in 1851, according to the Census, in a house in Chobham High Street together with his parents James and Damaris.

James IV (1812-18XX) Farmer of four acres. Grandson of Henry VII and son of his son James. Married Mary *Daborn* and they had six children: Eleanor b. 1833, Alfred b. 1834, died in 1835 and Frederick b. 1835, all baptised in Bisley, Emma b. 1838, George b. 1840 and James born (not baptised) 1843, the last three born in Chobham.

The story of the Street family was very difficult indeed to project in some reasonably coherent way because the sources were varied and needed a large amount of collation and co-ordination, but we hope that the result gives a reliable report of it.

Smither alias Smithers

A – **Larenc I** (161X-1655) His wife was Joan. We could not trace any children.

B –   **Henry I** (162X-1690) His wife was Elizabeth and their three children were: *Henry* b. 1656, John b. 1659, died a bachelor 1726, and *Richard* b. 1661. Father Henry's house had three hearths in 1664. He gave 2s. as his Present to King Charles II in 1661.

Richard I (162X-1676) His wife's name was Priscilla and they had four sons: *John* b. 1656, *Richard* b. 1661, Edward b. 1664, died three months old, and James b. 1666. Father Richard was named as Tythingman in the Hearth Tax returns of 1664, when his house was charged on one hearth.

C –   **Henry II** (1656-171X) Farmer. Eldest son of Henry I. Married Ann *Symonds* in 1695 and their six children were: Henry b. 1696, John b. 1797, *Richard* b. 1799, Ann b. 1702, Lawrence b. 1704 and Ambrose b. 1706, died two weeks after his baptism. Mentioned in the Association Oaths Roll of 1695. His brother was:

Richard II (1661-176X) Farmer. Married Elizabeth *Hudson* in 1698. Their five children were: *Richard* b. 1701, John b. 1704, died four days after his baptism, Elizabeth b. 1705, married Robert *Watts*, *John* b. 1708 and Mary b. 1711. In the will of Mary Hudson dated 1754 father Richard was called 'cousin'.

John I (1656-1725) Eldest son of Richard I. His first wife's name is not known but they had four children; *James* b. 1684, Mary b. 1685, died aged five, Mary b. 1691, died four months old, and *Richard* b. 1696. John married again after his wife's early death; his new wife was Mary and their son was John b. 1713. Mary died early also, in 1719.

D –   **Richard III** (1699-174X) Third son of Henry II. Married Ann *Street* at Windlesham church in 1728 and their seven children were: Ann b. 1729, Jane b. 1731, Elizabeth b. 1733, Hannah b. 1735, Mary b. 1737, Richard b. 1738 and Ann b. 1742.

James I (1684-1776) Yeoman. His wife was Jane who died a year before her husband, after the birth of five sons: *James* b. 1719, *Richard* b. 1721, *John* b. 1723 and *Thomas* b. 1738. In his will, dated 1775, father James gave a complete account of his sons and their children as beneficiaries.

Richard IV (1696-175X) Second son of John I. His wife was Mary and they had two daughters: Mary b. 1732 and Rachael b. 1740.

Richard V (1701-17XX) Eldest son of Richard II. Married a widow, Elizabeth *Turner* in 1733 and their son was *Joseph* b. 1733. His brother was:

John II (1708-17XX) Called 'blacksmith' in the will of Robert Watts, dated 1783, in which John got a 'clock'. His wife was Mary and they had six children: Henry b. 1736, a daughter (name illegible) b. 1739, James b. 1741, Richard b. 1743, Charles b. 1745 and Mary b. 1748.

E –   **James II** (1719-1805) Eldest son of James I. Married Marther *Cook* in 1757 and their two children were: Mary b. 1758 and James b. 1760. His three brothers were:

Richard VI (1721-17XX) Married Jane *Half-Acre* in 1743 and their son *John* was baptised in the same year.

John III (1723-1807) *OP 1792*. Married Sarah *Hathwed* in 1752 and their two sons were: *John* b. 1753 and *James* b. 1758. After the death of his wife, father John married again, to Mary *Grey*, in 1762 and they had eight children: Mary b. 1763, died a spinster 1842, John b. 1764, Mary b. 1766, *James* b. 1769, Henry b. 1770, Elizabeth b. 1772, another Elizabeth b. 1776 and Mary b. 1779. Both parents died in the workhouse.

Thomas I (1738-1810) Married Mary *Ottaway* in 1769 and their two children were: Thomas b. 1770 and Sarah b. 1772. Son Thomas died eight and a half years old. Both parents died in the workhouse, aged 72 and 80 respectively.

Joseph I (1733-179X) Husbandman. Only son of Richard V. Married Mary *Howard* in 1762 and their 10 children were: Ann b. 1764, *James* b. 1768, Sarah b. 1771, Elizabeth b. 1773, Sarah b. 1776, married Richard *Blake* 1791, John b. 1776, Harry b. 1778, Anne b. 1780, Jane b. 1783 and Richard b. 1786. In the will of Robert Watts, Joseph was called 'cousin'.

F –   **John IV** (1753-18XX) Elder son of John III. His wife was Ann and their only child was *William* b. 1773.

James III (1758-1791) Second son of John III. Married Elizabeth *Howard* in 1784 and they had four children: James b. 1785, died aged 13, *Henry* b. 1787, William b. 1789 and *George* b. 1792. Mother Elizabeth married again, after the early death of her husband, in 1797.

John V (1743-1807) Son of Richard VI. Married Elizabeth *Slyfield* in 1776 and their nine children were: Sarah b. 1778, William b. 1780, Hannah b. 1782, Ann b. 1784, Mary b. 1787, Jane b. 1789, Henry b. 1792, Mary b. 1794 and James b. 1796.

James IV (1768-1820) Eldest son of Joseph I. His wife was Jane and their two children were: Jane b. 1801 and *Charles* b. 1804.

James V Son of John III. (1769-1820) Married Sarah *Walker* in 1791 and their seven children were: Charlotte b. 1793, married James *Tunnel* 1817, Jane b. 1795, *James* b. 1798, Jane b. 1800, the twins Ann and Sarah b. 1803 and Milly b. 1807. Mother Sarah died before the baptism of her last child.

G –   **William I** (1773-183X) Son of John IV. Married Charlotte *Cocks* at Windlesham church in 1793. No children known.

Henry II (1787-18XX) Eldest surviving son of James III. His wife was Maria, born in Hampshire, and they had 11 children: James b. 1813, Eliza b. 1815, George b. 1817, died aged 10, Eleanor b. 1819, died 10 years old, Mary-Ann b. 1822, died two years old, Jane b. 1824, Ann b. 1829, Harriet b. 1831, died six months old, Louisa b. 1833, died two years old, Henry b. 1836 and Elizabeth born (not baptised) 1837.

George I (1792-18XX) Youngest son of James III. Married Mary-Ann *Attfield* in 1822. No children known.

James VI (1798-18XX) Labourer. Son of James V. Married Sarah *Grayson* in 1820 and their seven children were: Jane b. 1822, married Isaac *Gosden* 1845, Ann b. 1824, Harriet b. 1826, James b. 1829, William b. 1832, died nine years old, Henry b. 1835 and David b. 1838.

G –   **Charles I** (1804-18XX) Labourer. Son of James IV. Married Hannah *Hampton* of Horsell in Horsell church in 1829 and they had 12 children: Jane b. 1829, Sarah b. 1831, William b. 1832, Celia b. 1834, Elizabeth b. 1835, Richard b. 1837, Emma b. 1838, George b. 1840, James b. 1842, Henry b. 1844, Eliza b. 1847 and Ellen b. 1851.

Jewer alias Jure

A –   **George I** (160X-1677) His wife was Ann, who survived her husband by six years. We know of two sons: *George* born 163X (X) and Simon whose burial in 1682 was entered in the parish register.

B –   **George II** (163X-1712) We do not know the name of his wife, but their son was George b. 1656. Lived in 1664 in a house with one hearth.

C –   **George III** (1656-16XX) We have no details about this George other than his baptism but assume (X) that his son was *Robert*, born about 171X.

D –   **Robert I** (171X-1777) Yeoman (Little Heath Farm). His wife was Elizabeth and their two children were: Mary b. 1739 married John *Daborn* in 1764, and *Robert* b. 1742. Father Robert died intestate, at which date both widow and son Robert (described as 'yeoman') were mentioned.

E –   **Robert II** (1742-1808) Farmer (Brimshot Farm). Married Ann *Taylor* in 1769 and their son was *John* b. 1770. Mother Ann died one year before her husband who acted as witness to the will of Mrs. Jane Bailey, dated 1768. In the 1801 Census Robert's family was shown as sharing a house with the widow Burnett, a close relative of Mrs. Bailey.

F –   **John I** (1770-1831) Married the widow Mary *Baxter* née *Daborn* in 1810 and their only child was a daughter: Ann Maria b. 1812. In the 1831 Census they are shown as living at Chobham Park Farm which Mary's brother John Daborn ran. Father John died six months after the Census (where he was shown as 'educated') and his widow survived him by 17 years.

Here is the first of the 'post-1664' families.

Bailey

A –   **William I** (167X-17XX) Farmer from Chertsey. Married Ann *Symonds* in 1702 in Chertsey and their four children were: Edward b. 1703, Ann b. 1706, married John *Friend* 1729, Mary b. 1709 and Elizabeth b. 1716.

B –   **Edward I** (1703-1761) *CW 1738/9. OP 1742.* His wife was Ann and their four children were: Ann b. 1735, married Edward *Burchett* in 1754, *Edward* b. 1737, *Morrice* b. 1738 and Sarah b. 1748.

C –   **Edward II** (1737-1791) Yeoman. *CW 1769. OP 1764.* Married Jane *Stileman* in 1764. No children. In her will Jane Bailey left to her husband her manor of Stannards and Ford (1768). Jane died 1670 aged twenty-five. Edward married again, in 1781, Elizabeth *Jewer.*

        Morris I (1738-1805) *OP 1769. CW 1772, 1791/2.* Farmer. Married Elizabeth *Alexander* 1767 at Horsell church. No children known. In his will, dated 1799, John Alexander, Elizabeth's father, mentioned his only daughter as heiress next to his son-in-law Morris. In his will Morris mentioned, next to his wife, a nephew named Morris whom we could not trace elsewhere.

    It seems to be worth pointing out that the members of the Bailey family, in their short stay in Chobham, married into every one of the more important families of the parish, viz: Friend, Burchett, Stileman, Jewer and Alexander.

Howard alias Hayward

A –   **Henry I** (167X-1727) Married Ann *Grove* in 1705 and they had six children: *Henry* b. 1706, *John* b. 1708, Ann b. 1712, married Henry *Daborn* 1748, Thomas b. 1715, Richard b. 1719 and Sarah b. 1722.

        William I (168X-173X) His first wife was Ann and their two children were: Ann b. 1710 and Mary, baptised the same day as her sister but died aged three. Mother Ann died one month after the baptism of her daughters. William married again, in 1715, Elizabeth *Road* and their three children were: Elizabeth b. 1716, Mary b. 1719 and *William* b. 1722.

        Thomas I (168X-1749) We do not know the name of his first wife but their daughter was Hannah b. 1704. Thomas married again in 1718, Elizabeth *Homes*, and their six children were: Thomas b. 1719, Elizabeth b. 1721, Ann b. 1723, John b. 1725, Mary b. 1727 and James b. 1729. We found another *Thomas* born about 1706 who could have been a child of Thomas's first marriage.

B –   **Henry II** (1706-17XX) Eldest son of Henry I. Married Ann *Searle* from Horsell at Bisley church in 1732 and their daughter was Mary b. 1733. Mother Ann probably died soon after Mary's birth as Henry married again in 1734; his new wife was Sarah and their son was *Henry* b. 1735. His brother was:

   John I (1708-1749) His wife was Sarah who died aged 77 in 1787. Their son was John b. 1727 who was described in father John's will, dated 1749, as 'timber merchant in Woking'.

   William II (1722-17XX) Youngest child of William I. His wife was Mary and their five children were: Ann b. 1751, Henry b. 1754, John b. 1755, Mary b. 1756 and William b. 1766.

   Thomas II (1706-1786) (*See under* Thomas I.) *OP 1756, 1763. CW 1758/9.* His wife was Mary and their four children were: *William* b. 1732, *Thomas* b. 1739, Ann b. 1743 and James b. 1745. Father Thomas witnessed the will of Henry Dawkins, yeoman, in 1753.

   John II (1706-17XX) Father unknown. His wife was Katherine and their son was *Samuel* b. 1730.

   Richard I (171X-17XX) Father unknown. His wife was Ann and their seven children were: Ann b. 1738, *Richard* b. 1740, John b. 1742, Sarah b. 1744, died a spinster aged 29, *William* b. 1746, Mary b. 1747 and Hannah b. 1750. Young Richard was apprenticed on 29 July 1758 to Henry Attfield, cordwainer, until aged 24, for £6 (he was then 18).

C –   **Henry III** (1735-1801) Youngest child of Henry II. His wife was Mary and their three sons were: Henry b. 1768, *George* b. 1771 and Thomas b. 1775, died, five years old, after the death of his mother in 1780.

   Israel I (1747-1835) Father not known. His first wife was Martha and their daughter was Mary b. 1772, baptised after her mother's death. Israel married again in 1772 at Woking church, his new wife was Elizabeth *Sherrat* and they had six children; Elizabeth b. 1775, Israel b. 1777, *James* b. 1780, Ann b. 1783, Sarah b. 1786, died a spinster aged 38, and Jane b. 1789. Mother Elizabeth died aged 63 in 1810.

   William III (1732-18XX) Eldest son of Thomas II. Married Jane *Huntingdon* of Pirbright in Pirbright church in 1758. No children known. His brother was:

C –   **Thomas III** (1739-1814) Second son of Thomas II. Was parish clerk from 1788 to his death, succeeded by his son Charles. He was the vicar's partner in 1813 in their talk about the intended sermon on the collection for the school (*see below* p. 176). Married Frances *Edmead* at Winchester although both parties were from Chobham. They had 13 children: Richard b. 1766, died five years old, *Thomas* b. 1767, Mary b. 1768, *William* b. 1769, Frances b. 1771, died a spinster aged 30, Mary b. 1773, *James* b. 1775, *Richard* b. 1777, *Jeremiah* b. 1778, Anne b. 1779, Stephen b. 1781, Henry b. 1783, died five months old and *Charles* b. 1784.

   Samuel I (1730-17XX) Son of John II. (We only guess that he moved to Horsell, married there and had a son *John* baptised there in 1787.)

   Richard II (1740-17XX) Elder son of Richard I. Married Sarah *Tucker* in 1767. No children known. His brother was:

   William IV (1746-1832) Husbandman. *OP 1818.* Married Ann *Cole* in 1767 and their eight children were: John b. 1770, Jane b. 1772, Elizabeth b. 1774, James b. 1777, Sarah b. 1778, Henry b. 1781, Hannah b. 1784, died aged 12, and Ann b. 1789.

D –   **George I** (1771-1806) Bricklayer. Second son of Henry III. His wife was Mary and their only child was Henry b. 1805. Mary died in 1838, aged sixty-nine.

James I (1780-1845) Labourer. Second son of Israel I. Married Elizabeth *Loveland* in 1804 at Byfleet church and they had 11 children; Mary-Ann b. 1804, Henry b. 1806, William b. 1807, Eliza b. 1809, James b. 1812, Charlotte b. 1815, Frances b. 1818, Ann b. 1821, married James *Hampton* 1846 (after her husband's early death married again, in 1848, Henry *Rapley*), John b. 1823, *Thomas* b. 1824 and Stephen b. 1827.

Thomas IV (1767-18XX) Eldest surviving son of Thomas III. No other details. His four brothers follow:

William V (1769-1839) Farmer/carpenter (Wiggenors Farm in 1841 is the modern Grants Farm). *OP 1806, 1833. CW 1826/7, 1834.* Married Elizabeth *Draper* in 1793 and their seven children were: William b. 1795, Mary b. 1796, Ann b. 1798, *Edward* b. 1800, Elizabeth b. 1805, *Thomas* b. 1807 and *James* b. 1811. Mother Elizabeth died aged 46 in 1816 and William married again in 1825, Ann *Rogers*. No children. Father William acted as witness of the will of Henry Harris, collarmaker, dated 1803, and his brother-in-law James Draper named him executor in his will dated 1804.

James II (1775-18XX) Labourer. Next son of Thomas III. Known locally as 'soldier'. Married Sarah *Potter* in 1803 and their six children were: Ann b. 1804, John b. 1805, Sarah b. 1809, Charles b. 1811, James b. 1815 and Martha b. 1817.

Richard III (1777-18XX) Fourth son of Thomas III. His wife was Mary and they had two children; Celia born 1812, died before her baptism, and *Charles* b. 1813.

Jeremiah I (1778-1852) Carpenter/builder. Married Ann *Rogers* in 1810 Windlesham church and their two children were: Jane-Ann b. 1823 and William-Rogers, baptised together with his sister, but died three weeks old. Mother Ann died 1823 and was buried six weeks before her children's baptism. Jeremiah's second wife was Sarah *Street* from Laleham in 1825. No children. He witnessed the will of Thomas Wilkinson in 1833.

Charles I (1784-1849) Grocer. *OP 1843.* Followed his father Thomas as parish clerk in 1814 as mentioned by the vicar (*see below* p.176). Married Sarah and they had four children: Caleb b. 1807, *Samuel* b. 1810, Jemima b. 1813 and *Charles* b. 1816. Mother Sarah died 1821 aged 39 and father Charles married in 1825, Alice *Clunce* from Scotland, who was shown as 'Annuitant' in the 1851 Census (after the death of her husband). They had one daughter: Sarah born 1834. Father Charles witnessed the will of Thomas Mepham, dated 1836.

John II (1787-18XX) Labourer. Lived at Dolleys Farm, 1841-51. Born in Horsell, son of Samuel I. Married Sarah *Smith*, from Horsell, in Chobham church in 1811. Their five children were all baptised in Chobham: James b. 1814, Mary b. 1817, Margaret b. 1819, married William *Turner* 1835, Martha b. 1820 and *John* b. 1824.

E – **Thomas V** (1824-18XX) Labourer. Son of James I. In 1851, lived at Coxhill (Milford Green) with his married sister Ann, her husband, Henry Rapley, and their two children William and George.

Edward I (1800-18XX) Carpenter. Son of William V. We do not know his wife's name but their son was *Edward* b. 1821.

Thomas VI (1807-18XX) Carpenter. Next son of William V. Married Ann *Jackman* at Woking church in 1832 and their two children were: Mary-Ann b. 1834 and Frederick b. 1836.

James III (1811-18XX) Youngest son of William V. Carpenter. (In the Census of 1851, he was recorded as 'Carpenter – Master – employs two men'). Married Ann *Bolding* in 1835 and they had seven children: Sarah-Ann b. 1835, James b. 1840, Emily-Ann b. 1843, Ann-Elizabeth b. 1845, Jane b. 1847, and twins Alice and Frances b. 1849.

Samuel I (1810-18XX) Tailor. Son of Charles I. No further details.

Charles II (1813-18XX) Labourer. Son of Richard III. His wife was Catherine from Horsell and their seven children were: Mary born 1831 and Jane born, as was her elder sister, in Sunninghill, in 1836, James b. 1838, Charles born 1839, Richard born 1842 (the last two were apparently registered but not baptised in Chobham), Reuben b. 1847 and William b. 1850.

Charles III (1816-18XX) Grocer. Son of Charles I. Married Sarah-Ann *Neville* in 1850 and their child was Charles-Neville b. 1851. Sarah-Ann died four weeks before her baby's baptism.

John III (1824-18XX) Youngest son of John II. Married Mary *Gould* in 1849. No children.

F – **Edward II** (1821-1848) Labourer. Son of Edward I. His wife was Charlotte and their two children were: Mary-Ann b. 1845 and Alfred b. 1847.

Chittey alias Chitty

A – **John I** (167X-172X) His wife was Elizabeth and they had six children: *Richard* b. 1701, Jane b. 1706, married Joseph *Beauchamp* 1740, *James* b. 1710, *Edward* b. 1711, Mary b. 1712 and *John* b. 1713.

B – **Richard I** (1701-1759) His wife was Ann, their five children were: Mary b. 1734, died a spinster 1800, Richard b. 1736, died a bachelor 1791, George b. 1739, Sarah b. 1745, married Henry *Street* 1777, and *James* b. 1749.

Edward I (1711-1792) Farmer (Hookstone Farm). *OP 1741. CW 1745-7, 1761.* Married Margaret *Spong* 1735. Their four children were: *John* b. 1736, Margaret b. 1738, died a spinster 1823, *Edward* b. 1739 and Elizabeth b. 1741. Mother Margaret died in 1743 after four births in five years.

John II (1713-1779) His wife was Sarah and their only daughter was Sarah b. 1749.

James I (1710-1785) *OP 1738.* Married Jane *Friend* 1730 and their seven children were: Jane b. 1732, Margaret b. 1733, John b. 1734, Jane b. 1739, married Richard *Fladgate* 1769, Edward b. 1740, Hannah b. 1741 and Mary b. 1742.

C – **John III** (1736-1782) Yeoman. Son of Edward I. Married Elizabeth *Merlin* from Windlesham 1758 and their only son was John b. 1763. His brother was:

Edward II (1739-1793) *OP 1771. CW 1775, 1777.* Married Mary *Fladgate* in 1762 and their five children were: Mary b. 1767, *Edward* b. 1770, Sarah b. 1772, married Samuel *Mumford* 1791, Elizabeth buried 1781 (no baptismal date found) and Richard b. 1779, died a bachelor 1808.

James II (1749-1779) *OP 1774.* Son of Richard I. His wife was Mary and their three children were: Sarah b. 1772, Sophia b. 1776, died five months old and *James* b. 1778.

D – **James III** (1763-1825) Married Ann *Daborn* 1792 and their eight children were: Jane b. 1796, married James *White* 1817, Ann b. 1798, *William* b. 1801, Harriett b. 1803, married James *Heather* 1826, Hannah b. 1805, Phebe b. 1809, married William *Spong* 1827, James b. 1812, died (a cripple in the workhouse) 1836, and Charlotte b. 1816.

Edward III (1770-1838) *OP 1809.* Farmer (Hookstone Farm). Son of Edward II. Married Elizabeth *Stovell* from Bisley 1809 and their three children were: Margaret b. 1809, married John *Gosden* 1828, *Edward* b. 1813 and *John* b. 1814.

James IV (1778-1846) *OP 1814.* Gentleman at Pond Farm. Son of James II. His wife was Mary and their four children were: Mary b. 1799, died two months after her baptism, Maria b. 1802, died a spinster, Mary Ann b. 1805, died a spinster, *Richard* b. 1808.

E – **William I** (1801-18XX) Farmer (on four acres without labourer). Son of James III. In his
house lived Elizabeth Daborn, shown in the 1851 Census as husband and wife,
but in 1841 Elizabeth was shown as householder and we could not trace a marriage
in the Chobham register.

John IV (1814-1853) Farmer. son of Edward III. Married Mary Ann *Hone* 1842 and their son
John was not baptised until seven years old, in 1851. In his will, made two months
before his death, he established a trust for the benefit of his son John when aged
21, and appointed his brother, Edward, and William Hone as trustees. In the
1851 Census shown as farmer at Rounces Farm, farming 30 acres with one labourer,
who lived in the farm with his master. His widowed mother, Elizabeth, also lived
with her son. His older brother was:

Edward IV (1813-18XX) Farmer. *OP 1842.* Son of Edward III. Said to own Rounce Farm in
1851 when his brother, John IV, was probably too ill to run the farm (John died
1853!). Edward married Hariett *Viner* from Windlesham 1842. In the 1851 Census
Edward was stated to live at the Hookstone Farm with 70 acres employing three
labourers, two of whom lived in the farmhouse as well as a female house servant.

James-Richard (1808-18XX) *OP 1840.* Farmer (at Pond Farm). Son of James IV. Married
Ann *Baigent* 1848 and their two children were: Mary b. 1849 and Ann b. 1850.
James-Richard also had a third Christian name, Henry, and in 1851 lived at the
Pond Farm, shown as of 25 acres, employing one labourer who lived in the
farmhouse as well as a female house servant.

We have also found yet another Edward Chittey whom we could not place within our tree; he
would belong to generation D.

Edward V (1772-1806) Farmer at Leeds Farm (1801). No further details.

Collier alias Collyer

A – **Henry I** (164X-17XX) We only know of him through the register entries of his children's
baptisms. They were: Elizabeth b. 1672, Margret b. 1675, *Henry* b. 1676, *John* b.
1678, Richard b. 1680, Sarah b. 1682 and the twins *James* and *William* b. 1684.

Richard I (164X-1702) Father of 11 children: *Richard* b. 1670, John b. 1674, Henry b. 1675,
Joseph b. 1677, *Benjamin* b. 1679 and the twins Ann and William b. 1685, but Ann
died five years old, another son whose name was illegible b. 1688, and the twins
Jane and Sarah b. 1690, but Jane died two days after her baptism. Father Richard
was shown in the Association Oaths Roll of 1695.

Robert I (163X)-1719) His wife was Ann who gave him three children, of whose baptisms
two took place before 1654 but their burials are shown: James buried 1684 and
Henry buried 1690, a girl, Ann was baptised 1674. Mother Ann died 1685. Also
in Association Oaths Roll 1695.

B – **Henry II** (1676-17XX) Labourer. Son of Henry I. His wife is Elizabeth and they had eight
children; Elizabeth b. 1706, Ann b. 1708, *Henry* b. 1709, James b. 1712, Sarah b.
1713, Mary b. 1715, William b. 1720 and Jane b. 1724, married Richard *Lipscomb*
1751. His four brothers follow:

John I (1678-1766) Yeoman (Collingly Farm). He calls himself 'the elder' in his will in
which he also gives 'fifty deison of bread' to the poor of the village. His wife was
Grace and they had one son *John* b. 1723.

James I (1684-17XX) His wife was Ann and they had three children: James b. 1708, Ann b.
1710 and another *James* b. 1713. The first James might have died but his burial
was not found in the register.

William I (1684-17XX) James's twin-brother. His wife was Jane and their two children were:
William b. 1723 and *Richard* b. 1725.

Richard II (1670-1754) Labourer. Elder son of Richard I. His wife was Mary and their seven children were: Mary b. 1697, Elizabeth b. 1699, married Robert *Jewer* 1731, Richard b. 1701, died 12 years of age, Daniel b. 1703, William b. 1706, Joan b. 1709, died aged two and Henry b. 1713. Father Richard was mentioned in the Association Oaths Roll of 1695. His brothers follow:

Benjamin I (1679-1753) Farmer. He mentioned his wife Mary in his will as well as his brother Richard. They had three children; Mary b. 1719, married William *Towers* 1739, James b. 1724 and John b. 1726.

Charles I (168X-17XX) We could not determine his father (Richard I? *see above*). His wife was Ann and their only child was Richard b. 1730.

C – **Henry III** (1709-17XX) Son of Henry II. Married Jane *Collyer* from Bisley in Bisley church and they had five children; *Henry* b. 1739, *William* b. 1742, James b. 1745, John b. 1748 and Jane b. 1751.

John II (1723-1777) Yeoman (Collingly Farm). Son of John I. In his will he stated that the farm had been part of his 'mother's jointure'. His wife was Ann and their three children were: Ann b. 1760, married Robert *Dover* 1782, *Thomas* b. 1765 and *John* b. 1771.

James II (1713-17XX) Son of James I. Married Elizabeth *Gravett* 1736 and their three children were: James b. 1736, died unmarried aged 83, *William* b. 1738 and John b. 1741.

Richard III (1725-1786) Son of William I. Married Mary *Honer* 1770 and their three children were: *James* b. 1771, *William* b. 1772 and Richard b. 1786.

John III (1726-17XX) Son of Benjamin I. Married Mary *Jenneway* of Ripley 1750 and his wife died 1765 without having given birth to a child.

Charles II (171X-17XX) Married Jane *Spong* in 1741 who gave him five children: Jane b. 1742, Ann b. 1745, Charles b. 1747, Mary b. 1754 and James b. 1757. Father Charles was mentioned in the will of his brother, George, whom we could not trace otherwise.

D – **William II** (1742-1775) Cordwainer. Second son of Henry III. Married Elizabeth *Towers* in 1770 and they had four children: William b. 1770, James b. 1772, Jane b. 1773, married Richard *Lee* 1804, and Sarah b. 1775, baptised after her father's death. His older brother was:

Henry IV (1739-1774) Married Sarah *Lee* 1767 and they had three children: James b. 1769, Henry b. 1771 and Richard b. 1772.

Thomas I (1765-1840) Elder son of John II. His wife was Elizabeth and their only child was Mary Ann b. 1813.

William III (1738-1822) Son of James II. Married Ann *Harmes* 1763 and their six children were: William b. 1764, Ann b. 1765, married John *Hall* 1797, Elizabeth b. 1766, Mary b. 1771, *Henry* b. 1775 and Jane b. 1777.

James III (1771-1810) Yeoman (Pancras Farm). *OP 1792, 1797/8. CW 1795, 1799, 1803-8.* Son of Richard III. Married Sarah *Fladgate* 1793, their five children were: Sarah b. 1795, Mary b. 1796, William b. 1797, died a bachelor 21 years old, *Richard* b. 1800 and John b. 1803, died three months old. His brother was:

William IV (1772-1826) His wife was Mary and their three children were: Richard baptised in Woking 1796, Mary b. (again in Woking) 1797 and *William* b. 1798.

John IV (1771-1819) Second son of John II. Married Ann *Elson* in 1793 and their two children were: *William* b. 1801 and Sophia b. 1803.

E – **James IV** (1769-18XX) All we know about him was that he had a son *James* b. 1796.

Henry V (1775-1850) Son of William III. Married Ann *Taylor* of Pirbright in Woking church in 1801. Although he was described as labourer, his widow, in the 1851 Census was shown as 'ANNUITANT and Independent'.

William V (1764-1836) Married Mercy *Turner* in 1793 and their six children were: *John* b. 1794, Sarah b. 1796, married Samuel *Mumford* 1816, William b. 1798, died a bachelor at age 21, Jane b. 1802, Elizabeth b. 1805 and Henry b. 1808.

Richard IV (1800-18XX) Farmer (Pancras Farm. In 1835, also ran the Old Malthouse Farm for the Abdys.) *OP 1823. CW 1833.* Son of James III. His wife was Elizabeth who gave him two children: William George b. 1821, and Maryann b. 1826, died 13 years old. After his wife's death, Richard married again, Charlotte *Mumford*, who died without having given birth to a child, and Richard married, yet again, Emma from Chertsey; their two children were: Emma Mary b. 1838 and William James b. 1841.

William VI (1798-18XX) Labourer. Son of William IV. Married Eliza *Sleet* 1825 and their eight children were: George b. 1828, William b. 1830, Mary b. 1833, James b. 1835, Harriet b. 1838, Eliza b. 1842, Richard b. 1845 and Emma b. 1848.

William VII (1801-1841) Labourer. Son of John IV. Married Frances *Marr*, their five children were: Stephen b. 1829, David b. 1832, Abraham b. 1834, Eliza b. 1836 and Hester born 1849 (not in baptismal register).

F – **James V** (1796-18XX) Son of James IV. Married Maria *Rampton* in 1819 in Pirbright, their nine children were: Sarah b. 1821, Mary Ann b. 1823, Eliza b. 1825, died two years old, Maria b. 1828, James b. 1830, David b. 1833, John b. 1834, and Stephen and William not baptised but born 1840 and 1850 respectively.

John V (1794-18XX) Labourer. Son of William V. His wife was Sarah and we have no further information about John.

William VIII (1825-18XX) Married, 1846, Mary *Carter* from London and we have no further information about William, nor could we trace his father on the tree.

We have also found another member of this family who was from Pirbright, where also all his children were baptised.

Isaac (1805-18XX) Farmer (Boltinghouse Farm). His wife was Sarah from Billingshurst and they had five children: Esther b. 1832, Mary b. 1840, John b. 1844, Henry b. 1847 and George b. 1848.

Fladgate alias Fladgett

A – **John I** (164X-1709) His wife was Mary, they had five children; John b. 1670, *Henry* b. 1672, *Thomas* b. 1675, Mary b. 1678 and Edward b. 1680. Mother Mary died 1681 and father John married again but his second wife's name is not known; they had three children: James b. 1684, Frances b. 1686 and Richard b. 1689. John's second wife died two weeks after her third child's baptism, just before Edward, the fourth son of father John's first wife, died.

B – **Henry I** (1672-1?XX) Son of John I. His wife was Sarah and they had five children: twins *Henry* and Hannah b. 1718, Edward b. 1719, died two months after his baptism, Jane b. 1720, married William *Crane* in 1744 and died aged 75 in the workhouse, Edward b. 1722, died five days after his baptism. His brother was:

Thomas I (1675-1717) His wife was Sarah, they had six children; *Thomas* b. 1702, Sarah b. 1705, died three years old, Mary b. 1707, married George *Harms* 1740, Elizabeth b. 1709, married George *Woods* 1735, Sarah b. 1713, married Henry *Underwood* 1740, and Anne b. 1715.

C – **Henry II** (1718-17XX) Eldest son of Henry I. His wife was Elizabeth; they had seven children: Elizabeth b. 1745, Henry b. 1747, Sarah b. 1748, married John *Thomas* from Leatherhead 1769, Ann b. 1750, Mary b. 1753, Hannah b. 1755 and Thomas b. 1759.

Thomas II (1702-17XX) Son of Thomas I. His wife was Mary, they had five children: *William* b. 1726, *James* b. 1729, *Edward* b. 1731, *Richard* b. 1733 and a daughter, whose name was illegible in the book, baptised 1735.

D – **William I** (1726-17XX) Son of Thomas II. Married Mary *Field* in Farnborough in 1749. Witness of the will of Elizabeth Russell, dated 1757. Their son was *William* b. 1747. His three brothers follow:

James I (1729-1822) Yeoman. *OP 1768, 1798, 1801. CW 1770, 1790.* Married Mary *Yeowell* in 1764. At the Census of 1801, lived in Stanners Hill House (*see above* p. 23). They had six children: James b. 1766, Mary b. 1768, married Henry *Edmead* 1803, Sarah b. 1770, married James *Collyer* 1793, remarried 1811 William *Beauchamp*, *James* b. 1772, Thomas b. 1773 and Ann b. 1776. Mother Mary was a beneficiary of the will of Samuel Cobbett, dated 1785; she died 1795.

Edward I (1731-17XX) Married Sarah *Fritwell* in Bisley 1749. One daughter: Mary b. 1756.

Richard I (1733-1814) Farmer. *OP 1794, 1798.* Son of Thomas II. Married Jane *Chittey* 1769. They had one son: Richard b. 1770. Appointed executor in the will of John Roake, Gent, dated 1789.

Thomas III (17XX-1770) Yeoman. Married Ann *Worsfold* 1763 and in his will, dated 1764, made his wife executrix. (Note: we were unable to fit Thomas within our tree.)

E – **James II** (1772-1857) Yeoman (Lurkenshaw Farm in 1851). *OP 1815, 1827, 1843. CW 1845/6.* Son of James I. Married Elizabeth *Collins* in 1809 and they had five children; *James* b. 1811, Sarah b. 1812, William b. 1814, Richard b. 1816 and Henry b. 1818.

William II (1747-1808) Son of William I. Married Jane *Street* 1775 and their only child was Jane b. 1775, married James *Rogers* 1800, and died 1849.

F – **James III** (1811-18XX) Farmer (Bonsey Farm). Son of James II. Married Sarah *Daborn* 1833 and they had eight children: James b. 1831, William b. 1837, died aged five, Sarah Ann b. 1839, Richard b. 1842, Elizabeth Ann b. 1844, Edward b. 1846, Ann b. 1849 and Henry b. 1851.

Heather

A – **Henry I** (165X-17XX) The register shows three children: Henry b. 1681, Ann b. 1683 and Mary b. 1686. A son was entered only as being buried 1683.

B – **Daniel I** (166X-1724) Cordwainer. Married Ann *Gosden* in Farnborough 1699, a widow with one son *John* b. 1693 (who took the name Heather). Another three children: Ann b. 1701, Mary b. 1702, died five weeks old, and *Daniel* b. 1703.

C – **Daniel II** (1703-17XX) *CW 1729.* His wife was Mary with one son: John b. 1733. His elder brother was:

John I (1693-174X) Married Jane *Woods* in 1714 and they had four children: John b. 1715, *Richard* b. 1716, Jane b. 1717 and *Daniel* b. 1719. Mother Jane died 1720 aged only thirty-one. Father John remarried; his new wife was Elizabeth; no children.

D – **Daniel III** (1719-1771) Cordwainer. *OP 1755. CW 1767.* Married Elizabeth *Woods* in 1745; no children. His elder brother was:

Richard I (1716-1792) His wife was Ann with four children: a son, whose name was illegible in the register, b. 1739, Ann b. 1741, *James* b. 1744 and Richard b. 1748.

E –   **James I** (1744-1824) Married Mary *Hone* in 1764, described as husbandman in 1768 but a labourer at his burial, two sons: James b. 1769, died 11 years old, and *Daniel* b. 1776.

F –   **Daniel IV** (1776-18XX) Married Mary *Saunders* in 1797 in Byfleet, and had nine children: *James* b. 1799, Elizabeth b. 1802, married William *Pullen*, *William* b. 1801, Mary b. 1803, *Daniel* b. 1805, Sophia b. 1814, died aged three, John b. 1816, Isaac b. 1818 and Martha b. 1820, died two years old.

G –   **James II** (1799-18XX) Labourer. Eldest son of Daniel IV. Married Harriet *Chitty* in 1826; they had five children: Frederick b. 1826, Mary b. 1828, Sophia b. 1832, James b. 1835, Jemima b. 1841. Father James married again in 1852, a widow, Rebecca Grimsley née *Hall*; no children. His two brothers follow:

        William I (1801-18XX) His wife was Ann and they had six children; Henry b. 1830, died two months old, Mary Ann b. 1832, Sarah b. 1835, died two and a half years old, William b. 1839. Mother Ann died in 1839 only 27 years of age.

        Daniel V (1805-1838) Married Mary *Woods* in 1829, Daniel died in 1838 only 33 years old.

Try

A –   **John I** (166X-1724) His wife was Martha and their nine children were: *John* b. 1695, Elizabeth b. 1696, William b. 1697, Mary b. 1699, George b. 1702, died six weeks after his baptism, Ann b. 1703, Thomas b. 1705, George b. 1710 and Henry b. 1710.

B –   **John II** (1695-17XX) His wife was June and their son was *John* b. 1719.

        Richard I (169X-17XX) We could not find Richard's father but assume (X) that he was the eldest son of John I. Married Katherine *Field* in 1719 and their three sons were: Richard b. 1721, John b. 1724 and *Henry* b. 1726.

C –   **Henry I** (1726-1791) Married Ann *Friend* in 1759 and their two sons were: Henry b. 1760 and *John* b. 1761. There must have been a very close link between the Try and Friend families as a brother of mother Ann, James Friend, mentioned six members of the Try family as nephews and nieces and as beneficiaries of his will.

        James I (1742-1817) We could not establish James's father and only know of him that his wife was Sarah. No children known.

D –   **John III** (1761-1819) Farmer (Lovelands Farm). *OP 1805.* Married in 1796 the widow Hannah *Gosden* née *Loveland* and their son was *James* b. 1798.

E –   **James II** (1798-18XX) Farmer (Scotts Farm) *OP 1828. CW 1843/44, 1848-51.* Shown in the 1851 Census as living in Scotts House, farming 95 acres with three labourers (two of whom lived in the house in addition to a governess and a female house servant). His wife was Esther who died shortly before the 1851 Census and they had four children: James b. 1841, Ann b. 1843, Esther b. 1845 and Sarah b. 1851, after the death of her mother. Sarah was in fact baptised on 30th March and the Census shows her as of 'no age'.

        James III (1771-1846) 'Independent' in 1841 Census. *OP 1816, 1831.* Married Sarah *Marter* in Windlesham church in 1807 and we found no children. In the 1841 Census he was shown as 'senior' and he lived in Scotts House until his death when James II moved in. In 1841 two 'male' servants and a female servant live in the house with the owners.

Mumford

A –   **William I** (1718-1798) He was mentioned in the will of Sir Anthony Abdy dated 1774 as 'my late servant when in Essex'. His wife was Hannah and their son (X) was William b. 1764.

Samuel I (172X-179X) Likewise mentioned in Sir Anthony Abdy's will, as follows: 'I give to Mr. Samuel Mumford twenty pounds and I beg the favour of him to make out the accounts of the several persons for whom I am concerned and I direct my executors to pay him a gratuity for the same'.

We feel that it was necessary to insert here a brief résumé of the happenings in Chobham when the last of the Thomas family had died and left his House (Chobham Place) and the grounds to his cousin Mary who had married Sir Anthony Thomas Abdy of Albyns in Essex. The Sir Anthony Abdy whose will we have quoted above was the grandson of Mary's husband and had inherited their Chobham estate. We can now continue with the Mumford family:

B – **William II** (1764-1827) Son (X) of William I. Married Elizabeth *Harvey* in 1795 at Windlesham church. Their daughter was Charlotte b. 1796 and their only son was John b. 1801. Mother Elizabeth died 1819 and William married again. His new wife was Abigail, who had no children, and she died before her husband in 1825, aged forty-four. William had witnessed the will of Samuel Cobbett, yeoman, in 1785.

Samuel II (1771-18XX) *OP 1795, 1800, 1815 and 1827. CW 1796, 1801-14.* We have called him 'the grand old man of Chobham', as he held an official position a record number of times, probably with the support of the new vicar. Samuel Mumford had apparently inherited the accounting gifts of his father as we find him engaged on every occasion when a large estate had to be administered on the death of an owner who left no will. In 1813 he was called 'farmer' but in the 1851 Census he was shown as 'Fundholder'. He married Sarah *Chittey* in 1791 at St Margaret's, London, and their six children were: Sarah b. 1792, married John *Sanders* 1812, Mary b. 1793, died five months old, *Samuel* b. 1795, *William* b. 1796, *James-Edward* b. 1797 and Mary Ann b. 1799, died three weeks old. Mother Sarah died four months after the birth of her last daughter (having given birth to six children within seven years). Father Samuel married again in 1801, Catherine (Kitty) *Collyer* at Horsell church and they had eight children: Mary b. 1801, married Mr. *Thompson* in 1820 but died two years later, John b. 1802, died a bachelor 1847, Henry b. 1803, Ann b. 1806, Charlotte b. 1805, married Richard *Collyer* 1828, but died without children 1833, Frederick b. 1808, Hannah b. 1809, married William *Luker* 1828 and Thomas b. 1811, died six years old. Mother Catherine died 1817 aged 39 and Samuel married again in 1824. His third wife was Mary and their two children were: Sarah b. 1825 and George b. 1829. Father Samuel was appointed executor in the will of Dr. Robert Harrup, the first Chobham surgeon, dated 1821. He lived in Brook Place in 1831.

C – **Samuel III** (1795-1851) *OP 1835. CW 1822-24.* Lived very much under the shadow of his father (Samuel II). Called a 'gent' when asked to act as trustee in the will of Ann Rapley dated 1830. In the 1851 Census, he called himself 'Landed Proprietor' and lived in Grants House (*see below* p. 137) with a gardener and a female servant. Married Sarah *Collyer* in 1816 but no children have been traced in the parish register. Sarah survived her husband by 18 years and was named as witness in the will of John Swaine, servant in husbandry, dated 1818. His two brothers were:

William III (1796-18XX) Shown as 'nursery labourer' in the 1851 Census. Married Frances *Harvey* in Sunbury. Middx. in 1817; Frances could have been a relative of William's aunt Elizabeth (the wife of William II) as both ladies were shown as 'born in Chobham' and there was at the time only one such family in the village. That might be the reason why they married so far away from Chobham. They had six children: Frances b. 1818, married Thomas *Haynes* 1842, Ann b. 1821, Sarah b. 1823, married Henry *Hockley* 1844, Samuel b. 1828, *John* b. 1832 and Jane b. 1840. Although we could not find a marriage of son John we did find the baptism of George, son of John and Jane Mumford, on 3 August 1851. (*see below* – John I.)

James-Edward I (1797-1871) Farmer and miller (Emmetts Mill). *OP 1830.* His wife was

34.   The old Emmetts Mill before restoration.

35.   Emmetts Mill after it had been restored in 1916.

Elizabeth and they had three children: Thomas b. 1823, Elizabeth b. 1825 and John b. 1827. Both husband and wife died in Horsell where they were buried. James-Edward was asked to act a executor in the will of John Souter, butcher in Chobham, dated 1834, and was witness of the will of John Daborn, dated 1827. His wife came from Bagshot, where their first child, Thomas, was baptised, but the other two children were baptised in Chobham.

D – **John I** (1832-18XX) Son of William III. ('Farmer's son' in 1851.) Lived in New House Farm with a male servant.

The name 'Grants House' raises a puzzle: it appears, for the first time, in 1820 in the Land Tax Lists where it quite distinctly replaces the property's old name 'Broadfords'. On the map of 1872 the two names are shown quite clearly on the opposite sides of the road as is the position today. But 'Broadfords' is said to have been owned by relatives of the British Prime Minister, Sir Robert Walpole (1730 to 1741), and is today a distinct separate entity from Grants Lands, opposite. The tax lists show 'Broadfords' as owned by the Chittey Family from 1780 onwards, who sold it to Samuel Mumford senior in 1801 and it was with him that the change of name took place.

Soan alias Sourn

A – **William I** (172X-178X) His wife was Mary and their seven children were: James b. 1747, died a bachelor 1791, *William* b. 1748, Sarah b. 1750, Thomas b. 1752, George b. 1754, John b. 1756 and Abraham b. 1758. His son was:

B – **William II** (1748-1828) Married Elizabeth *Knowles* in 1774 and their three children were: *William* b. 1775, *James* b. 1776 and Sarah b. 1777, died six weeks old. His two sons follow:

C – **William III** (1775-1840) Farmer. *OP 1802, 1805, 1819, 1838. CW 1804, 1828-32.* Married Ann *Lee* in 1800 who died three and a half years after the marriage without children. William married again; his new wife was Elizabeth and their 12 children were: Frances b. 1807, died a spinster 1834, *Elizabeth* b. 1808, Jane b. 1810, *William* b. 1811, James b. 1814, Alfred b. 1816, Palacia (Paulina) b. 1817, *Joseph* b. 1820, Martha b. 1822, died aged 14, Mary b. 1823, died two months old, Maria b. 1825 and Mary-Ann b. 1828. Father William was the first of the family as tenant at Shrubbs Farm (a property of the Abdy family).

James I (1776-1844) Farmer. *OP 1817, 1805.* Second son of William II. His wife was Sarah and their two children were: Elizabeth b. 1798, married twice: William *Wallis* 1825 and James *Daborn* 1845, and Sarah b. 1802. (Records show that the brothers William III and James I jointly ran the Shrubbs Farm for the Abdys.)

D – **William IV** (1811-18XX) Farmer. Son of William III. Married Susannah *Richardson* 1836 and their seven children were: Edward b. 1837 (his father at his baptism was described as 'baker'), Susannah-Elizabeth b. 1840, Emma b. 1842, Mary-Elizabeth b. 1844, Jane b. 1846, Anne b. 1849 and Jessie b. 1851. William followed his father as tenant on Shrubbs Farm. In the 1851 Census he was shown as farming 94 acres with three labourers, one of whom lived in the house as 'lodger' (as did Susannah's father).

Joseph I (1820-18XX) Farmer (Home Farm). Married Eliza *Turner* in 1842 and their seven children were: Elizabeth b. 1842, Matilda b. 1843, William b. 1845, Lucy b. 1846, Joseph b. 1848, John b. 1849 and Eliza b. 1850. Father William was shown as 'labourer' at the baptisms of the first four children and then as 'farmer'! His elder sister was:

Elizabeth (1808-18XX) Shown as 'School Mistress' in the 1851 Census, when she lived with her youngest sister Mary-Ann in a house in the High Street. In 1841, shortly after the death of their father William III, she and her brothers William and Joseph lived in Shrubbs Farm.

Nesmith

This family arrived in Chobham in 1740, when James Nesmith married Mary Bartholomew, the daughter of John Bartholomew, the owner of Hatchgate Farm which James farmed for his father-in-law. We shall see that this family deserves inclusion here, as their members held official posts in the village on many occasions. We suggest starting with members of the Bartholomew family as they, too, became important members of the community.

Bartholomew

John (1696-1776) Yeoman. Married Mary *Cox* from Thorpe at Little Bookham in 1722 and their six children were: Mary born 1722 (X), married James *Nesmith* in 1740, John born 1724 (X), died a bachelor 1796, Sarah born 1728, died a spinster 1783, Ann born 1730 (X) married Henry *Hone*, Catherine born 174X, married John *Chitty*, and Charles born 1742, who died and was buried in Windlesham 1818.

Henry (170X-1786) His son Henry built the Baptist Chapel in Westend in 1806 and father Henry left his farm (name unknown) to James Nesmith who referred to it as 'my uncle's'. So Henry could have been John's brother.

Nesmith

A –   **James I** (1716-1789) We have heard above that he married Mary *Bartholomew* in 1740 and their seven children were: John, Mary, Ann b. 1748, married John *Longhurst*, Elizabeth, *James* b. 1751, William and *Francis* b. 1752.

James II (1746-1812) We do not know his relationship to James I, but he married Jane *Merryett* in 1778 and their five children were: *Thomas* b. 1778, Robert b. 1780, Henry b. 1782, *George* b. 1783 and Ann b. 1786, married James *Lipscomb* 1813.

B –   **James III** (1751-1805) *OP 1779, 1796, 1802. CW 1782, 1797/8, 1803.* (Our records do not allow us to say whether it was James II or James III who held all these posts!) Married Hannah *Russell* in 1779, who died five years after her husband at the early age of 52. They had two children: Amey b. 1779, who died aged five and Sarah b. 1793, who died seven years old.

Francis I (1752-1802) Youngest son of James I. Married Elizabeth *Sedgewick* in 1807 and their four children were: Ann, Amy, Sarah b. 1793 and *James* b. 1786.

C –   **Thomas I** (1778-1846) Eldest son of James II. Married Mary *Bliss* in 1809 and their two children were: Mary b. 1810 and Thomas b. 1814.

George I (1783-1854) Married Elizabeth *Merrick* in 1813 and their three children were: George, Elizabeth and Jane.

James IV (1786-1835) Farmer (Hatchgate Farm). Only son of Francis I. Married Mary *Merrick* from Stanwell Middlesex in 1807 and their eight children were: Francis b. 1808, died a bachelor 1846, Mary b. 1810, Ann b. 1815, died a spinster 1839, *Henry* b. 1817, Charles b. 1819, Martha b. 1822, died just over one year old, John b. 1824 and Ellen b. 1826.

D –   **Henry I** (1817-1870) *OP 1847.* Married Elizabeth *Howard* in 1847 and helped his widowed mother (who in the 1841 Census was shown as 'farmer') at Hatchgate Farm. The couple had four children: Elizabeth b. 1849, Henry-George b. 1851, Emma b. 1852 and Charles b. 1855.

Note: Many of the details of the Nesmith family were not found in the Chobham records and we owe much to the research of the latest members of that family.

Gosden

A –   **James I** (1707-17XX) His wife was Elizabeth and their six children were: *John* b. 1732,

Edward b. 1735, a daughter (name illegible) b. 1737, Morice b. 1739, Elizabeth b. 1743, married William *Waller* 1765, and *Joseph* b. 1745.

B – **John I** (1732-17XX) Eldest son of James I. Married Hannah *Reed* in 1768 and they had one son Edmund b. 1771. Hannah died 1789.

Joseph I (1745-18XX) Third son of James I. Married Mary *Mote*, a widow, in 1770 and their son was Joseph b. 1771.

James II (172X-17XX) We could not trace his father. Married Sarah *Martin* in 1753 and their daughter was Sarah b. 1754.

John II (174X-17XX) His wife was Sarah and their son was *John* b. 1768 (again we could not trace John's father).

George I (173X-17XX) Married Ann *Giles* in 1768 and their two sons were: *George* b. 1768 and *Isaac* b. 1770.

Robert I (175X-18XX) His wife was Elizabeth and their son was *Robert* b. 1788. (No link within the tree).

George II (174X-1792) *OP 1776, 1792. CW 1773, 1790.* Married Hannah *Loveland* in 1772, and their seven children were: Henry b. 1778, *Thomas* b. 1780, Morris b. 1783, Jacob b. 1786, Edward b. 1789 and the twins Elizabeth and Sarah b. 1792; Elizabeth married William *Hampton* 1812 and Sarah married Thomas *Glazier* 1813.

C – **John III** (1768-1846) Son of John II. Married Mary *Reed* in 1816; no children.

George III (1768-18XX) Elder son of George I. His wife was Elizabeth and their two sons were: *George* b. 1806 and James b. 1810, died a bachelor aged 22.

Isaac I (1770-1842) Farmer (Bullrosen Farm). *OP 1821.* Married Sarah *Saunders* in 1792. Their nine children were: *James* b. 1792, *Isaac* b. 1795, Elizabeth b. 1797, Mary Ann b. 1799, *William* b. 1804, *John* b. 1806, Daniel b. 1808, Jacob b. 1811, died six weeks old, and Henry b. 1813, died aged three. Father Isaac was shown first as 'shopkeeper' and later as 'farmer'.

Richard I (176X-18XX) Married Charlotte Rowe in 1798. No further details.

William I (177X-1847) His wife was Elizabeth and their daughter Ann, b. 1798, married Richard *Bowyer* in 1823. We could not trace William's father.

Robert II (1788-1847) His wife was Mary (from Horsell) and they had eight children: Stephen b. 1813, died 10 years old, *Allen* b. 1815, Frances b. 1817, died aged one and a half, *Isaac*, b. 1822, Henry b. 1825, Charles b. 1827, Mary b. 1828 and James b. 1831.

Richard II (1768-1829) (No trace of his father). Married at Horsell, Elizabeth *Spooner* from Horsell in 1787 and their six children were: Elizabeth b. 1789, married Anthony *Fisher* in 1808, Allen b. 1790, *Richard* b. 1792, James b. 1793, died two weeks old, Amelia b. 1795, died a pauper and spinster aged 17, and James b. 1797. Mother Elizabeth died 1799 and father Richard married again; his new wife was Ann and they had one daughter, Sarah b. 1804.

Thomas I (1780-18XX) Shoemaker. Son of George II. Married Ann *Hill* at Windlesham in 1804 and their six children were: Hannah b. 1805, Eliza b. 1807, Stephen b. 1809, Charlotte b. 1812, married William *Hill* in 1834, *Arthur* b. 1815 and Thomas b. 1825.

D – **Stephen I** (1803-18XX) Labourer. Married Ann *Hayward* in 1824 and their nine children were: Stephen b. 1824, died five weeks old, *Isaac* b. 1825, Eleanor b. 1828, died aged seven weeks, Joseph b. 1829, Stephen b. 1831, Charles b. 1834, died aged two months, Henry b. 1835, Eliza b. 1838 and Margaret b. 1841. (We could not find Stephen's father).

George IV (1806-18XX) Farmer (Fellow Green Farm). *OP 1850.* His wife was Catherine and they had five children who were registered but not baptised. George born 1843, Walter born 1846, Job born 1848, Catherine born 1849 and John born 1850. George was the elder son of George III.

James III (1792-18XX) Labourer. Eldest son of Isaac I. His wife was Maria and their four children were: Martha born (not baptised) 1831, William born 1833, Elijah born 1836 and Daniel baptised 1838. His three brothers follow:

Isaac II (1795-18XX) Farmer (Hooklane Farm). Witness of the will of James Heather in 1824. Second son of Isaac I. Married Jane *Godfrey* in 1818 and they had eight children; Elizabeth b. 1819, Ann b. 1820, Sarah b. 1822, married James *Daborn* in 1849, Mary Ann b. 1824, Jane b. 1826, Margaret b. 1830, Isaac b. 1833 and Jacob b. 1836, died aged one and a half.

John IV (1806-18XX) Farmer (tenant at Rounce Farm). Witnessed of Thomas Turner's will in 1844. Married Margaret *Chittey* at Bisley church in 1828 and their three children were: John b. 1830, Ann b. 1833 and Elizabeth b. 1835. Mother Margaret died 1839 (only 30 years old) and John married again: his new wife was Mary and their one son, Isaac, born (not baptised) 1842. (Rounce Farm was owned by the Chittey family.)

William II (1804-18XX) *OP 1845.* States 'carpenter' in 1841 and 'farmer' in Census of 1851. Had taken over the Westend Nursery in 1838 but had moved again by 1851 to Watts Farm. Married Agnes *Eacott* of Bisley (their marriage was not shown in the parish register but as their children were entered in the West End Baptist chapel records, we assume that they were married there as well). Their children were: Sarah born 1831, William born 1832 and Hester born 1834 – the next children were registered by the new registrar of births: Stephen born 1837, Emma born 1840, John born 1841 and Agnes born 1850.

Isaac III (1822-18XX) Labourer. Second surviving son of Robert II. Married Jane *Smithers* in 1845 and their three children were: Eliza born 1846 (not baptised), George b. 1847 and Francis b. 1850. His elder brother was:

Allen I (1815-1839) Eldest surviving son of Robert II. Married Sarah *Sleet* in 1837, who remarried after the early death of Allen. They had one son: William b. 1838.

Richard III (1792-1826) Second son of Richard II. Married Sarah *Wells* in 1808 and their four children were: Rebecca b. 1807, Elizabeth b. 1808, James b. 1811 and Sarah b. 1813, died aged two and a half. Daughter Rebecca died aged four. Mother Sarah died 1816 and Richard married again. His new wife was Amelia and they had five children: Mary b. 1817, *John* b. 1819, Richard b. 1821, Caroline b. 1823, married Henry *Burchett* 1839, and Frances b. 1825. Father Richard died 1826 aged thirty-five.

Arthur I (1815-18XX) Labourer. Second son of Thomas I. His wife was Eleanor from Worplesdon and their three children were: (all born and baptised in Bisley) Ann b. 1841, George-Goodwill b. 1843 and Arthur-David b. 1845.

E –   **Isaac IV** (1825-18XX) Labourer. Eldest son of Stephen I. His wife was Esther from Pirbright. No children known.

John V (1819-18XX) Eldest son of Richard III's second marriage.

James IV (1811-18XX) Labourer in 1841, but 'Grocer and Farmer' in the 1851 Census. Married Hannah and they had five children: James b. 1841, Charles born 1844 in Chobham, Susan born in Windlesham 1847, Elizabeth born in Windlesham 1848, and Elizabeth born in Chobham 1850.

Ottaway alias Otterway

A –   **George I** (171X-17XX) Married Elizabeth *Gunner* in 1735 and their seven children were: George b. 1736, *Richard* b. 1738, *James* b. 1742, Elizabeth b. 1745, James b. 1747, Jane b. 1752 and Sarah b. 1754.

B –   **Richard I** (1738-18XX) Married Susannah *Wellbeloved* from Windlesham in 1762 at Bagshot church and their six children were: Susannah b. 1766, Mary b. 1767, Richard b. 1769, Elizabeth b. 1772, William b. 1774 and Jane b. 1777, died aged one year. Mother Susannah died in 1780 and father Richard married again in 1784; his new bride was Mary *Baker*.

John I (1742-1828) Labourer. Married Martha *Tapley* in 1770 and their seven children were: *John* b. 1770, Hanah b. 1772, *George* b. 1774, *Thomas* b. 1777, James b. 1780, *William* b. 1783 and Jane b. 1787, married William *White* in 1817 and, after her husband's early death, Robert *Hopkins* in 1831.

Henry I (1764-1835) Father unknown. Married Alice *Tikener* in 1789 and they had 10 children: *Henry* b. 1790, *James* b. 1792, *John* b. 1795, William b. 1797, Charlotte b. 1800, Elizabeth b. 1803, died four days after her baptism, Mary b. 1804, married Daniel *Underwood* 1819, Frances b. 1807, Eliza b. 1810, married Carmi *Cobbett* 1838, and *Stephen* b. 1812. In the 1851 Census, mother Alice is shown as 'farmer of 29 acres employs 2 labourers at Penfold Farm'. The two labourers lived in the farm and, in 1841, a 'nurseryman' was shown as living in.

C –   **John II** (1770-18XX) Labourer. Eldest son of John I. Married Jane *Howard* and their eight children were: James b. 1799, Thomas b. 1801, Jane b. 1802, Hannah b. 1808, married Thomas *Crane* 1833, Jemima b. 1811, Louisa b. 1813 and *John* b. 1815. In the 1841 Census Lucy, an illegitimate child of Jane, also lived in her mother's house. Four of his brothers follow:

George II (1774-18XX) Labourer and sawyer in 1840. His wife was Sarah and they had one daughter Hannah b. 1798. Mother Sarah died only 32 years old in 1810 and George married again. His new bride was Sarah *Munday*, whom he married in 1810 only seven months after his first wife's death. The second Sarah gave him nine children: Martha b. 1811, died aged six in 1817, *Charles* b. 1813, *Arthur* b. 1816, Stephen b. 1818, died a bachelor aged 20, Harriet b. 1821, died aged two, Caroline b. 1824, died five months old, Joshua b. 1825, Harriet b. 1828 and William b. 1832.

Thomas I (1777-18XX) Labourer. Married Lydia *Sale* (Searle?) in 1802 and their eight children were: Jane b. 1803, another Jane b. 1805, married William *Crane* 1825, William b. 1806, *Joseph* b. 1808, Elizabeth b. 1811, Mary b. 1815, *William* b. 1819 and Frances b. 1823.

James I (1780-18XX) Labourer. His wife was Margaret from Benson, Oxon. No further details.

William I (1783-18XX) Labourer and, in 1831, shown as brickmaker. His wife was Elizabeth. No other details known.

Henry II (1790-18XX) Farmer ('of 11 acres' in Mincing Lane, as shown in 1851 Census – *see also* p. 151). Eldest son of Henry I. Married Ann *Collyer* in 1815 and their only child was Henry b. 1819, died aged 16. Three of his brothers follow:

James II (1792-18XX) Blacksmith ('farmer of six acres' in 1851 Census). *OP 1842*. Married Ann *Hughes* in 1816 and their four children were: Ann b. 1816, married George *Lee* 1845, Charlotte b. 1818, William b. 1820, died 18 months after his baptism, and James b. 1823, died aged eighteen. We did not find the burial of father James's wife but he married again in 1838. His new bride was Ann *Swift*, a widow, and they had one son, Stephen born 1838 (apparently not baptised).

John III (1795-18XX) Farmer ('of 36 acres, employs 1 labourer and two sons', as shown in the 1851 Census at Halebourne Farm). *OP 1849*. Married Elizabeth *Arlet* from Yateley, Hants in 1827 and their three children were: John b. 1828, Frederick b. 1830 and Mary b. 1834. Father John's father-in-law, a labourer, left Elizabeth £40, as to his three other children!

Stephen I (1812-18XX) Carpenter. Youngest and 'late' son of Henry I. Married Mary *Baigent* in 1840 and their son Henry was b. 1841.

D – **John IV** (1815-18XX) Labourer. Youngest son of John II. No other details.

Charles I (1813-18XX) Woodsawyer. Eldest son of the second marriage of George II. Married Elizabeth *Hewitt* in 1840 and their four children were: James b. 1840, Stephen b. 1842, Caroline b. 1849 and Charles born 1850 (apparently not baptised).

Arthur I (1816-18XX) Woodsawyer, like his elder brother (in his father's trade!). His wife was Sophia from Shepperton, Middlesex, and their three children were: Henry b. 1843, Martha b. 1844 and Sophia-Jane b. 1847. (In their baptismal entries Arthur was shown as labourer.)

Joseph I (1808-18XX) Labourer. Second son of Thomas I. His wife was Sarah and their five children were: James born 1839, Eliza born 1832, William born 1834, George born 1844 and Robert born 1846. (None of the children was shown in the baptismal register of Chobham.) His younger brother was:

William II (1819-18XX) Labourer. Married Mary *Taylor* in 1845 and their three children were: William b. 1846, James b. 1848 and Eliza b. 1850.

We also found two youths whom we could not fit within our tree: John aged 17 and Richard aged 10, both shown as labourers in the 1851 Census. In addition there was also an entry in the 1851 Census which we feel ought to be shown in this family in spite of the 'odd' Oatway spelling:

Robert (1785-18XX) He came from Cutcombe in Somerset and was shown as: farmer (at the Folly with 30 acres). His wife was Frances from Tiverton, Devon, and they were listed with four children: Jane aged 13, Mary aged 11, Thomas aged seven and Elizabeth aged five (ages as in 1851).

Mepham alias Macham, Mackham, Meacham

A – **Richard I** (173X-1795) His wife was Elizabeth and they had three children: Richard b. 1756, Elizabeth b. 1760 and *Thomas* b. 1763.

B – **Thomas I** (1763-182X) His wife was Mary and their three children were: Elizabeth b. 1795, died a spinster aged 43, Charlotte b. 1796 and James b. 1799.

William I (174X-182X) Married Ann *Wye* in 1774, who died in 1821 aged ninety. No children known.

David I (1752-1821) Married Ann *Strudgett* in 1776 and they had eight children; *David* b. 1777, *Thomas* b. 1779, Elizabeth b. 1782, died a spinster 1840, James b. 1786, died 'in a quarrel in Twickenham' aged 26, *Richard* b. 1789, William b. 1793, died three weeks old, *Henry* b. 1794 and *Isaac* b. 1797.

C – **David II** (1777-183X) Married Harriet *Handasyd* in Windlesham church in 1809. No children known. Eldest son of David I; his four brothers follow:

Thomas II (1779-1845) Farmer at Lucas Green Farm, Westend. *OP 1824*. Married Elizabeth *Turner* in 1801 and their 12 children were: *James* b. 1801, Mary b. 1803, Martha b. 1806, *Richard* b. 1808, William b. 1810, died two years old, Sarah b. 1813, married Henry *Sherwood* 1832, Jane b. 1815, *George* b. 1817, Elizabeth b. 1820, Hannah b. 1824, married James *Arlett* from Bisley 1839, and Charlotte (Catherine) b. 1826. Father Thomas was appointed executor in the will of the widow Elizabeth Puddick in 1840.

Richard II (1789-18XX) Labourer. Married Ann *Prince* in 1812. No children known.

Henry I (1794-18XX) Labourer. Married Mary *Waller* at Horsell church in 1820. Their nine children were: *Henry* b. 1822, James b. 1823, Mary b. 1826, married Henry *Chapman* in 1853, Richard b. 1828, died aged five, Martha b. 1831, died three years old, Thomas b. 1833, George b. 1836, Eliza born 1839 and Harriet born 1842. (The last two children registered but not baptised).

Isaac I (1797-18XX) Labourer. Married Mercy *Lucock* of Pyrford in 1818, their 12 children were: John b. 1820, died 14 years old, Jacob b. 1821, died 12 years old, Jane b. 1823, married Henry *Daborn* 1844, Martha b. 1825, died aged nine, Eliza b. 1827, died aged seven, Isaac b. 1829, Thomas b. 1831, Charles b. 1833, died 11 months old, Mark b. 1835, Ellen born 1839, Emma born 1841, and John born 1845; the last three were registered but apparently not baptised.

D – **James I** (1826-18XX) Labourer. Married Jemima *Stevens* in 1848 and their daughter was Emma born 1858 (not baptised). James was shown as of Windlesham, and at his marriage his father, Alfred, brickmaker, was noted as witness.

Richard III (1808-18XX) Farmer (Washford Farm). Second son of Thomas II. Married Hannah *Holmes* in St Mary's, Guildford, in 1836 and their three children were: James b. 1838, Jane born 1841 and Martha born 1849. The children were registered but apparently not baptised. His brother was:

George I (1817-18XX) Farmer (Hooklane Farm) and local preacher. Married Mary-Ann *Cox* in 1840.

Henry II (1822-18XX) Labourer (but in 1851, 'farms seven acres'). Son of Henry I. Married Jane *Tickner* in 1849 and their daughter Jane was baptised 1850.

Tickner alias Tikener

A – **John I** (165X-17XX) Married Elizabeth *Hone* in 1678. Only one daughter is shown in the register but we suspect that they had one son, (X) John. Their daughter was Elizabeth b. 1683.

B – **John II** (168X-17XX) We have no further details.

C – **John III** (171X-17XX) Again a guess (X) but his brother James whose burial in 1807 aged 80 has been found.

James I (172X-1807) Married Mary *Hall* (X) in 1749. The names of four sons have been found in other parishes but one of them was buried in Chobham in 1825 aged 70, thus born around 1755. His name was *John*.

We found two more men and two women who fit into this generation.

William I (173X-17XX) Married Mary *Jones* in Horsell church in 1758 and, again, we assume that they had a son *William* born perhaps 176X.

Richard I (172X-1796) Married Jane *Sullenge* in 1756 and their six children were: *Richard* b. 1759, Mary b. 1762, James b. 1764, William b. 1766, Alice b. 1770 and *James* b. 1776.

D – **John IV** (1755-1825) Son of James I. Married Ann *Cocks* in 1785 and they had eight children: Ann b. 1786, Elizabeth b. 1787, John b. 1788, Hannah b. 1791, *James* b. 1792, *William* b. 1798 and *Henry* b. 1800. Mother Ann died seven months after the birth of her last child. Father John married again, in 1804, Sarah *Hill*, a widow who only lived four more years.

Richard II (1759-1828) Eldest son of Richard I. Married Elizabeth *Hine* in 1789 and their five children were: Elizabeth b. 1790, *John* b. 1792, Mary b. 1795, Ann b. 1798 and Alice b. 1801. His youngest brother was:

James II (1776-1847) Labourer. Married Elizabeth *Bullen* in Shere church in 1808. Their three children were: James b. 1811, William b. 1813, died four days after his baptism, and Mary b. 1814.

William II (176X-18XX) Labourer. Son (X) of William I. Married Jane *Henten* in 1784 and their 11 children were: William b. 1785, Richard b. 1787, John b. 1789, died four months old, Sarah b. 1790, James b. 1793, Jane b. 1795, Mary b. 1797, Letitia b. 1800, Isaac b. 1802, Elizabeth b. 1805 and Henry b. 1807.

E – **James III** (1792-18XX) Labourer, (shown in 1851 at Focklesbrook Farm). Second son of John IV. Married Sophia *Lee* in 1817 and their 10 children were: James b. 1818, died aged 14, *John* b. 1820, William b. 1822, *Henry* b. 1824, *Stephen* b. 1826, Mary-Ann b. 1828, Hannah b. 1830, Morrice b. 1832, Charles b. 1834 and Ann b. 1843. (In the 1841 Census Morrice's place has been taken by Maria!)

Henry I (1800-18XX) Youngest son of John IV. Married Ruth *Underwood* in 1822 and their 10 children were: *Henry* b. 1822, *Thomas* b. 1824, Jane b. 1826, married Henry *Mepham* in 1849, John b. 1828, James b. 1830, died 10 years old, Daniel b. 1833, died eight years old, Sarah b. 1836, Ann b. 1840, Mary b. 1842 and Harriet b. 1845.

F – **John V** (1820-18XX) Coal and corn labourer. Eldest surviving son of James III. Married Ann-Charlotte *Woods* in 1844 and their four children were: Charlotte b. 1845, James b. 1847, John b. 1849 and William b. 1851.

Henry II (1824-18XX) Labourer. Second son of James III. Married Rebecca *Daborn* from Horsell in 1850. Children not known.

Stephen I (1826-18XX) Next son of James III. Married Jemima *Lunn* in 1850. Also a labourer.

Henry III (1822-18XX) Labourer. Eldest son of Henry I. Married Sarah *Burchett* from Woking 1843. No children known.

Thomas I (1824-18XX) Labourer. Second son of Henry I. Married Charlotte *Champion* from Windlesham in 1847 and their two children were: Charlotte b. 1848 and Ruth b. 1850.

Rapley

A – **William I** (162X-1673) Married Jane *Hone* in 1667 and one daughter, Jane is shown as buried in 1691.

The name Rapley now disappears from the register until four generations later when we again find a William. We jump generations B, C and D.

E – **William II** (1755-1819) Labourer. His wife was Ann who was mentioned in his will of 1818. They had one son *William* born in 1783 in Horsell. Mother Ann survived her husband by 28 years, and witnessed the will of John *Swaine*, dated 1818.

F – **William III** (1783-18XX) Shoemaker. Married Elizabeth *Carpenter* at St Martha's in 1805 and they had 14 children: William b. 1805, Mary Ann b. 1807, James b. 1809, Charlotte b. 1810, Sarah b. 1812, *George* b. 1813, *John* b. 1815, Jane b. 1817, *Henry* b. 1818, Frances b. 1820, Richard b. 1822, Charles b. 1824, Stephen b. 1826 and Maurice b. 1827. Father William's mother, Ann, lived with her son's family according to the 1841 Census.

John I (178X-1840) Labourer. Married Phebe *Harcourt* in 1810 and their five children were: *James* b. 1811, Harriet b. 1819, died a spinster aged 21, *Indigo* b. 1825, William born 1834 and another James born 1839. (The last two boys were apparently not baptised.) Note that in 1839 mother Phebe was 46 years old!

James I (1794-18XX) Labourer. Married Jane *Hampton* in Woking in 1816 and their 10 children were: *William* born 1818 in Horsell, Stephen b. 1817, Arthur b. 1820, Hannah b. 1823, John b. 1825, Reuben b. 1827, Esther b. 1829, Eleanor b. 1831, died aged three, Joseph and Mary (twins) b. 1833.

G – **George I** (1813-18XX) Labourer. Second son of William III. Married Frances *Ridger* in 1833 and their five children were: Hannah b. 1834, died 17 months old, Mary b. 1835, Charlotte b. 1837, Sarah b. 1839 and George b. 1841, died 11 months old. Mother Frances died three months before the burial of her last child. His two brothers follow.

John I (1815-18XX) Shoemaker. Married Hannah *Pharo* from Ash in Woking in 1837, and their four children were: William b. 1837, James b. 1840, George born 1844 and Frederick born 1847 (the last two boys were apparently not baptised).

Henry I (1818-18XX) His wife was Ann *Hampton* (née *Howard*) and in the 1841 and 1851 Censuses they were recorded living with Ann's brother, Thomas, a bachelor. They had two children: William b. 1848 and George b. 1850.

James II (1811-18XX) Labourer. Son of John I. Married Martha *Hayward* in 1840 and their five children were: Henry b. 1841, Harriet b. 1843, James and Martha (twins) b. 1847, and George b. 1850. His brother follows:

Indigo I (1825-18XX) Married Frances *Crane* in 1847 with two children: Frances b. 1848 and Ellen b. 1850.

William IV (1818-18XX) Labourer. Son of James I, born in Horsell as stated in the marriage entry. His wife was Ann and they had four children: Jane b. 1841, William born 1844, Mary Ann born 1846 and James born 1848. (The last three children were apparently not baptised.)

Crane

A – **John I** (168X-17XX) Married Mary *Child* in 1714. No further definite details.

Nicholas I (169X-17XX) His wife was Jane and their daughter was Mary b. 1729.

B – **John II** (172X-18XX) Son (X) of John I. Married Mary *Beldam* from Pirbright in 1755. No further details.

William I (172X-18XX) Married Jane *Fladgate* in 1744 and they had three children: Jane b. 1746, married Benjamin *Haynes* 1769, Ann b. 1748, married James *Taylor*, 1774, and Samuel b. 1749.

C – **John III** (1751-1820) Married Ann *Clifton* in 1774 and their 12 children were: *William* b. 1774, *James* b. 1776, *Henry* b. 1780, Ann b. 1782, Elizabeth died unbaptised 1783, Susannah b. 1784, married Thomas *Wells* 1805, Joseph b. 1786, died aged 10, Stephen b. 1788, died one and a half years old, Ann b. 1790, *Samuel* and *Stephen* (twins) b. 1792 and Sarah b. 1795, married John *Giles* 1813.

Joseph I (176X-181X) Perhaps (X) son of William I. Married Sarah *Churchill* from Chertsey in 1785 and their nine children were: William b. 1786, Elizabeth b. 1788, married John *Gould* 1812, James b. 1791, Sarah b. 1793, married Robert *Hopkins* 1816, Mary-Ann b. 1796, *Joseph* b. 1798, Hannah b. 1801, married Edward *Evershed* 1820, *John* b. 1803 and Stephen b. 1807.

D –   **William II** (1774-1834) Labourer. Married Sarah *Gosden* in 1796 and their five children were: Sarah b. 1798, married James *Glazier* 1818, Charlotte b. 1801, *William* b. 1803, Elizabeth b. 1805 and *Henry* b. 1819.

James I (1776-186X) Married Amelia *Daborn* in 1796 who died aged 21, two years after the marriage. James married again in 1799, his new bride was Mary *Mitchell* who died, without having had children, aged 63 in 1831. James married again in 1832 the widow Mary Clemens who died in 1845, aged 76.

Henry I (1780-186X) Married Hannah *Challingham*, in East Molesey church in 1804 and their seven children were: Mary-Ann b. 1805, Frances b. 1807, married James *Budd* in 1826, Martha b. 1808, Henry b. 1810, Stephen b. 1816, Samuel b. 1820 and Eliza b. 1823, married James *Hall*.

Stephen I (1792-18XX) Labourer. Married Elizabeth *Gothard* in 1814 and their nine children were: Elizabeth b. 1815, married John *Smith* 1836, George b. 1817, name illegible b. 1819, Eliza b. 1822, Sarah b. 1832, died nine years old, Stephen b. 1825, James b. 1828, died 11 months old, Maurice b. 1830 and Mary b. 1833.

Samuel I (1792-18XX) Labourer. Twin-brother of Stephen I. Married Mary-Ann *Jeffries* in 1824 and their eight children were: Mary-Ann-Elizabeth b. 1825, James b. 1826, *Charles* b. 1827, Esther b. 1829, Arthur b. 1831, Charlotte b. 1833, Caroline b. 1835 and Sarah b. 1838.

Joseph II (1798-18XX) Labourer. Married Elizabeth *Hunt* in 1820 and their 10 children were: Miriam b. 1820, married William *Stevens* 1840, *William* b. 1822, Lois b. 1825, married William *Taylor* 1844, Celia b. 1828, Stephen b. 1830, died five months old, Elizabeth b. 1831, Hannah b. 1833, Harriet b. 1837, Amelia b. 1839 and George b. 1841.

John IV (1803-18XX) Brother of Joseph II. Labourer. Married Sarah *Hampton* in 1827 and their six children were: Sarah b. 1827, Eliza b. 1829, Jane b. 1831, died aged four, Frances b. 1833, Elizabeth b. 1836 and Stephen b. 1839.

E –   **Henry II** (1819-18XX) Labourer. Second son of William II. His wife was Mary-Ann from Egham and their six children were: Charlotte b. 1839, Mary b. 1841, died two months after her baptism, Harriett b. 1843, Sarah b. 1846, Emma b. 1848 and Ellen b. 1850. His elder brother was:

William III (1803-18XX) Labourer. Married Jane *Otterway* in 1825 and their 10 children were: John b. 1825, died within two years of his baptism, Harriet b. 1829, William b. 1831, Hannah b. 1835, James b. 1837, died seven days after his baptism, Caroline b. 1839, Joseph born 1843, Eliza born 1845 and George born 1847. (The last three children were apparently not baptised.)

Charles I (1827-18XX) Second son of Samuel I. Shown as 'General Servant' in the 1851 Census. We do not know his wife's name but his son was Henry-Charles b. 1850.

William IV (1822-18XX) Labourer. Eldest son of Joseph II. Married Mary *Shorter* in 1844 and their two girls were: Mary born 1844 and Esther born 1846. (Both apparently not baptised.)

Thomas I (1812-18XX) Labourer. Father unknown. Married Hannah *Otteway* in 1833 and their six children were: Stephen b. 1835, Jane b. 1838, Lucy b. 1840, Sarah b. 1843, John b. 1845 and Emma b. 1847.

James II (1809-184X) Labourer. Father not known. Married Louisa *Chisman* in 1830 and their six children were: Thomas b. 1832, Eliza b. 1834, James b. 1836, Harriet b. 1840, William born 1844 and Esther born 1850. (The last two children were apparently not baptised.)

John V (1823-18XX) Bricklayer. Father not known. Married Eliza *Lee* in 1850 and their two children were: Eliza born, not baptised, 1849, William b. 1851.

Shorter

A –   **William I** (171X-1784) His wife was Sarah and their nine children were: Thomas b. 1742, Sarah b. 1745, Elizabeth b. 1747, *Henry* b. 1750, *Robert* b. 1752, *John* b. 1755, James b. 1758, Ann b. 1760 and *Stephen* b. 1764.

B –   **Henry I** (1750-1829) His wife was Mary and their 10 children were: Henry b. 1772, Mary b. 1774, *James* b. 1775, Ann b. 1778, Sarah b. 1782, William b. 1785, Hannah b. 1788, died 10 months old, *Allen* b. 1790, Jane b. 1793 and John b. 1796. His three brothers follow:

    Robert I (1752-1828) Married Elizabeth *Leadbeater* in 1775 and their four children were: *Ephraim* b. 1776, the twins Elizabeth and Ann b. 1778, both died within three weeks of their baptism, and Jane b. 1779.

    John I (1755-18XX) His wife was Mary and their only child was *Henry* b. 1780.

    Stephen I (1764-1841) Married Sarah *Gray* in 1785 and their six children were: Mille b. 1785, Frances b. 1787, died aged two and a half, Rebecca b. 1789 died six months after her baptism, *Stephen* b. 1790, another Frances b. 1793, died aged 13, and yet another Rebecca b. 1796, died two weeks after her baptism. Mother Sarah died in 1812 aged only 49. Father Stephen married again; his new bride was Sarah who bore him nine children: Sabina b. 1815, Frances b. 1816, Charity b. 1819, died aged 11, Naomi b. 1821, Winifred b. 1822, Clarissa b. 1823, Richmond (a girl) b. 1825, Olive-Matilda b. 1827 and Spencer-Haley b. 1829.

C –   **Allen I** (1790-1829) Son of Henry I. Married Jane *Stovell* in 1813 at Bisley church and their nine children were: Elizabeth b. 1813, *Allen* b. 1815, William b. 1817, John b. 1820, Jane b. 1822, died aged 13, Martha b. 1825, died aged 15, Mary b. 1827, married William *Crane* 1844, William b. 1828, died two and a half years old and Sarah (baptised after her father's death) b. 1830, died six weeks after her baptism. His elder brother was:

    James I (1775-18XX) Labourer. His wife was Sarah whom he married in 1798 and their five children were: James b. 1799, died a bachelor aged 31, *John* b. 1802, Sarah b. 1805, Mary b. 1809, Eleanor b. 1813.

    Ephraim I (1776-18XX) Son of Robert I. His wife was Elizabeth and their only child was Elizabeth b. 1799.

    Henry II (1780-1856) Son of John I. Labourer. Married Mercy *Tunnell* in 1802 and their seven children were: *John* b. 1804, *Henry* b. 1805, Martha b. 1807, Isaac b. 1811, George b. 1813, William b. 1815, died three months after his baptism, and Charles b. 1817. Mother Mercy died in 1819 aged 38 and father Henry married again. His new bride was Sarah *Harden*, their marriage taking place in Ash in 1827. They had four children: Frederick b. 1828, Hannah b. 1831, Jane b. 1833, died one year old, and Richard b. 1835.

    Stephen II (1790-18XX) General Dealer (horse dealer in 1831). Married Sarah *Stevens* from Pirbright in Pirbright church in 1811 and their nine children were: Elizabeth b. 1811, *Stephen-Frederick* b. 1816, Margaret-Matilda b. 1818, Mary Ann b. 1821, Frances b. 1824, died aged 19, Thomas b. 1827, Hannah b. 1831, married Thomas *Mose* 1851, Ann b. 1834 and William-John b. 1835.

D –   **Allen II** (1815-18XX) Labourer. Married Mary *Watts* in 1843 and their three children were: Allen born 1844, Mary born 1848 and Jane born 1850. (They were apparently not baptised.)

John II (1802-18XX) Labourer. Eldest surviving son of James I. Married Sarah *Knight* in 1824 and their six children were: Sarah b. 1830, Henry b. 1833, Eleanor b. 1835, John b. 1837, Charles b. 1842 and Emma b. 1845.

Henry III (1805-18XX) Labourer. Second son of Henry II. His wife was Jemima and they had six children: Ann b. 1838, Martha b. 1840, Charles b. 1843, William b. 1845, Emma b. 1848 and George b. 1851. His brother was:

John III (1804-18XX) Labourer. Married Martha *Howard* in Horsell in 1826 and their five children were: John b. 1827, Martha b. 1829, died aged 15, Henry b. 1832, died aged seven, Mary b. 1835 and William b. 1838. In 1851 the family lived in Chertsey.

Stephen III (1816-18XX) Labourer in 1841 but 'General Dealer', like his father, in 1851. Married Mary-Ann *Taylor* in 1847 and their daughter was b. 1848 as Mary-Ann-Hannah.

Searle alias Sale

A –   **William I** (167X-17XX) His wife was Anne and their two children were: William b. 1697 and Anne b. 1699.

Thomas I (16XX-1728) His wife was Mary and their four children were: Ann b. 1707, Joan b. 1709, William b. 1712 and Henry b. 1715.

B –   **James I** (17XX-18XX) We could not establish his father. His wife was Ann and their four children were: James b. 1735, Henry b. 1736, William b. 1739 and Mary b. 1749, married John *Roake* 1778. Father James witnessed the will of Thomas Loveland, yeoman, in 1797, and also the will of Henry Slyfield, yeoman, in 1774.

We also found in the Bisley registers an entry of a marriage of a couple of Chobham residents dated 26 September 1734.

James II (171X-17XX) His wife was Mary *Longhurst*, also from Chobham.

Thomas II (172X-17XX) His wife was Elizabeth and their only child was Richard b. 1746.

C –   **Charles I** (174X-18XX) Again we were unable to ascertain his father but he married Mary *Collier* from Horsell in Horsell church in 1770. No children known.

D –   **William II** (1755-1833) His wife was Elizabeth and their five children were: Elizabeth b. 1777, James b. 1779, Sal b. 1780, John b. 1789 and Samuel b. 1797, died aged fourteen.

This was the first of four Williams whose parentage we could not find but who fell into this generation.

William III (1760-1835) Married Sarah *Cobbett* in 1779 and their six children were: William b. 1781, *James* b. 1784, *Morris* b. 1787, Charlotte b. 1789, married William *Sleet* 1815, Lucy b. 1792, married Thomas *Tucker* 1809 and Henry b. 1794.

William IV (1775-1833) Married Sarah *Howard* at Byfleet in 1799 and their eight children were: Ann b. 1799, Mary b. 1800, Sally b. 1803, Jane b. 1805, died nine months after her baptism, *Benjamin* b. 1806, Martha b. 1807. James b. 1810 and William b. 1813.

William V (17XX-17XX) His wife was Judith who died in the Chertsey Union House in 1846 aged 95. Their only child was William b. 1791.

Now we return to our normal method:

E –   **James III** (1784-18XX) Carpenter. Second son of William III. Married Susannah *Rapley* in 1808 and their nine children have been found in the Baptist (Westend) chapel: *James* born 1810, Charlotte born 1812, Esther born 1816, buried aged seven in the chapel grounds, Aron born 1818, Martha born 1820, buried aged three and a half in the chapel grounds, Rhoda born 1824, and another Esther born 1827. James had married in St Lawrence church! His brother was:

Morris I (1787-18XX) Married Ann *Cobbett* from Bisley in Bisley church in 1807 and their first child was b. 1810. The following children were found in the Westend Baptist Chapel records: Nathan born 1812, Morris born 1816, Joseph born 1817, Sarah born 1818 and Frances born 1822.

Thomas I (1748-1850) Labourer. As with the four Williams, (*see above*) we could not trace his father but, again, we could find their years of birth as their burial entries showed the age at death. His wife was Ann and their five children were: Louisa b. 1810, married James *Gibbons* 1839, *Henry* b. 1812 (from this birth on, father Thomas was shown as 'Shop-keeper'), Jane b. 1815, Celia b. 1817 and Martha b. 1819, died four years old.

F –   **Benjamin I** (1806-18XX) Labourer. Son of William IV. His wife was Elizabeth and their four children were: Charles b. 1826, Charlotte born 1833, Arthur born 1834 and Susannah born 1837. The last three children were not found in the Chobham baptismal register.

James IV (1810-18XX) Master-bricklayer. Son of James III. Married Sarah *Church* in 1833 who, in 1851, was shown as 'bonnet-maker'. They had three children: George b. 1835, died aged four and a half. Sarah b. 1839 and Mary b. 1841.

Nathan I (1812-18XX) Cordwainer. Son of Morris I. His wife was Mary and their three children were: Mary born 1838, Martha born 1849 and Ann born 1851. Nathan witnessed the will of James Lucock, farmer, in 1839.

Henry I (1812-18XX) Farmer (of six acres in 1851). His wife was Eliza and no children are known. Eldest son of Thomas I.

Sleet

A –   **John I** (169X-176X) His wife was Ann who died a widow in 1774. Their two children were: *James* b. 1722 and *Joseph* b. 1725.

B –   **James I** (1722-1800) Wheelwright. Married Sarah *Johnson* in 1756 and their daughter was Elizabeth b. 1765. James witnessed the will of Richard Lee, farmer, dated 1773.

Joseph I (1725-17XX) Married Elizabeth *Dawborne* in 1747 and their four children were: John b. 1748, *Joseph* b. 1749, Elizabeth b. 1751 and *James* b. 1754. We have also found two more members of the family who (X) could be sons of Joseph I: *Henry* b. 1756 and *William* b. 1759.

Elijah (17XX-17XX) The marriage entry in the Chobham register shows him to be 'from Woking' and we have no means of establishing his father. He married Mary *Daborn* in 1763. No other details.

James II (1730-18XX) Married Elizabeth *Chitty* in 1762 and their daughter was Hannah b. 1771.

C –   **Joseph II** (1749-1832) His wife was Elizabeth and their two sons were: *Henry* b. 1781 and *Joseph* b. 1786.

James III (1754-1841) Married Sarah *Casell* in 1782 (from Old Windsor) and their three children were: *James* b. 1783, Sarah b. 1785 and Henry b. 1787.

Henry I (1756-1829) Married Elizabeth *Spooner* in 1781 and their seven children were: Henry b. 1783, died a bachelor 1805, William b. 1786, again died a bachelor in 1816, James b. 1788, Elizabeth b. 1791, died aged 16, *John* b. 1792, Ann b. 1795 and Sarah b. 1798.

William I (1759-18XX) His wife was Sarah and their only child was *William* b. 1790.

D –   **Henry II** (1781-18XX) Married Amelia *Shorter* in 1813 and their three children were: Frances
        b. 1813, Paulina b. 1820 and Henry-John b. 1824. His younger brother was:

Joseph III (1786-18XX) Married Elizabeth *Cooper* in 1822 and their only child was Joseph
        born, not baptised, 1829 and who died aged six.

James IV (1783-18XX) Labourer. Son of James III. Married Jane *Martin* in 1806 and they
        had seven children: Eliza b. 1808, James b. 1809, Henry b. 1812, Rebecca whose
        baptism was not found and who died aged 14 in 1829, *George* b. 1814, Marianne
        b. 1819 and Emma b. 1821.

John II (1792-18XX) Labourer (lived at Langshot Farm, 1851). Married Mary *Cook* in 1825
        and their seven children were: William b. 1826, Elizabeth b. 1828, John b. 1831,
        Mary b. 1833, Jane b. 1835, Ann b. 1839, and Elizabeth born (apparently not
        baptised) 1847.

William II (1790-1851) Married Charlotte *Searle* in 1815 who died in the following year aged
        twenty-six. William married again in 1818, his new bride was Sarah *Bageant* from
        Windlesham who gave him seven children: William b. 1819, Sarah b. 1821,
        married Allen *Gosden* 1837 and, in 1842, James *Taylor* after the death of her first
        husband, Charlotte b. 1823, died three weeks after her baptism, Henry b. 1825,
        Elizabeth b. 1827, Harriet b. 1829, Hannah b. 1832, died 15 months old, and
        James b. 1834.

E –   **George I** (1814-18XX) Labourer. Son of James IV. Married Elizabeth *Vince*, from London,
        in 1849 and their daughter was Jane-Louisa b. 1850.

   Now that we have finished our task of describing the development of a number of families
in Chobham, we feel that our concentration on this subject enables us to say something of
the ways and reasons why and how our families developed.

   First, we will demonstrate one aspect of family fortune by comparing two families and
their ways of dealing with their property. We want to select the Attfield family who held,
from Henry VIII's time until around 1700, two of the largest farms in the Westend of
Chobham. After that date they disappear from our records, the reason for which, we feel is
the way they acted in financial affairs. Henry Attfield of Millwards is reported to have been
involved in a number of attempts to raise credits, whilst Henry Attfield of Fellow Green

Henrie Feilde of Millwards and Henrie Feilde of Velley (Fellow) Greene recorded among
those participating in the lottery of 1567.

made a large number of bequests in his will to 'be paid out of my freehold'. The family
name reappears again only in 1858 when Sir William Abdy is asked to grant the tenancy
of one of his farms to the family. To complete this picture, we must admit that we were
unable to fit the many 'Field-brides' who were, in fact, really 'Attfields' into our family
tree.

The other family we wish to discuss in this connection is the Beauchamp family where we can point to opposite methods for preserving the family fortune. Phillipp, a member of the fifth generation, had two sons. The older of them married at only $17\frac{1}{2}$ years of age and showed, apparently, signs of lack of responsibility, so father Phillipp disinherited him and left his considerable landed estate to his second son, Anthony. That father Phillipp was indeed keen to preserve his family's standing is shown in that he left generous sums to his two daughters with the proviso that the amounts should be cut to one tenth if they married against their mother's wishes. Phillipp's younger brother, although shown as 'yeoman', apparently decided that his branch (as the cadet branch) should turn to a handicraft activity to avoid the necessity for demanding a part of the family's landed estate. His son, Martin, became a carpenter but he was to maintain the respect their family had enjoyed in the village and was one of the first non-farmers to be elected as churchwarden, in 1760 and again in 1761.

It will also be of interest to see how a poor family dealt with the problems arising from having to make a will; John Ottaway, labourer at Borough Hill, made his will in 1813, going on to live another 15 years to reach the age of 82. In it he bequeathed to his wife Martha 'plate, linen, china' and other household items together with an annual rent of £12 (after his death his estate was valued at 'less than £20'). To each of his five sons he left a quarter acre of his freehold, to his eldest son, John, the messuage he occupied himself, and to each of his still-living children (including one girl) £2. His daughter apparently had already built a cottage on her quarter-acre plot after her marriage in 1817.

Now we want to turn to another subject. Building up family trees by its very nature stresses the importance of the male members, as the survival of a son to marriageable age is the only guarantee of the continuation of the family name. In this connection we have had to restrict a wife's contribution to her natural role as mother. But we feel we can additionally show the vital influence of the female members in assisting their husbands; this is particularly clear in cases where a member of a labouring family, perhaps having shown qualities as a good worker and thus recommended to a new owner who lacked local knowledge, married the daughter of an established farmer's family.

Our first example is the Lee family; here the first Henry made in his will a large number of bequests which, apparently, were met by the sale of his farm. His and his brother William's descendants had to wait a long time to recover their standing in the village. William's great grandson had to wait for his chance until a non-resident man purchased the Biddle Farm and was looking for a reliable tenant. William Lee was the person recommended for the job. When the new owner asked him to run the farm as a nursery, we can be sure that the influence of William's wife, Catherine, was of great importance. She was the daughter of John Rogers, a member of a very old and respected family of farmers, who had apparently had a better education and was thus able not only to be an efficient housewife but was also in a position to support her husband in the new venture. That he made a success of the task – or perhaps we should say 'they' – was shown in that for although he had no chidren himself his cousin's boys, whom he trained, were accepted to follow him as tenants in the nursery.

Another example of a rising family is the Daborns. We will show that their rise started with the marriage of William to Mary Rogers, a sister of Catherine whom we mentioned in the previous paragraph. William's nephew, John, had also married into an old farming family in the person of Mary Jewer, a member of a family highly respected in the village. When Lord Bulkely (*see above* p. 29) looked for capable tenants for two of his farms, he appointed William and John Daborn, who after his Lordship's death, continued running the farms for their new owner. Perhaps we should add here that the two farms were the largest in Chobham, one of 170 acres and the other well over 100 acres.

But it was not only as supporters of their husbands that wives are shown. There are a number of cases where a man died leaving his widow to carry on his trade. John Beauchamp, a sawyer and farmer, died in 1840 and in the 1841 Census his widow was described as 'farmer', and she had to look after their seven children, the oldest of whom was 27 and the youngest thirteen. Henry Otterway, farmer at the Penfold Farm, died in 1835 and, in the 1841 Census, his widow was described as 'farmer of 29 acres, employing 2 labourers'. William Howard, farmer and carpenter, had died in 1839 and his widow was, in the 1841 Census, described as farmer of Wiggenors Farm. William Harris, a saddler, died in 1845 and his widow in 1851 was described as 'saddler, employs 3 men'.

In our emphasis on the 'Old Families' we must have created the impression that these families kept the election of parish officials exclusively to themselves. So we feel it will be useful to quote as an example a rather different instance: Robert Nix from Souldon, Oxfordshire, having applied for relief was in consequence transferred back to his home village in April 1831; however, the 1831 Census, taken in May of that year, shows him as a labourer residing in Chobham with his wife and two children, both of whom had been baptised in Chobham. At the baptism of his further two children in 1832 and 1834, he is still shown as labourer, but from 1837 in the baptismal register he is named as 'farmer' and shown in the Censuses of 1841 and 1851 farming the 'Lane End Farm' (otherwise 'Gosdens Farm'), owned by the Collier Family. In 1841 Nix was elected Overseer of the Poor.

On page 382 of his *The Family, Sex and Marriage in England 1500-1800*, Professor Lawrence Stone points out that certain demographic facts can only be laboriously extracted from parish registers of marriages and baptisms and, further, that privacy for families who lived, worked, ate and slept in one or two rooms was impossible; we feel that our research had given us ample opportunity to amplify these comments.

First, concerning the question of privacy, we want to mention the details of the Hearth Tax returns of 1664 which show that among the 143 families in Chobham, not fewer than 57 lived in cottages with one hearth only, of which number 38 had been judged as inhabited by families too poor to be charged the Tax.

In order to come closer to the second suggestion, we have extracted from all our family records those with five and more children to work out the time difference between the first and last baby's baptisms. Here are the figures at the basis of this analysis: the number of families in this category was 317, 32.5 per cent of all the marriages shown in the parish registers. (The latter total was 973 – *see page* 68.) The total of children in those families was 2,308, which represents 60.2 per cent of all the baptisms registered between 1654 and 1851 (3,797). The number of 'woman years' between the first and last babies' baptisms was 4,639, which gives a figure of nearly exactly two years between pregnancies. To show how reliable our figures are, we have divided the total of all pregnancies by the total of families (3,797÷973), which gives 3.9 baptisms as the overall average of baptisms in all families. To try to produce a control for our figures we divide the number of baptisms not included in our analysis (3,797 less 2,308 = 1,489) by the number of families not included (973 less 317 = 656) which gives a reasonable average of 2.25 for these 'not so productive' families; the average number of pregnancies in our sample families (2,308÷317) was 7.25, while the average number of pregnancies in all families (3,797÷973) was 3.9.

We hope that we have given proof of the reasonable reliability of our analysis so that we can return to the demographic realitites of our village's life. If we assume an average age of brides at marriage of 22-23 we cannot be far out from the facts as otherwise a duration (7.25 x 2.00) of 14.5 years of reproductive activity would bring us to the upper limit of female fecundity. In fact a rather large number of women experienced their last pregnancy in their forties.

36.   Medhurst's shop (now a chemist's), with the post office to the right.

37.   An old postcard of the postman and his horse-drawn delivery cart.

We must also not forget the general circumstances of our village society: the small number of unmarried women over the age of 24 (in 1801 19, but rising to 61 in 1841) which restricted the assistance available from that source. That the frequent pregnancies resulted in the early deaths of many wives is borne out by the numbers of widowers (in 1841 38, starting with one each in the age groups 30-34 and 40-45 and then rising to reach seven among men over 80). But, on the other hand, we must also point to the number of widows, who were obviously often left alone with young children (starting with one or two in age groups 20-24 to 45-49 then increasing to nine in the age group 70-74 and six at over 80). No help was apparently available from the older daughters within the family: our figures for 1841 show that the number of girls at ages up to nine was larger than that of the boys, but decreased clearly in the later age group when compared with the boys' numbers. Many of the older girls, i.e. those of 12 or more, had left their homes to go into service possibly in the village, but at times further afield, even as far as London. Perhaps at times a number of elderly widows, named as 'dames' in the poor-overseers' reports, were paid for assisting younger wives. But we must also stress the fact that we have, up to now, overlooked incidences of miscarriages and stillbirths of which there is only one case mentioned in the 200 years of entries in the registers. Our records also show the small number (69) of female servants who were obviously working in the houses of gentlemen, richer farmers and traders so that the average wife had to rely on herself under difficult conditions. But perhaps we should also add that the large families were found at all levels of society i.e. among farmers, traders, craftsmen and labourers.

Two newcomers to the village, though not shown amongst the old families, ought to be mentioned here as they brought new 'trades' to the village. Daniel Adey, *stationer*, arrived in 1825 and after his death in 1838 was succeeded in his shop by Thomas Medhurst ('Master Printer, Stationer & Druggist employs 2 men and two boys' – according to in the 1851 Census) to whose son, William Aubrey, born in 1845, we owe the many postcards depicting the village at about the turn of the century (1901). The name of Robert Harrup, a *surgeon*, appears in the reports of the overseer of the poor from 1795 , he treating inmates of the workhouse. His will provides a good idea of his personality: he gives 'the sum of fifty pounds to be paid to my late servant Hannah Moody, not as a legacy or donation but for wages which I stand indebted'. He goes on:

> To my daughter Hannah Street the sum of ten pounds and to my two other daughters Margaret and Richmond all and every rest of my personal estate, goods, chattels etc. I make the difference between them *solely* on the ground of her not standing in such want of pecuniary aid as her two sisters and not from any malice or dislike.

But we also know more about our surgeon from the book of Charles John Shore, second Baron Teignmouth (*see also* p. 172):

> Our Doctor, skilled in Pharmacy, was a tall, stout man, wearing pig-tail, a widower living in the village with his three daughters. The misadventure of eloping with the Lady . . ., wife of a Scottish laird, reconciled him to a life of obscurity.

Dr. Harrup died in 1825 and his 'mantle' was taken over by Joseph Hewer, surgeon, who is shown in the 1851 Census as living at 'Windsor Road, North of Chertsey Road' with his second wife Elizabeth, whom he had married in 1836 in Chertsey (after his first wife's death in 1833), with their two youngest children (of the four older ones, one had died on the day after her baptism). The Census also shows his qualifications as 'Medicine M.R.C.S., L.A.C.'. In his house lived another surgeon, in addition to a young visitor, a cook, nurse, groom, housemaid and page, all born in Chobham and surrounding villages.

Here is yet another new occupation: John Saunders (whose widow describes herself as 'pauper, Postman's widow') worked normally as a farm labourer, but his son born in 1817 gives, in the 1851 Census, his trade as 'Letter deliverer' – the Penny Post had been introduced in 1850.

Here we stop looking at individual people in our village and turn our attention to how all these people acted in running their community.

The signatures of 19 members of the vestry, 1737.

Chapter Six

The Farmers Run the Village

We have come a long way from the days of A.D. 673, when the small settlement between the two bournes was given to the Monastery of Chertsey, to the Census of 1851, when the village had grown to 429 houses with a population of 2,069.

The settlement, together with the Abbey, was twice destroyed: first by the Danes and then by the Normans after 1066, after which we hear for the first time of the church of St Lawrence which in the Domesday Book is still only referred to as a 'chapel'. In the nearly nine hundred years under the supervision of the Abbey's abbots, the Benedictine monks had taught the villagers the art of husbandry so as to feed themselves and their families from the produce of their ground, although the Black Death of 1348 interrupted such development. We have heard that in the following scarcity of labour the inhabitants of the Hundred of Godley rose as 'the Confederation of serfs in Chobham, Thorpe and Egham' in 1378, formed soon after the benevolent prelacy of Abbot Rutherwyk had ended in 1346. Little was found in old documents to report on the following 200 years until Henry VIII set his eyes on a part of Chobham as a perfect spot for a hunting lodge and deer park, which he obtained in 1537 in the course of the Dissolution of the Monasteries. In 500 acres of ground surrounding the old manor-house he created a deer park where several times he hunted wild boar. His royal successors did not share his interest in Chobham and the house and park changed hands until finally the whole manor became part of the Onslow estate in 1752; the family provides today the lords of the manor of Chobham.

In the absence of a resident lord of the manor we suggested that the inhabitants of the second big house, Chobham Place, must be considered as the village's squires. We found, however, that the interests of the resident family, well into the beginning of the 18th century, were concentrated on their lands in other parts of the country so that they only interfered in Chobham business when acting as J.P., such as when the overseers of the poor presented their annual report or in some case of difficulty.

It was only natural, therefore, that the other educated person in the village, the vicar, took a leading role in village affairs. But from our list of incumbents (*see above* p. 52) we have seen that no vicar before 1575 held his post for long enough to have had much influence. On the other hand we have also seen that John Haywood (vicar from 1575 to 1595), coming from a background much like that of his parishioners, was probably unable or unwilling to impose his ideas on his parish. His successor, however, Thomas Taunton, vicar from 1595 to 1649, had both the length of service and the experience as a former schoolmaster to see that his parishioners were properly looked after according to the existing laws. And the extant early accounts of the churchwardens dated 1635 and 1639 throw a light on the wardens' work and attitudes. Taunton's successors, two covering 16 years and thus unable to show their influence in the difficult years of 1649 to 1665, were followed by the Rev. Christmas. His stay in Chobham was cut short for family reasons so we have to wait until 1691 and the arrival of William Oates, of whose work we have given a few examples; he was able to occupy the vicarage for 39 years, when his stay was abruptly ended in 1730 after a period when he influenced his parishioners considerably. This proved to be most important as his successors for the next 70 years did not live within their parish so that the parishioners had to look after affairs themselves. Fortunately we have been able to find a number of documents to show how the men, after being elected by the vestry as church-wardens or overseers of the poor, did perform their tasks.

It was for that reason that we gave so much space to show which families provided the men to run the village, starting in Henry VIII's time when we found the earliest list of inhabitants which, with later details, enabled us to determine the history of their families, then reporting on the families which appeared in the village in Queen Elizabeth's time and thirdly those later arrivals who took over the burden of parish office from the older families. We found that in these 70 years no one family had kept the running of the parish to themselves and documents show that vestry meetings were always attended by a number of persons who had been officials before and, when necessary, were always at hand to assist the office-holders in difficult or time-consuming duties. That the range of families from whom officials were elected covered the whole community has been proved by using the Muster List of 1583 which gave a complete list of men in the village and again by using the Hearth Tax list of 1664 which offered a similar basis.

In the next paragraphs we want to give examples of how the churchwardens and overseers of the poor managed; but before we do that we also want to show as best we can what life was like in the days of Queen Elizabeth I, for which we have some good sources. Imagine that the year is A.D. 1583. One quiet Sunday evening we come out of the church after evensong and for a moment look down the Street – no cars to be seen nor heard; we lean on the churchyard wall and close our eyes but not our ears; we hear what the parish constable has to say.

> Maye yt please your Worship those be to advertyse yow of the Woordes that one Sybell Whytinge did speke agaynst certen honest women of Chobham:
> Fyrst that Jone Morer a wydow women was an old bawde and also dyd threaten to beate her –
> Further she did threten Jone Hiller that she wolde beate her and that she wolde make one hand having a lame hand as short as the other –
> Further she did threaten Anys Holis and that she wolde bate her –
> Further she did beate Ales Burchet at Thomas Tayler's gate and toke Cowe donge and sayde that she wold make her receyve the Communyon with it, and wyped yt about her face –
> Further she hathe beaten three wyves already –
> Further she hathe called Thomas Morer Cokold and sayd that his wyfe is a whore –
> Further she hath called Lorans Lord thefe and sayd that she wolde thrust a knyfe in him or his wyfe yf eyther of them cam out a dores –[1]

The statement was signed by An Hollis, Jone Heller, Allis Burchatt, widow, and Jone Morer, widow.

Here is another incident, but this time concerning only male offenders, which can be dated as occurring within perhaps ten years of the previous uproar; in this case the constable was rather more outspoken:

> To the right worshipful Sir William More Knight. This is to certify your worship that upon Monday being the 26th Day of February ther came to me John Woodes beinge constable of Chobham; one Elysander Farman and with him another of his fellows and they sent for me in the alehouse and ther requested of me 18 shillings 6d which was spent in chardges with Carriage of the man Mussell to your Worship and so to Jayll at London and the sayd Elysander Farman dyd ask me whether I would deliver the money or not and I sayd I would not without the Consent of my neghbors and with that the sayd Elysander Forman Drewe his dager and beat me and hurt me and I the sayd John Woodes constable brake away from them and came into the street and chardged my neghbors to ayd me in the quennes majesties name and some did and some would not for the sayd forman had his sworde and dagar bent agaynst me and I beinge connstable chardged them to deliver ther wepons and the sayd the would not I syd to them will ye nether obey the quennes majestie nor her offycers and the sayd no and therwith I criede Donne with them the be Rebelles and with that I toke a stafe and stroke at the, but the could not for one Henry wye alehouse keeper conveed them to ther howses

so that we could not have them to bring unto your worship Thus having to trouble your worship at this tyme.

Wyttness to these John crosse tethynge man and Robert Norwood Anthony Whytinge Roger Tetley John Eyde with others.

By your loving frendship to commande Henry Rogers Henry Hedge Henry Try William Bulling John Waphott Thomas Taylor thomas pritchard Thomas Lane Thomas sponge and John Millis cravinge Your worshipes Frendship in our behalfe and the queenne majestie officers that the may not be so over bourne for if the be we shall gett non to bear the office.[2]

But this is not enough of sad happenings in the village or regarding villagers; in the *Calendar of Assize Records, Surrey Indictments*, we found the following cases where Chobham people were either culprits or victims:

1. Wye, Stephen, husbandman, and Bedell, Lawrence, yeoman, of Chobham, indicted for grand larceny. A Grand Jury presented that on 3 November 1575 at Chobham they stole 2 silver spoons, a silver ring and a silver pin and £22 in money from John Smyth of Sonning Hill, Berks., husbandman. Total value £22 13s. 4d.
   Wye found guilty: to hang. Bedell is at large.

2. Hartopp, John, of Oxford, Gent., indicted for highway robbery. On 23 May 1586 he assaulted Richard Baynes in the highway at Chobham and stole from him a gelding (£10) and 15s. in money.
   Verdict unknown.

3. Skynner, John, silk weaver of Chobham, indicted for burglary. On 20 December 1587 he burgled the house of Roger Shere at Chobham and stole 30 ells of Lockram, two ells of holland, 20 ells of canvas and one yard of velvet, total value £2 18s. 4d.
   Skynner found guilty: to hang.

4. Grigg, Robert, of Farnham, and Eles, William, of Chobham, labourer, indicted for grand larceny. On 18 January 1588 at Chobham they stole two oxen (£8) from Richard Lee, Gent. Wood, John, of Chobham, tanner, was indicted as an accessory.

5. Quick, Robert, of Chobham, tailor, indicted for grand larceny. On 22 April 1595 at Chobham he stole four geldings (£13 6s. 8d.) from William Sumner.
   Guilty: to hang.

6. Wood, John, of Dorking, shoemaker, indicted for grand larceny. On 18 October 1593 he broke into the house of Richard Beckenstall at Epsom, and stole £7 in money, six gold rings, a silver ring, a coral and silver bracelet, a bundle of bugle lace, 12 handkerchiefs, three falling-bands, a pair of sheets, two silk girdles and three ruff bands. Total value £6 15s.
   Guilty: to hang.

7. Glover, Hugh, of Chobham, labourer, indicted for petty larceny. On 17 November 1596 at Chobham he stole a sheep (10d.) from John Houghts.
   Confessed: whipped.

8. On 4 December 1580 Cooke, John, and Hyckes, William, both yeomen of London, assaulted an unknown man in the highway at Chobham Heath and stole from him £3 in money.
   Cooke confessed: to hang.[3]

We have given all these examples to show that the village officials be they constables, tythingmen or churchwarden or (later) overseers of the poor, faced very difficult tasks which, as constable John Woodes said, without support from higher authority would have made it impossible to find men to undertake the offices. However, there is one bright thought in that in 1595 a new vicar arrived in Chobham in the person of the Rev. Thomas Taunton, who in his 54 years as vicar led his flock and his wardens in coping with any problems they may have had to face. His three successors were not as lucky as their stay at the vicarage together only lasted 42 years. The next vicar, William Oades (1691-1730) was, as we have said before, the last incumbent to reside in the village. Thus the churchwardens and overseers of the poor were left to face alone the problems created by their brothers and sisters in the village. This is now what we are going to describe.

We found no proof that Chobham had nominated overseers of the poor in accordance

An account of the charges

About the amending & repairing

of the Church

Imprimis Eleaven hundred of Boards at divers
shillings and sixpence the hundred ...

Item for slitt stuffe and lead & three quarters ...

Item for vij oak boards at xvjd the board comes
to ...

Item for one hundred of Plankes ...

Item for glasing the Church windowes ... iiij vjd

Item paid to Christopher Hopkins for xxvij dayes
worke at viijd the day ... xxxij viij

Item paid to him for his boyes worke for xxiiij
dayes worke a halfe at vjd the day
comes to xijs iiij

Item to Thomas Hopkins for xxij dayes worke
at viijd the dayes ... xxij

Item paid Mathew Chapman for three
hundred of nailes & five plates at
iiijd a poure ... iiijs iiij

Item paid to william forte for forging of
three hundred of bords from John mill
and for forging of a ton of stufe from the mill
viij

38. Part of John Biddle's 'Account of the Charges About the amending & repairing of the Church'. This document is dated 1635 and is the oldest extant churchwarden's report.

with the 1597 Act but the earliest note of their existence is an indenture dated 1683 in which
a poor child of the parish is placed as apprentice to a brickmaker in Chobham, a document
which also bears the signature of Anthony Thomas, J.P. (of Chobham Place). We must
wait until 1732 before we find the annual reports of the overseer, both his receipts and
payments. The churchwardens' accounts of earlier dates show that in 1635 John Biddle,
churchwarden, had divided his report into two parts: 1. The accounts of the expenditure on
mending and repairing the church and 2. other expenditure, among which we find: paid at
'severall times to pore 18d' and, again, 'I gave 5s worth of bread to the pore', which show
that at that time the churchwarden filled some of the overseer's roles. At the same time we
ought to report that, in 1632, a letter was addressed

> To the Churchwardens and Overseers of the parish of Chobham. According to certain new Instructions
> given by the ffeoffees and Executors of Henry Smith Esq., deceased, concerning the distributing and
> accompting for the benevolence bestowed by the said Henry Smith for the releife of the poore of the
> Towne. These are to admonish you that you made ready your accompts fairly written for mee when
> I come for them which shalbe within fourteene daies after Easter next. And that you have ready also
> to deliver mee a true copy of the rates of your able Inhabitants made unto the Justices. And also
> the bond of your Churchwardens and Overseers made unto your Mynister. And moreover I am
> commanded to refuse all accompts which are not true, or which are not in every point exact and
> farmall according to this and former instructions given mee answerable to the deeds of uses. And if
> the accompts be not ready when I call for them without further attendance I am appointed to
> retourne your Towne defective whereby they shall lose the next years benevolence. And more if any
> pretend ignorance of the deeds of uses they are to take notice thereof at their peril. And this much
> I am enjoyed to signifie unto you by the ffeoffees and Executors of Mr. Smith.
> 29th September 1632   M.G. Weston

To explain to what the preceding quotation refers we must, again, turn to our trusted source,
John Aubrey, who on page 219 in vol. III of his *Natural History of Surrey*, reports:

> On a parchment, in a frame, in the church in (old) Woking, is an Account, that Henry Smith, Esq;
> by a deed, dated 26 January, 1626, 2 Carol I, gave several large Sums of Money to be employed for
> the Maintenance of the Poor of several Towns and Parishes in the County; with which his Feoffes
> purchased the Manour of Warburton in Sussex, of which the several Annual Payments following
> are made to the Parishes under-mentioned: (Amounts totalling 160.0.0). These Parishes are in
> Number 38.

These distributions are still performed today.

Mr Weston appears to have assumed that Chobham had already appointed overseers of
the poor but as we said we found no *local* evidence of their election before 1683. We have
copied this document because it shows in so many words what the parish officials were
expected to know about their village. Again, in 1639, we find a churchwarden's bill for the
repairing of the church, a quite detailed account showing a list of materials purchased and
the names of Chobhamers who who either supplied some of them or did some of the work:
the bells are mentioned and the glazing of the church windows and other repairs.

One of two apprentice indentures dated 1639 and witnessed by Thomas Taunton, the
vicar, shows 'that John Chapman, son of John Chapman of Chobham hath putt himself
Apprentice to Daniell Sidell, yeoman of Chobham', which is followed by a detailed
enumeration of both the master's and apprentice's duties. The other indenture, very much
on the same lines, shows that Richard Smith, son of Henry Smith is apprenticed to John
Spott, bricklayer of Chobham. (Both apprentices came from 'able' families.)

Further early documents show the range of actions the churchwardens were expected to
deal with. In 1662 John Marshall, Rector of Ilminster in Somerset, signed a receipt for
8s. 10d. ' .pon the Brief for the Fire of Ilminster'. For the same year we also find the receipt
of Thomas Underwood for 8s. 'received by vertue of His Majeties Letters Pattents produced

To the Churchwardens & Overseers of the
Parish of Chobham

According to certein new instructions given by the Feoffees
& Executors of Henry Smith Esqr, deceased, concerning the
distributing & accompting for, the benevolence bestowed
by the said Henry Smith for the releife of the poore of yo[ur]
Towne. These are to admonish you that you make ready
yo[ur] accompts fairely written for mee when I come for
them, or if it be within fifteene daies after Easter
next. And that you have ready also to deliver to mee
a true Coppy of the rates of yo[ur] able Inhabitants made
unto the Justices: And also the bond of yo[ur] Churchwardens
and Overseers made unto yo[ur] Minyster. And moreover
I am commaunded to refuse all accompts which are not
true, or which are not in every point exact & formall
according to theis & former instructions given, moore
answerable to the deede of Mr Smith. And if the accompts
be not ready when I call or call for them w[i]thout further
attendance I am appointed to returne yo[ur] Towne deferties
whereby they shall lose the next yeares benevolence. And
more if any pretend ignorance of the deede of Mr Smith they
are to take notice thereof at their pill. And thus much
I am enioyned to signifie unto you by the Feoffees
& Executors of Mr Smith.

Nich Weston

29° Septem
1632

39. Mr. Weston's appeal in 1632 to the Chobham parish officers to prepare their report which he required before he could distribute the Smith's Charity.

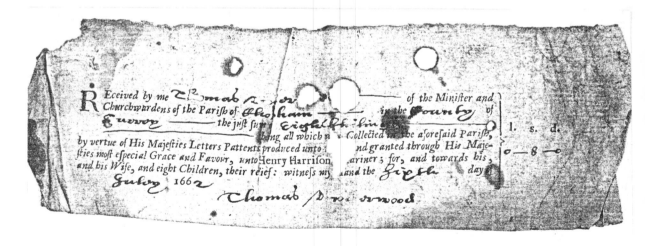

day nor night absent — him self, but in all things as an honest and faithfull Apprentice shall and will demean and behave himself towards his said Master and all his during the said Term. And the said Master his said Apprentice in the Art during the so term — — — which he now use they — shall teach and instrict, or cause to be taught and instructed by the best way and manner that he can; finding and allowing unto the said Apprentice, sufficient, wholesome Meat Drink, Apparel, Washing, Lodging, and all other Necessaries fit for an Apprentice during this so term for the true performance of all these covenants & agreem: either of the said Parties bindeth himself to the other by these presents —

In Witnes whereof, the said parties to these Indentures, interchangeably have set their Hands and Seals, the first — — — day of December — — in the — third — Year of the Reign of our Soveraign Lord and Lady William and Mary by the Grace of God, of England, Scotland, France and Ireland, King and Queen Defender of the Faith, &c. Annoq; Dom. 1691.

Sealed & delivered in the presence of

Ralph Sucmer Daniel: Biddle:

John Marsh   the mark of Hen: Gro

40. Two old documents relating to Chobham: (*above*) an apprenticeship agreement dated 1691 and signed by Daniel Biddle; (*below*) a receipt for 8 shillings granted as relief to Henry Harrison in 1662.

Received by me Thomas a jor   of the Minister and Churchwardens of the Parish of Chobham   in the County of Surrey   the just sum Eight shillings   l. s. d.
being all which n   Collected in the aforesaid Parish, by vertue of His Majesties Letters Pattents produced unto   nd granted through His Majesties most especial Grace and Favour, unto Henry Harrison   ariner; for, and towards his,   0 — 8 — 0
and his Wife, and eight Children, their relief: witness my   and the fifth   day
July 1662   Thomas Underwood

unto and granted unto Henry Harrison, mariner, for, and towards him and his wife, and eight children'.

A will dated 1659 shows the influence of the 'new times' in that it does not begin, as was normal in royal times, with a statement of the regnal year. But otherwise it is perhaps surprising that the upheaval of the years 1649 to 1660 seems to have left little impression after its end. The vicar took up again his old duties and the villagers seem to have settled down – they had to look after their livelihood and had perhaps not much time and energy for political considerations. The King, Charles II, continued – as far as the villagers were concerned – as his father had done and 55 men contributed £25 11s. 2d. between them when, in 1661/2, they were asked for 'a free and voluntary present to the king' (see above p. 28). But this time the demand affected, against the advice of the king's grandfather, James I, even lowly persons such as labourers.

In 1688, we have a chance to see how much was in fact collected as parish rates: a penny rate was earmarked for the church and the work of the churchwardens, and three farthings for poor relief. It seems that, from 1656, the two accounts were kept separately. But we must not forget that the officeholders had to continue with their ordinary work – the only charge they made for themselves was in the early years 1s. when they spent a day on parish matters which, in later years increased to 2s. 6d. While it is true that their spelling and grammar was often faulty even if their hand was fluent: in one instance the writer, coming across the word 'coroner' for the first time spelt it 'Crowner'; three years later, he had learnt the correct way! In many cases the parish clerk transcribed their reports before they were shown to the J.P. (Such lack of academic achievement, however, did not prevent them from fulfilling the very-often quite complicated duties of the post.)

We have now reached the year 1664 which we have mentioned several times as a year the Hearth Tax was collected.

> These are to give notice that the Officer, or Officers, appointed to collect and levy his Majesty's Duty of Hearth-Money, intend to be at Chobham in this county, upon or about the 7th day of November in order to the viewing and numbering of the Fire-Hearths and Stoves, in the respective houses therein (wherein all Constables and such like his Majety's Officers are to be ready to assist them as the Law directs;) And to the demanding and receiving of all Moneys due to his Majesty for the said duty, at and before the feast of St Michaell last past. And all Persons concerned in payment of the said duty, are desired to have ready their last Acquittance, and to provide Money for discharge thereof accordingly; That so themselves and the Officers may be put to no further trouble; dated the 1st November 1678.   signed William Chary, Collector.[4]

We might make an attempt at estimating Chobham's population at that time based on this list of householders. We had said (see above p. 11) that there were around 400 people in the parish in 1583, but now we have a sounder basis for our estimate. The total of householders in 1664 was 143, suggesting a population of approximately seven hundred. Using the method which W. G. Hoskins recommends in his Local History in England, taking the total of baptisms in the ten years nearest to the time sought and multiplying the annual average by 30, we find that the number of baptisms between 1661 and 1670 was 228, implying a probable population of 684 in the village at this period. So we can, with some certainty, accept a figure of 700 for Chobham's population in 1664.

But back now to our parish officials: between 1664 and 1695 we find no less than 13 apprenticeships for poor Chobham boys arranged by the parish officials and there were six more between 1700 and 1755. Two more problems to engage the attention of the officials were the establishment of the rights of settlement of persons arriving in the village and asking for relief. In such cases the overseers would apply to two Justices of the Peace to establish whether the immigrants had the right of settlement in another parish and, according to the decision or finding, a letter to the 'home' parish of the people would be sent to recover any expenses made for them and the newcomers might be sent back there. At the same time persons with the right of settlement in Chobham will have been taking the same steps elswhere and our officials will have had to accept and deal with the wanderers.

In the period from 1700 to 1730 twenty cases of outward movements and 13 of inward moving people are shown in the records. We must underline that in many instances whole families had to be moved which led at times to some difficult decisions. However, numbers of such cases increased manyfold in the following 70 years: parish records show no less than 86 cases in these years. Such actions would in our eyes appear to be cruel and selfish but it was the job of the wardens and overseers to look after the people of their own parish, where the numbers of poor people requesting relief grew steadily.

Yet another very worrying problem were the cases of illegitimate children. In every case the father of the child had to be ascertained and made to contribute to the cost of the upbringing of his child. Again, here the help of J.P.s had to be sought where the men were found unco-operative. We have counted such cases: between 1700 and 1730 there were seven instances, a number which increased to 29 over the next 70 years.

In addition to these problems was, of course, the old problem of the poor: we have heard that as far back as in the 14th century Abbot Rutherwyk was praised for 'setting the poor to work' and, again, that Thomas Cromwell offered daily sustenance to some 200 poor people. We have very good records of amounts collected and spent in our village from 1732 onwards and we must underline the fact that the amount of poor rate to be paid by each villager/householder was set by decision of the vestry; in fact it was the farmers who determined how much each should pay and they themselves, when overseers of the poor, distributed the money as they thought fit.

We know the sums involved from 1769 onwards: the average from 1769 to 1780 was £220 annually collected, increasing in the next ten years (1781-1790) to £321, again rising to £371 in the next five years. When the total needed rose within two further years (1796-7) to £480 the vestry decided in January 1798 to halve the poundage and double the basic value of property, thus obtaining the same amount in the end. Perhaps the reason for this financial 'dodge' is illustrated in Manning and Bray's comment:

> About the year 1790 the poor were maintained by three sixpenny rates in a year. In the terrible years of 1799 and 1800, 8s. in the pound answered the purpose, when many Parishes raised 18s. and some much more.[5]

In modern terminology one would call this a 'fiddle' but apparently the Chobham farmers thought it to be a good idea! We ought to add here that the total collected in 1799 was £768 and in 1800 no less than £1,702. Of the 229 families enumerated in the Census of 1801, no less than 109 were 'on relief'.

This general outline of the problems facing our officials ought now to be followed by individual examples of some of them. But first we shall quote from documents and this one, dated 1737, arouses our interest:

> The said William Harvest for and in consideration of the summe of one hundred and forty pounds of lawful money to be paid to him by monthly payments by the overseers of the poor of the said parish and their successors . . . That he does herewith promise and agree with the said Churchwardens Overseeres and Vestry to provide for, keepe and maintain at his own proper costs and charges all and every such poor person and persons as now are or shall happen to become chargeable, with all necessary Victualls Drink Clothing Washing Lodging Firing and Tendance and to bury them when dead at his own costs and charges for the consideration aforesaid. And the said William Harvest doe hereby promise to procure one or more fitting persons to be bound with him for the due performance of this agreement and to direct them in the intended workhouse as a master and overlooker. And the vestry doe appoint the two churchwardens to be overlookers in the workhouse.[6]

The agreement is signed by 19 members of the vestry.

From that date we were able to find annual agreements, sometimes extended to over two or three years, with local persons to act as workhouse-masters. The amount payable remained the same until 1786 as can be seen from the overseers annual reports. In many instances, however, the parish supplied the workhouse with necessary items of food or clothing. We have not been able to find any provision made for the erection or otherwise of the workhouse until 1784 when we find an inventory of goods at Chobham workhouse which mentions a number of rooms, with 14 bedsteads, and a kitchen and washhouse. This house served until 1790 when it burnt down and another was built by a local carpenter/builder at a cost of £570 which was covered by an annuity of £400 from a Mr. Cummins; we find the monthly repayments of the annuity in the overseers' account.

In 1739 a general meeting of the parishioners was called to discuss the increasing instances of turf and peat being cut without permission and sold to people in adjacent parishes. An appeal was made for informers to act and for successful informations a sum of 40s. was to be paid. Two or more copies of the agreement to be made and publicly posted within the parish. The proclamation was signed by 13 inhabitants.

Quite a different matter also calls for our attention. The overseers have complained to two J.P.s that the father of an illegitimate child who had agreed in an earlier session to pay 1s. 6d. per week was now heavily in arrears. The J.P.s command the overseers to apprehend the culprit and bring him before them as soon as possible (1747 and 1749).

1741: An indenture to put William Ricketts, a poor child of the parish, as apprentice to a victualler at Egham; the officials also undertake to provide the apprentice with coat and waistcoat, doeskin breeches, stockings and shoes at the start of his work and his new master promises to supply him with the same articles at the end of his apprenticeship.

1751: A statutory declaration of John Hollis, butcher, of Chobham, in which he declares his willingness to give the churchwardens and overseers of the village a bond amounting to £100 as a guarantee for his payment of 6d. weekly for the upbringing of his grandson John Hollis as long as the boy remains chargeable on the parish, the grandfather clothing his grandson initially.

1757: The churchwardens and overseers of the parish of Ockham have contacted those of Chobham for their permission for a young mother to come and live in Chobham in the house of her mother and at the same time offering a bond for £20 to be assigned to the Chobham officials.

1760: A young woman expecting an illegitimate child of a father, also of Chobham, intends to await the birth at the house of her mother in Frimley, before returning to Chobham with the baby. In this case the magistrate is Sir Anthony Thomas Abdy (of Chobham Place) and both parishes agree.

1764 and 1766: We précis these two documents because they give a picture of what happened to young persons and their work experience.

1. Thomas Draper states that at nine years of age he worked for a yeoman in Woking for four years, at 13 he worked for a yeoman at Walton, the following year again for a farmer in Woking. The next year he was hired by a gentleman in Woking for a whole year, but fell ill after six months when he went to stay with friends for a fortnight. He returned and completed his year but was not paid his full wages on account of his illness. He then was hired for a year by a yeoman in Horsell but his master 'became poor and left his business' without paying the boy his due wages. The happy ending of the story: young Thomas married and had two children.

2. Our next case concerned a girl born in Chobham. She states that at the age of 16 she was hired by a yeoman in Chertsey with whom she stayed for two years, before moving to a brickmaker in the same town. After one year she was hired by a yeoman in Woking and after a year moved again to Thorpe – in this way she had not gained any settlement rights. No decision is shown to have been made by the J.P.s so that her birth would have governed her rights in Chobham.

These were examples of routine matters which engaged our officials' attention but we have noted a number of 'petty' incidents which are shown in the overseers' books but are not necessarily supported by other documentary evidence.

1773: Bond to Kingston attending justices and getting Isaac Spooner out of gaol – £1 15s. 1d.

1774: Licence to marry T.S. £1 8s. parson & clerk 15s. Other expenses at the 'sun' 17s. 8d. likewise ring 10s. 6d.
    Mr. Nugent's rate forgiven him being a SHUFFLER.

1776: Mrs. Giblett to learn Mary Everett make mantua

1777: Getting Mrs. L. to Bethlem 10s. 6d. and

1778: Bringing Mrs. L. back from London

1779: Subsistence: for T. Boyer of Stoke family; him going substitute for Richard Shorter £3 16s. 6d.

The Examination of Anne Wye of the Parish of Chobham Single woman taken on oath the 1st of January 1760 before Sr Anthony Thomas Abdy Bart: one of his Majestys Justices of the Peace for the said County

This Examinant on her oath saith that she is a Parishoner of the Parish of Chobham in the said County, that about fifteen months ago she became quick with Child & that the said Child was begotten by Robt Knight of the said parish of Chobham Labourer, That about six or seven weeks before she was brought to bed, the said Robert Knight perswaded her to go to his mothers. who is now the wife of Richard Freeman of the Hamlet of ~~Bisley~~ Frimley in the said County, That she accordingly went to the house of the said Richard Freeman & was there delivered of a male Bastard Child named William, That she continued at the house of the said Richard Freeman for the space of five weeks after she was deliverd of the said Child and then returned with her Child to the said parish of Chobham And this Examinant saith that the said Robert Knight is the father of the said Child and that she was delivered of the said Child in the house of Richard Freeman in the said Hamlet of Frimley

This Examination was taken on oath the day & year abovewritten before me

the mark ✝ of
Anne   Wye

Anty Thos Abdy

41. The examination in 1760 of the mother of an illegitimate child before Sir Anthony Thomas Abdy of Chobham Place to decide the future residence of mother and child.

1780: Ben Hay family six times in six weeks running him being eloped 5s. 2d.

1781: Ring and expense married Jas Maunt and licence £4 10s. 9d. again Keeping Ben Hays family four weeks pay him being listed in the Militia – Dame Savage for making poor gowns 5s. 6d.

1783: Mrs. Hartwell for children schooling £1 5s. 11d.

1784: Gave Reed children on coming to Workhouse 1s. (H Reed poor)

1785: Mr. Gayton overcharged, house empty [this was the vicar]

1786: Attending bench, delivering in the account of the state of the poor. (Was this, perhaps, a requested contribution to the great work of Sir F. M. Eden – *The State of the Poor* of 1797?)

1787: Returning John Case to his parish – half clothing Elizabeth J. to go to service – writing militia list

1788: Warrant to apprehend James Carter – expenses going after him – Spent meeting Mr. Carter & his friends at the *White Hart* to make up the affair, meeting them at Staines to make up – paid the nurse towards nursing the child two weeks – total costs about 18s.

1790: Gave J. H.'s daughter 10s. 6d. to go to service

1791: Meet T. H. take bond of indemnification for his bastard

1792: John Smith half pay to his substitute in militia

1794: Paid the whole expenses and other charges providing volunteers for the Navy £29 7s. 2d. – paid Barnes overseers for wife of militia man serving for Richard Stevens.

1795: Putting out the workhouse fire 3s. beer 11s. 8d. – collecting timber and tiles when workhouse was afire 6s. – a man falling ill on road 3s.

1796: Paid towards the time for not finding a man for the army £22 8s. 10d. Expenses to London to attend sessions on Trimbly's account re finding man for navy two years ago 15s. 6d.

1797: There is a list of names for whom apparently substitutes for militia had to be found.

The above notes are only a small extract of the great variety of action taken by the overseers in those years. Here is an example of an entry in the register:

Henry, ELEDGAMATTE son of Eamey Bedford baptised 8.8.1762

And some extracts from churchwardens accounts of a rather 'lighter' nature:

Paid the ringers on Thanksgiving Day concerning the Plott
Paid for beere & Tobacco for the ringers the first time Mr. Zouch came over
Paid for a barrell of beer for the ringers on the Kings Coronation Day
Paid unto Ed Stimpson for Beere on Gunpowder Treason Day
Paid the Ringers the Queen's Birthday
Paid the Ringers November 5th
Paid for Bread & Beere & Tobacco when they went the procession

We have by now given a goodly range of examples of the duties and tasks of the parish's officials but feel that two more problems require our attention. Old Chobham documents contain a complete set of Land Tax lists from 1780 until 1832 which show for each property 1) the name of the proprietor; 2) the name of the occupier and 3) the amount of assessment. These assessments were made by two assessors, usually two of the most respected inhabitants, who had to assess how much of the total of £543 14s. of the parish assessment had to be paid by each property. As an example we can quote the opening page of the 1801 assessment which gives the names of William Beauchamp and Samuel Mumford as assessors, two names which we shall meet again when we talk about the churchwardens and overseers of the poor around that time.

The importance of the lists is for us the fact that we can establish that, for example, in 1780 the proportion of properties owned by non-resident men was around forty-five per cent, which can be compared with the figure of 31 per cent calculated from the lists for 1800. Here we can quote Dorothy Marshall in her *Industrial England 1776-1851*:

The greater part of the land was farmed by tenants rather than by occupying owners, who by the end of the eighteenth century had become a minority.[7]

The details shown in the 1851 census forms enable us to compile the figure for 1850 which

County of *Surry*,
for the *Parish* of
Chobham
in the *said County*.

An Affeffment made for granting an Aid to His Majefty by a LAND TAX, to be raifed in Great-Britain, for the fervice of the Year 1801, in purfuance of an Act, paffed in the Thirty-eighth Year of the Reign of his prefent Majefty, and of another Act paffed in the Thirty-ninth Year of His faid Majefty's Reign, intituled, "An Act for making perpetual, fubject to Redemption and Purchafe in the Manner therein ftated, the feveral Sums of Money now "charged in Great-Britain as a LAND TAX for one Year, from the 25th Day of *March* "1798," and alfo of another Act paffed in the Forty-firft Year of His faid Majefty's Reign, "for continuing and granting to His Majefty, a Duty on Penfions, Offices, and "Perfonal Eftates."

Affeffed by us, *W. Beauchamp* ASSESSORS.
Saml Mumford

No	Name of Proprietors.	Names of Occupiers.	Rents.	Sum Affeffed and Exonerated	Sums ASSESSED.		
1	Tedy Sr 10th Bart	Mefsrs Soane			12	1	6
		Himself			6	14	0
		Do for Home Farm			2	16	6
		Willm Hammond			8	19	0
		Himself			1	16	0
		Henry Gunner			4	17	0
		For Birketts			1	11	6
	Elfield Henry	Richard Lee			12	0	0
		Stephn Shorter			4	15	0

T. Jones, Printer,
138, Fetter-lane.

42.   The front page of the Land Tax Assessment of 1801.

show that the proportion of non-resident owners had then fallen to 26 per cent. The place of the absentee owners was taken over by their former tenants who must have profited considerably from the rising prices of their land's produce. We want to suggest that it was the product of this rise in social standing and the consequent rise in home comforts that enabled or rather encouraged a greater distinction between farmers and labourers, contrary to the olden days when all men considered themselves as almost equal.

There is yet another document which attracts our attention:

The bounds of the parish of Chobham in the County of Surrey, as taken by the direction of the

Parishioners in their Perambulation of the said bounds, May 26th and 27th, Anno Domini 1786 agreeable to the old writings of a Perambulation taken in the year 1595 carefully inspected and compared with the present bound marks by the Parishioners and the then officiating curate to the Rev. George Gayton, Vicar of Chobham and Rector of Bisley. Attached: a true copy of the old perambulation in A.D. 1595 Witness Thomas Snelling, Curate of Chobham. [A later line has been added:] by Mr. Collyer of Pankhurst, 15.11.1864.[8]

This seems the right moment to quote the utterings of various people who describe the general position in the country; here is part of a letter written by Lord Teignmouth in 1791:

Nothwithstanding the excessive taxes, the country throughout exhibits the appearance of the greatest opulence; and whenever you return you will see the advance of luxury greater than your imagination can form. Every one now lives in style. The grocer's wife has her routs; the butcher's misses flaunt in Indian muslins; the tailor has his chariot. But there is, with all this, great internal wretchedness amongst the labouring class, and particularly the cultivators of the soil. Fortunately, however, the same spirit of profusion gives a spur to benevolence; and I am well convinced, that without its operation a third of the nation could not subsist at all . . .[9]

Yet another voice can be quoted, that of the highly regarded Sir F. Morton Eden, from his great work *The State of the Poor* issued in 1797:

In consequence of the very great price of bread-corn during the whole of 1794, the distresses of the Poor were unusually great, and the sums expended on their relief beyond all former example. If, however, we except the late period of scarcity (which was such as had not occurred for nearly a century before) it is believed that no period during the present reign [George III's] can be adduced in which the condition of day labourers was not much more comfortable than that of the same class of people in what are often called the 'good old times' of former reigns.[10]

And here is the judgement of a late 19th century historian, J. E. T. Rogers, who wrote in his *Six Centuries of Work and Wages (The History of English Labour)* written in 1884 (on page 64):

I am convinced that at no period of the history for which authentic records exist, was the condition of manual labour worse than it was in the 40 years from 1782 to 1824, the period in which manufacturers and merchants accumulated fortune rapidly, and in which the rent of agricultural land was doubled.

Here is an earlier report from a practical man, the steward of Lord Hardwicke's estate in Gloucestershire, written in 1766:

The high price of provisions was felt by all with this difference that the rich received a reciprocal advantage in the advance of their incomes whilst the poor had no other recourse than in the advance of their wages. Their clamours raised to procure these were artfully turned to the cause of the other . . .[11]

We feel that these contemporary statements describe the general situation adequately; but here is an extract from a modern writer on our subject; Dorothy Marshall in her *Industrial England 1776-1851* wrote as follows, describing the situation in Chobham very well indeed:

. . . and where there was no resident squire, the parson was likely to be the most influential person in the parish, unless he also was non-resident, in which case his power filtered down to his curate-in-charge. . . . there were always some clergymen who ruled their flock with benevolence and devotion and more who, being kindly men, did what they could to ameliorate the condition of the poor, running schools and dispensing charity. In this respect the evangelical clergy had a good record; they at least cared that their parishioners should find salvation.[12]

And a final extract, from A. T. Hart's *The 18th Century Country Parson*:

In any case the French wars made trade difficult, and in 1800 the price of wheat rose to 137/- a quarter. Squires, the bigger tenant-farmers and the country clergy benefitted enormously from these changes; but not so the agricultural labourers who found that their small wages did not rise with prices. Furthermore, because of the strict Laws of Settlement, they were unable, freely, to move from parish to parish in search of better conditions.[13]

We must now return to our village and continue our story to show what happened after the entry in the visitation book dated April 1800: 'George C. Gayton, minister, dead'. The four churchwardens, those retiring and the newly confirmed men, must have heard the announcement but were, obviously, more interested to hear that the new vicar would be the Rev. Richard Cecil, who would move to Chobham on the 14 July, and that a new curate, the Rev. Daniel Wilson, was to take up residence soon. There can be no doubt that they were rather surprised also to hear Cecil would reside in the village only for three months during the summer every year, but they must have considered this as a great improvement compared with the past practice.

43. Rev. Charles Jerram, vicar of Chobham 1810-34.

The new curate proved to have been a good choice – he was to become Bishop of Calcutta – and did what he could to prepare the parish for the arrival of their new vicar, whose first reaction to his new parish we have already described (*see* pp. 60-1). Mr. Wilson only stayed until 1803, to be followed in the curacy by two men who each only stayed one year. But in 1805 the vicar heard that Charles Jerram, the curate of Sutton, Lincs., whom he had recommended to Simeon at Cambridge and who had proved a very good choice in his work there, was looking for a change.

On the occasion of the Jubilee, 25 Oct 1809 when King George III entered his 50th year of his reign, £63 1s. 6d. was collected and given in bread and beef to 150 families in the following scale:

Man & wife: 1 loaf, 4 lbs beef
Man, wife & 8 children: 4 loaves, 12 lbs beef.

But first back to our churchwardens and their duties which they had, of course, to carry out as before the change at the vicarage. In addition to their routine tasks, a completely new job had to be tackled: the first census of population ordered by an Act of Parliament had to be carried out by the wardens in the absence of the vicar. We are very fortunate indeed in Chobham that the original copies of the enumeration sheets have been preserved. The top sheet reads:

Surrey: Hundred of Godley, Parish of Chobham signed by Saml. Mumford, and John Hone.
This Account was taken the 11th and 12th Day of March 1801, by Samuel Mumford and John Hone.
An account of the Population of the Parish of Chobham in the Hundred of Godley, County of Surrey taken in furtherance of an Act made in the 41st Year of the Reign of King George the Third and entituled "An Act for taking an Account of the Population of Great Britain and of the Increase or Diminution thereof". 31. Decr. 1800[14]

The total of people in the village was 1,176, living in 229 houses. It will be of interest to hear that the proportion of non-resident landowners who were shown to have owned 45 per cent of all farming land had now, by 1801, gone down to 31 per cent.

We are now coming to the arrival in Chobham in 1805 as the new curate of the Rev. Charles Jerram. He states, as is reported in his memoirs, that at first he took up residence in Chobham House where Mr. Cecil had lived during his stays in the village. He describes his position thus:

> Now let me present myself, in my house in Chobham, with ten pupils of the most respectable families, placed under my charge, two churches, demanding of me four sermons each week, except during the three months in each year, whilst his health continued tolerably good, when Mr. Cecil came to reside on his livings. Next, having to shepherd two flocks, scattered over a very wide extent; to visit them when sick, and to minister both to their temporal and spiritual wants; and also to attend to the numerous incidental circumstances which are continually requiring the care of a parochial minister . . .[15]

44. Hassell's 1824 drawing of Chobham House, home of Rev. Charles Jerram.

He continues:

> . . . Next, with regard to the pastoral part of my ministerial office, finding it impracticable to visit my flock from house to house, I adopted the following substitute. Every Tuesday evening I arranged with some or other of my parishioners to take tea with them, leaving them to select any or none to join the tea-party . . . These were considered highly priviledged meetings, both by the person, who received me, and those who attended them . . .[15]

It must be clear that such meetings could only be arranged in the houses of the richer farmers and tradesmen thus counteracting one principle he had established in his previous parish:

> Everything of a parochial nature was in disorder. A few individuals carried everything before them. A system of favoritism on the one hand, and of oppression of the poor on the other, prevailed; and though many saw and lamented this state of things, none had either sufficient courage or influence to get themselves against it.[16]

But it would appear that in Chobham the parish officials had, in their long period of sole responsibility for the whole community, found a sound method of running the village's affairs for the benefit of all its inhabitants. Here, again, are Mr. Jerram's words about his relations with his flock:

> While I was at Sutton I had a great deal to do with parochial affairs and parish vestries. When I went to Chobham I seldom attended a vestry; by enjoying the full confidence of three or four of the most influential parishioners, I could always carry the measures I desired, through them. When attending vestries, one is always sure to come into collision with rude and obstinate men, who pride themselves in the brief authority with which such occasions invest them, in showing their independence and their superiority, by saying offensive things with the intention of affronting their minister.[17]

These extracts will create the impression that Jerram had feelings of superiority over his parishioners. Yet he makes a most interesting comment later:

> But apart from the parochial advantages from being on friendly terms with some of the leading persons in the parish, there is also a great comfort, of a social side, from their familiar intercourse . . . I believe that there are few parishes which do not possess some individuals whose familiar intercourse is worth cultivating, men of sound sense and strong minds if not of polished manners certainly not vulgar – kind, social and hospitable; the female inmates of these families are modest, unassuming, obliging, of decent education and ready to engage in any prudent measure to promote the welfare of their neighbours in which their minister might wish to employ them. From long experience as a clergyman, I have found many of this description, and desire here to record with thankfulness the numerous instances in which I found their cheerful co-operation with me in the furtherance of the great objects which I have endeavoured to promote of the greatest benefit. I will add, moreover, that I have found in such families an agreeable retreat, when weary and exhausted with my ministerial labours, and whose society and cheerful conversation has been truly refreshing.[18]

It will be interesting to hear the impression Jerram made on other people; here are the remarks of one of his pupils, later the second Lord Teignmouth:

> Mr. Jerram received twelve pupils whom he attached to himself by the affectionate warmth of his sympathies, the fervour of his religious zeal, and the undisguised frankness of his deportment. He was short and stout, his complexion florid, and his expression bearing with kindness and intelligence. One defect impaired the influence of his many admirable qualities, and taxed the strength of his religious principle – a singularly choleric temper . . . On one notable occasion we saw him returning with his wife, a perfect ball of fire, fresh from a peculiarly irritating adventure. Meeting on the bridge near his house a hawker, selling pernicious tracts and forthwith arraigning the stranger, he was posed by the simple interogation: 'Pray, who set you up as a scarecrow to the parish?' To insure his being better prepared in future for such encounters he took out a commission of the peace.[19]

The reader will ask now, why we are giving so much space to the curate and have really said little about the vicar, the Rev. Richard Cecil? We can, however, explain that Cecil had, by the contents of his sermons and the way in which he pronounced them put the church again into the centre of the village's life. He is said to have, quite early, been able to preach to an audience of five hundred. We have already heard that he lived in Chobham only for three months in the summer so that, obviously, contacts beyond his sermons and services in the church could not be many. But, as we have also heard already, Cecil had, in addition to his much-admired sermons, introduced some practical measures of aid to poor parishioners such as he had practised in his London parish. In Chobham he was to introduce his ideas within weeks of taking up his duties. The records show that in 1800 six parishioners benefited from the product of the collection of sacraments money, a number increased to 10 in the following year and reaching 28 in 1803. It seems that Jerram took over this idea very efficiently as the number of beneficiaries never fell under thirty in any one year but reached over sixty in 1814 and afterwards. These lists of poor parishioners are the only record of some inhabitants' nicknames, such as 'Pipkin' for Isaac Harding, 'Pug' for Henry Shorter, 'Puff' for James Smith, 'Ratter' for James Taylor, 'Brute' for John Taylor, 'Sir Isaac' for William Searle, 'Soldier' for James Lee, 'Friar' for James Smither and, as we have said in the family tree of the Slyfields, 'Crock' for John Slyfield; the name 'General Monk' though mentioned could not be fitted to its bearer. In time this voluntary contribution to poor parishioners, especially those with large families, was properly established as the 'Chobham Benevolent Fund' with a firm list of contributors as shown in 1841.

The Rev. Richard Cecil fell very ill in 1808 so Jerram had to bear the whole burden, and when Cecil died in 1810 the Rev. Charles Jerram was apointed the vicar of Chobham, but not the rector of Bisley. (We have not explained that Bisley was also under the care of the Rev. Cecil and thus had to be covered by Jerram in his boss's absence.) The Thornton Trust handed that parish over to one of its members, the Rev. John King, who, as there was no suitable house for him in his new parish, took up residence in Mr. Jerram's house in Chobham. We have not said very much about the parish of Bisley but cannot forego the opportunity of telling a story which the young Lord Teignmouth relates:

> The Situation of the church of Bisley was most retired, a favorite resort of owls, who might be heard hooting by day. On one occasion, when we were present, Mr. Jerram's preaching was disturbed by snoring. He more than once appealed to the supposed sleeper, and at length peremptorily intimated that, unless the good man or woman to whom he attributed the interruption, were awakened, he must discontinue his sermon. 'Sir,' explained a man in a remote part of the church 'it's a "howl"'.[20]

The way in which we have described the new vicar will give the impression of a self-righteous man not easily prepared to change his mind once he had decided an issue. However we found the following note in the register book:

> At a meeting of the Minister & Churchwardens held this 31st day of Jany. 1827 for the purpose of distributing the contributions of the Sacraments during the last year – It having been stated that various complaints have been made by the poor that the money which had been allowed them to expend in clothing in the parish of Chobham has not always been laid to the best advantage, being that they have no choice when to lay out the said money. – Resolved that hereafter tickets be allowed to each poor person to go to such shops in the parish of Chobham for articles of clothing as they may think proper. signed: Chs. Jerram, Wm. Howard. Hy Edmead.

Having mentioned one of young Lord Teignmouth's notes, we feel that further remarks of his will set the scene of Chobham in the early 19th century:

> The retired village of Chobham, an oasis in a desert, could be approached, except from the south, only by sandy roads traversing the undulating ridges and skirting the lonely meres of Bagshot Heath, a dreary region, although much of it has since been enclosed, but still available for the military manoeuvres. [This was written in 1878, after the 1853 camp.][21]

But he cannot refrain from recalling some village gossip:

> An 'omnibus' – ere vehicles bearing this well-known name came into fashion – called the 'Chessy Hoy', was the only regular conveyance between London and Chertsey, the nearest post town in that direction. A stage-coach pursued another route. Twice a day a roll or other sort of bread was packed in a pocket of this vehicle, destined for the breakfast and tea of the Duchess of York at Oatlands; and it was usual for passengers to take it out of the paper envelope, and pick off a piece, that they might boast of having shared the meal of Her Royal Highness, whose relish for London baking was fortunately not abated by the knowledge of such unseemly manipulation.[22]

And here are more personal memories:

> The parish was not wanting in the usual complement of 'characters'. . ... Our farmers could boast of a noble specimen of stalwart and high-souled humanity in the person of good Sam Mumford, who when the French were expected, was seen furbishing his musket resolved to take the life of Nap, even at the cost of his own. A more conspicuous contrast could scarcely be conceived between this individual and a very corpulent and gluttonous publican who 'ate himself poor', and who, though his house overlooked the church yard, declared his determination never to enter the church except on his bier.
> The church choir occupied the front seat of a spacious gallery commanding a view of the long

45. The famous 'Clump' on Chobham Common.

central aisle of the church. It consisted of performers on a variety of instruments under the direction of a good-humoured, self-important tailor, who, by no means forgetful of his weekly vocation, would rise from his seat and, standing beside his violon-cello put his hands in an attitude of self-congratulation when a special specimen of his handiwork made its appearance.[23]

And here is yet another bit of the young man's reminiscences:

A solitary hut ensconced in the heath, was tenanted by a squatter named Jack Sprung, 'the Chobham snipe-shooter', who got his living by his gun. He was but once seen at church during divine service, viz on a Thursday evening; but, being intoxicated, and talking loudly, he was transferred to the stocks, placed, as formerly was the case, at the gate of the graveyard, and thence, as he vociferously complained of the treatment by which his desired hearing of the Word of God had been rewarded, to a more distant lock-up.[24]

The following story comes from yet another *local* source:

Frequently 'Crazy Jack' would be arrested for drunkenness and clapped into the stone prison (the lock-up) to sober up, but inevitably appeared before the Chertsey Petty Sessions in an even worse state than when arrested. No bottle was ever found inside the jail, and apparently there was no way of getting liquor into the man; but a mischief-maker by the name of 'Bill White' was responsible, for the 'maskelynes' act. He would get a bottle of beer and a long rye straw and creep up to the local 'Hoosegow'. Under the cover of darkness he would pass one end of the straw through the keyhole and put the other into the bottle. 'Crazy Jack' would be ready and willing to suck the fluid through the straw.

We have now reached 1810 with the Rev. Charles Jerram the vicar in Chobham, just in

46. Chobham's old lock-up.

time to receive the directive to carry out the next census of population. This time the title-page reads rather differently: 'Population of the Parish of Chobham, taken by the Revt. Charles Jerram, vicar; Samuel Mumford and William Beauchamp, Churchwardens, May 27th 1811'. These two men had been overseers of the poor in 1800 when Mr. Mumford became churchwarden, a post he held until 1814; William Beauchamp held his office from 1805 until 1811. To hold these posts for such a long period was a new development, probably introduced by the vicar to ensure continuity. The top sheet of the list also says: 'Copy of Return sent to the Magistrates from the Parish of Chobham on Account of the Population taken May 27th 1811': the number of enumerated persons had grown in the 10 years to 1,329 and the number of inhabited houses to 259. The number of people in the workhouse which had been 40 in 1801 was now down to 17. We have also found, once in 1801, the purchase of rice and potatoes for the workhouse, an experiment which was apparently not repeated.

In 1809, on the occasion of the 50th birthday of King George III, a collection for the poor was held and a total of £63 1s. 6d. collected, which was distributed in the form of beef and bread to 150 poor families (*see* p. 170). So we see that the work of the overseers had to go on, although the vicar criticised the existing system of parish relief severely in a paper sent to Samuel Thornton, the M.P. for Surrey (as we have heard, the youngest son of the philanthropist John Thornton of 'Clapham Sect' fame). Thornton had settled in Chobham and is known to have served as J.P. in matters relating to the village.

Yet another subject which, as a teacher, was much in the mind of the new vicar, was the education of the young, and in 1813 he decided to preach a sermon on behalf of a parish school:

> On the morning appropriated to the charity sermon, on meeting the parish clerk in the vestry, who was a very respectable tradesman, far advanced in years, and wore a neat brown wig, and had some oddities of manners about him, I said 'Well, Mr. Howard, what do you think we shall collect this morning?' '. . . as much as fifteen pounds might be collected. I mean myself to give half-crown.' '. . . Why, I shall expect you to give a guinea' . . . I believe he did contribute that amount, and his worthy son, who succeeded him as clerk, did, I know, at every anniversary of the school sermon, put down his guinea on the plate. The actual collection amounted to something more than thirty-six pounds. I mention this with some minuteness as it was the first experience in the memory of the people of an attempt to raise money for a parochial purpose in a sermon; and I record it not as a solitary instance of their liberal contributions . . . For let it not be supposed that the Chobham congregation, generally, was affluent. There were only two independent gentlemen at that time in the parish. The rest were farmers, and little tradesmen; but I have many times witnessed more than one of those farmers put on the plate two or even three sovereigns each, and few of the tradesmen would pass without leaving upon it either a sovereign or half a one . . .[25]

We feel that we have said enough of the vicar's ideas and methods but would like to quote a comment by Robert Southey from his *Letters from England*, dated 1807, which seems most appropriate here:

> . . . The sermon seems to be regarded as the most important part of the service; children are required to remember the text, and it is a regular thing for the English to praise the discourse when they are going out of church, as it is to talk of their health immediately before, and of the weather immediately afterwards.[26]

As a teacher himself the Rev. Charles Jerram was, of course, keen to see started some good instruction for his parishoners' children. These are his first thoughts when coming to Chobham:

> When I first entered on my curacy, I found a prosperous and well attended Sunday School; but there were only two or three day-schools for children, taught by dames; and a lower scale of instruction than was carried on in them cannot well be conceived.[26]

And here are the impressions of John Blackman when he recalled his own experience as a pupil in such an establishment:

> As soon as I was able to walk, I was sent to a dame's school to learn, to the extent of the old lady's abilities, the alphabet and to spell and pronounce monosyllables. She was very poor, and resided in a lovely, thatched cottage across several fields, and her charge per boy was threepence per week. She was known as 'Old Sally Artful' but her real name was Hartwell. Her fictitious name however seemed appropriate for she had a knack of giving a sly pinch, or an unexpected prick with a pin, whenever our eyes were off the primer. At other time inattentive scholars would be brought round by a short lug of the ear. I soon outgrew the limits of the dame's knowledge, and was removed to the national school in the village, where I made some progress in such elementary education as the school afforded . . . The favourable reports which my village tutor frequently gave of my mental progress, induced my father to take me from school earlier than he otherwise would have done 'for fear', as he said, 'you will learn too much'. At the age of nine, therefore, my school days ended, and I was marched into the fields to render my feeble assistance in the way of farmwork.[28]

After these very telling extracts from John Blackman's book, *The Story of my Life*, which we owe to the kindness of its editor, R. J. Turner, John's descendant, now living in New Zealand, we feel that it will be useful to proceed with further extracts when he describes what life was like in Chobham in his boyhood:

> My grandfather, Thomas Blackman, was a Berkshire man born near Reading. He passed the prime of his life at Knaphill as 'mine host' of the 'Barley Mow' tavern. [Barley Mow Lane can still be

Vicarage Road, Chobham.

47. Vicarage Road, with the school building on the left.

seen in Knaphill on the road to Chobham.] At Knaphill, my father, James, and his seven brothers and sisters were born. I was born of worthy parents, July 13 1819 – the birth-year of Queen Victoria – at an old fashioned prettily situated farmhouse – still known as 'Blackman's farm [now under its older name 'Fowlers Well Farm'] in Chobham. The house occupies a secluded position about half a mile north of the village and its church.

My father managed our farm in Chobham for a scholarly yeoman [Samuel Cobbett – *see* p. 127], and after his death rented at a nominal rental the homestead and its surrounding 70 acres.

My father was a quietly disposed man with a limited knowledge of the world and, apparently, without a desire to know anything of its doings beyond the confine of his farm and crops, excepting the current prices of corn as reported in the market column of the 'Reading Mercury' and 'County Chronicle'.

The soil of Surrey parishes is as varied as the varying scenery in their midst. In the confines of my native village, one man's garden produces some kind of fruit or vegetable, which a neighbour's garden fails to produce, and hence a mutual exchange takes place, which tends to foster good feelings amongst farmers and cottagers.

The several events which break the monotony of the year are The Whitsuntide Club Feast when the members come forth in their white smock frocks, best corduroys, and blue and orange rosettes. The triennial beating of the parish bounds is dying out, but at one time it was a great event, accompanied with roisterous conduct and much beer.

The horse-races at Ascot Heath, a few miles away, were not without their lively influence in the

48. Fowlers Well Farm House painted by John Blackman before 1840. This house was home to James Blackman and his family from about 1790 until 1840.

49. Fowlers Well Farm House in 1985.

village. In 1829, when I was ten years old, my father promised us children a treat to see the gentleman of the age, King George the Fourth, and the sights of what our minister termed 'Vanity Fair'. We went to witness the races against which the parson Rev. Charles Jerram invariably preached a warning discourse on the previous Sunday in accordance with his sense of duty.

The day I remember, was remarkably fine and the scene entirely new. At noon, the Royal procession passed slowly up the course amid hussahs and waving of handkerchiefs, and there in his low bodied carriage I saw King George the Fourth, with a silver star on his breast, and the future queen of England, Victoria, by his side.[28]

But now, we must come back to our own story and report the news in our village. On 28 May 1821 the third census was taken but, unfortunately, the detailed enumeration sheets have not survived. On one sheet of the 1831 census a note is added: 'Population of Chobham taken in 1821 was 1719 and the number of inhabited houses 306', showing a steady increase, if slow growth.

The churchwardens and overseers of the poor had still to carry on with their old-established duties: we found a document showing that a widow who had applied for relief in Chobham was examined by two J.P.s, namely Charles Jerram and Samuel Thornton, who found that she had a legal settlement in Banstead and was to be removed and conveyed to that parish. In a second examination, however, the widow was found unfit to travel but three months later she was sufficiently recovered and she was taken to Banstead. Another instance of a woman found in Egham who had a settlement in Chobham is given below; we provide the whole story as entered on the report:

Father of the Child, Wm Froud of Egham, promised marriage two or three times; works on the Bromell Hut Mill for Mr. Haggener; lodges at Th. Luff – Mrs. Baker new the connection Mrs. Kemp Do., Used to come to her Father's house. Stephen Bath Bricklayer saw us together on the 24 day of Oct. 1834 the day it happened half May 1833 left Chobham Michaelmas. went to Mr. Haggener at Staines lived 7 months, left Haggener about 9 months ago. – April 8th 1835 the child born.

A second entry reads as follows:

On the 13th February 1832 I went into the Service of Mr. Richardson publican at Chobham as his indoor servant I was hired by the year at £5 a year I served under such hiring in Chobham for 15 months and then left his Service and received my wages. I lived in no service since or done any act to acquire a Settlement subsequently I have received relief from the parish of Egham.[29]

For the census of 1831 much more detailed instructions were issued from London and in Chobham the operation was divided into four districts: Valley End, East End, West End and Folley End. This time, house names were shown and the sheets show more details than in earlier years. The population had again increased and now numbered 1,837, living in 349 houses. Even the description of occupations was more detailed; for example farmers were subdivided into those working with labourers and those without.

In 1834 the Bishop of Winchester offered to The Rev. Charles Jerram the Rectory of Witney, in Oxfordshire, which was a much more valuable living than that of Chobham. The vicar's thoughts in answer to this offer were:

There was the dilemma of leaving Chobham without providing a successor, who should preach the same doctrines, and adopt a course of pastoral offices corresponding with those to which the people had been accustomed. The most feasible way in which these objects might be accomplished, seemed to be, by procuring if possible, for my son the next presentation to the living; and on mentioning this to the Bishop he thought there would be no great difficulty in carrying this point.[30]

Here is the text of a memorandum:

James Jerram MA, was instituted to the vicarage of Chobham, April 21st 1834, on the Presentation of his Father, the late Vicar, to the Rectory of Whitney in Oxfordshire by the Bishop of Winchester, the 3rd of March 1834.

So father Charles left Chobham in April 1834 to be succeeded by his son James. After 29 years in the parish, first as curate under Mr. Cecil and then as vicar, the parting must have been equally hard for the vicar as for the villagers, who had become used to their vicar's strong leadership and personality.

But even a more severe break with the past was the introduction in 1836 of the New Poor Law, which established a union of parishes with guardians in charge who were to take over the provision for the poor people in the member-parishes; Chobham was to close its own workhouse and all 'in-door' relief was to be carried out in the workhouse at Chertsey. A solicitor's bill, addressed to the Union's newly apointed Clerk shows the difficulties arising from the changeover:

> The Parish of Chobham, To Clerk, Mr. Glazebrook: 1837, Feb 4: Attending Mr. Adey the Overseer advising in consequence of the Poor persons in the Workhouse refusing to quit and taking Instructions to commence proceedings against them – Drawing General Notice to quit. – 5 fair copies. – Letter to the Overseers therewith and with Instructions. – March: Letter to the Overseers respecting the proof of Service of the Notices ——   S 17 10d.

To read today the very complex and detailed instructions of the guardians we wonder how the local overseers could follow them. They contained several pages in small print about how the annual accounts of local actions for the benefit of poor inhabitants by way of 'out-door relief' had to be laid out; every item of expenditure had to be shown under a number of 'subheads'. The guardians did not stop at issuing definite orders to the local overseers, such as this:

> Chertsey Union, to the Overseers of Chobham. Gentlemen I am desired by the Board of Guardians, to request that when you feel it necessary to relieve tramps, that you will only give them orders for night lodging and a Loaf of Bread. – No other relief, such as suppers breakfast, Bacon etc. etc. can be allowed.
>
> I am Yours obediently   H. G. Grazebrook, Clerk. Sept. 30, 1840[31]

Moreover, we must point out that under the 1834 Poor Law Act, outdoor relief (to persons not living in the workhouse) was only allowed with the nearly-unobtainable permission of the union Guardians. Here again the *Chronicle* has something to add:

> By the exertions of Mr. James Jerram, the worthy vicar, ways and means have been obtained to alleviate the distress of the wives and families of the poor. Many an honest labouring man has been compelled from want of employment to go to the Union in Chertsey, when he is paid for his labour 6d. a day from seven in the morning in grinding bones, and upon quitting the place at night a loaf of bread, to take home to a family of a wife and, in some instances four or five children.

Thus the implementation of such instructions, and of the changes arising from the creation of the new Poor Law Unions, was somewhat eased by the attitude of the new vicar who, contrary to his father's ideas, decided to attend vestry meetings as often as possible; in the extant vestry minute books he is shown as chairing every meeting which he attended.

When we described various happenings in Queen Elizabeth's time we also mentioned a few cases of highwaymen within the village bounds or at Bagshot Heath which was infamous for such assaults. How this reputation had been maintained over the intervening 250 years can be seen from a remark communicated to us by a former vicar of Chobham:

> My great grandfather, who was vicar of Southstoke, Bath, had visited Chobham in 1832, to preach for the British and Foreign Bible Society. He was picked up off the Stage Coach at Bagshot. My grandfather, on being offered the living of Chobham in 1879, inquired of the old chap if he would advise him to take the living. The answer was 'Dear Herbert . . . under no circumstances take the living of Chobham, the place is full of Highwaymen'.[32]

We also know of one Chobham man who, in 1834, was transported to Tasmania having been found guilty of holding up a traveller on Bagshot Heath.

The introduction and creation of the General Register Office in 1837 and the appointment of local Registrars of Births and Deaths must have created quite a lot of raised eyebrows in our village. From our family trees we have noticed that a number of children were no longer shown in the church register book as baptised when their birth had been registered. Such procedure must have led to quite some argument between parents and the minister who found it hard to explain the purpose and consequences of the changes brought about by the dual system of entering events. On the other hand the creation of the G.R.O. and appointment of local registration officers relieved the local officials and the minister of the onerous and time-consuming duty of holding the Census in 1841. This year the parish was divided into five enumeration districts, with the High Street affording the north-south divide and the Vicarage and Chertsey Roads the border between north and south. The enumerators were instructed systematically to visit each house so that their records form a reasonable record of one house following its neighbour.

The total of population in 1841 was 1,989, a rather small increase since 1831, with 378 inhabited houses. We can also say that of the total number of 1,989 inhabitants, 1,763 were stated to have been born in Surrey. It is perhaps of interest to hear that nearly 50 per cent of the population were under 20 years of age and eight per cent over sixty. The number of widows and widowers seems to be rather high: of the males 13 per cent of once-married men were widowed and of women the percentage was over 15 per cent. The official Enumeration Abstracts for the 1841 Census contain a marginal note:

> The return for the Parish of Chobham includes 23 persons in barns and tents. Ten persons have emigrated since 31st December 1840.

But the *County Chronicle* shows two entries which give further details of emigration:

> 19 Jan 1841. Twenty agricultural labourers and artisans, all young men, with three females left Chobham in the last week for London under the care of Mr. George Lee, the recruiting officer in this district, and were put on board the Moffat, Captain Gilbert, for Australia. Another party is collecting to proceed shortly to the same place.
> 2 Mar 1841. On Monday last another detachment of young men and women, altogether 32, left this village as settlers in Australia to embark on board the Earl Grey, Captain Mollison.

But neither in the researched vestry-minutes nor the churchwardens' or overseers' reports could we find supporting payments to emigrating persons or families, which is rather surprising as these records show so many different details of assistance to the village poor.

This seems to be the right point to say more about emigration in general: In the Registar-General's report in the 1851 Census we found a table giving the numbers of emigrants for England and Wales in the years 1825 to 1851. In these 26 years a total of 2,622,617 emigrating persons have been counted; comparing decennial figures we find an increase between 1831 and 1841 of 42 per cent and for the next ten years (1841 to 1851) the increase was not less than 136 per cent. On the basis of our count for the first quarter of 1841, we think we can be entitled to predict for Chobham perhaps a total of 250 emigrants for 1851.

When reading the vestry minutes of that time we find that in nearly every meeting a list was produced of inhabitants who were considered unable to pay the poor rate for submission and approval by the magistrates. Here is a document dealing with a man who was considered able but refused to pay his rate. It reads:

> Richard B. an inhabitant and occupier of a house in Chobham as duly assessed and rated for and towards the necessary relief of the poor in that parish in the sum of 4 shillings, that the sum was demanded of him but that he refused to pay. After having been duly summoned to shew cause why he had refuseth to pay but has not appeared. The overseers are then required to make distress of the goods of R. B. and if the sum owing plus 3 shillings 6d plus reasonable charges for taking the distress are not paid within 5 days to sell the distressed goods and pay the overplus to R. B. But if no distress can be made they should certify the same to the magistrates to end that forther proceedings may be had as the law appertains.   signed 23rd day of February 1842.[33]

Such proceedings filled quite a part of the overseer's time; here is an annual report of travelling expenses of Henry Nesmith, overseer in 1847: 'Attending seven meetings at Chertsey, attending Bench four times and once to the Auditor from October to April = 12 instances total expenses £1.15s.'.

50. The travelling expenses of Henry Nesmyth countersigned by the other overseers of the poor, 1847/8.

But this seems to be the right place to change the topic under discussion basing it instead on this comment in Cesar de Saussure's *A Foreign view of England in the Reign of George I and George II*, dated 1725-1729:

The English are very fond of a game called cricket. For this purpose they go into a large open field, and knock a small ball about with a piece of wood. I will not attempt to describe this game to you, it is too complicated. . .[34]

We had already related some newspaper reports on this subject (*see above* p. 45) and will give some more here. We are now in the year of our Lord 1845, when we read in the *County Herald* dated 17 May.

> A respectable Cricket Club has at length been established here which bids fair to give the county some excellant players, the practice being carried on with some considerable spirit. The members, although not numerous, have been well selected and very great praise is due to Mr. Jones of the White Hart Inn for the perservering activity displayed by him in promoting the interests of the Club. – The ground at Little Heath, is pleasantly situated, has been put in good order and a great deal of sport is expected during the season.[35]

So, in 1846, two matches were played against clubs from other villages and in August we hear that a return grand match was played between the *gentlemen* of Chobham and Odiham: then follows the names of 11 gentlemen of Chobham. Now we recall that the Rev. Charles Jerram, when describing the result of his sermon on behalf of a school in Chobham in 1813, pointed out that his audience, besides two gentlemen, were mostly farmers and small tradesmen. And then we read that in September 1846 a match was played between the married and single gentlemen of the neighbourhood: 11 married and 10 single men were mentioned. We shall see who they were to find out how this change came about in our village: among the 11 players in August were six names whom we can identify as gentlemen from the surrounding area; the other five were the village doctor, one draper in the high street and his son and one farmer and the doctor's son. Yet in September we found: three farmers, two farmer's sons, one doctor and his son, six tradesmen with two of their sons, one miller, one blacksmith, the tenant of the *White Hart* and three gentlemen. Thus we see that there were now in the village a number of men who could leave their farms or other occupations to attend the practice sessions and matches thus deserving the name of gentlemen (defined in the *Oxford English Dictionary* as: 'men of wealth and leisure').

We have gone into such detail to show how far Chobham has changed in the 29 years of the vicarship of the Rev. Charles Jerram, to whose ideas and attitudes we have devoted a considerable amount of space. By showing his preference in visiting the better-housed members of the community and by insisting that the officials stayed in their post for a considerable time he transformed these from old-fashioned but conscientious leaders of the farming community. Perhaps it was partly also the impressions created by Jerram's students:

> Always, among my pupils I found two or three most ready to call upon a poor person whom I had pointed out; and not only to administer the relief I sent, but to add something from their own pecuniary resources; and it was not seldom that I learned that they had gone with a loaf under their arm to assist an industrious man in providing for a large family.[36]

We can only guess what such contacts of the villagers with number of well-dressed and well-spoken young gentlemen would have been when hear what William Marshall says in his *Agriculture in the Southern Counties* of 1799:

> The farmers (the higher class excepted) are as homely, in their dress and manner, as those of the more recluse parts of the kingdom, and are far less enlightened and intelligent than those in many parts of it. The reason is, they live chiefly among themselves, as a distinct community, retaining much of the character, probably of husbandmen of former times, and holding their prejudices as fast, or at this time perhaps faster, than those of the most distant provinces.[37]

It was not only the influence of the vicar himself but also of the members of his family who are said to have had their share of contacts with the villagers; here is the testimony of young John Blackman whom we have quoted before:

> A kind-hearted lady of the village also took a lively interest in my welfare. She further encouraged me with many kind words and much good counsel which I trust have had a salutary influence on my subsequent career. The husband of this lady was the Rev. Charles Jerram who was vicar of Chobham for thirty years. On her death she was mourned by the whole parish, and especially by

those who had been grateful recipients of her gentle ministrations and unobtrusive Christian charities.[38]

And here is what father Jerram said about his daughter:

> . . . during the last winter months up to the end of March my daughter was almost daily visiting the cottages of the distant poor of this parish . . .[39]

The term 'gentlemen', as used by the newspaper, is really a confirmation of the great transformation in the village that had taken place in the years of the Rev. Charles Jerram as vicar, which development had been encouraged also by his son when succeeding him in the vicarage.

Here is a copy of the minutes of a vestry meeting held on 9 February 1849:

> It was moved by Lord Vaux & seconded by Mr. Gude that a paid Constable shall be appointed for the parish of Chobham at a salary of fifty-two guineas a year. Carried unanimously. Resolved by acclamation that the thanks of the Vestry are prominently due and hereby presented to the Right Hon. Lord Vaux of Howarden for his persisting efforts in protecting the property of the Parish. – Resolved that the thanks of this meeting be given to the Rev. James Jerram for the keen interest he has exercised for the benefit of the Parish and for his able application in the chair upon the present occasion.[40]

The 'present occasion' is described in the *County Chronicle* of 3 April 1849, which reads:

> The late incendiary fires. It will be seen by a reference to the files at the Surrey assizes, that James Stevens and William Smith pleaded guilty to setting fire to some buildings in this parish and were sentenced to transportation for life. We are now enabled to give the confession of Stevens, which was taken by the Magistrates. The said James Stevens saith as follows: I wish to state about all the seven fires . . . The next was Mr. Gude's fire. We then ran home. The next fire was at Mr. Collyer's. I then struck a match and Smith held a bit of paper. We then ran away into the fields and waited for about half an hour. We then returned to the fire and stopped there for about two or three hours. We went away to a rick of hay which belonged to James Hull. We then went into the High Road and after we went home. The next fire was the parish fire. The next was Hodd's; then we proceeded to Lord Vaux's and set that on fire. We could not get out of the gate and jumped over into the road. I was then shot as described by Lord Vaux.
>
> Stevens then wrote a most humble letter to Lord Vaux, in which he refers to the trouble caused to his old parents and, that in the three months he had spent in prison he had come to repent and deplore the madness of his deed. He ends with imploring His Lordship to recommend him to the merciful consideration of his Judges.[41]

We must admit that we could not find details of the final result of this case. But what we do feel is necessary here is to show what we know about the two movers of the appointment of the constable: Lord Vaux had purchased the Highams Lodge (we discussed the members of his household earlier, *see* p. 40) in 1842 and it is doubtful whether he would have taken part in vestry meetings unless it was thought necessary after the arson cases in the village. Mr Gude, on the other hand, had moved into Chobham in 1829, when he bought two farms; he resided in one of the farmhouses and describes himself as 'Land Owner' in the 1851 Census but not as 'farmer' – he had appointed tenants to both his farms to run them for him. It is not to be wondered that, under the chairmanship of the young vicar, the meetings were now better run and the gentlemen among the farming community gave them a more refined style, as the minutes show.

Perhaps we ought to say something about the other eleven men who attended the meeting: Thomas Hudson, aged 49, grocer and farmer; John Lipscomb, aged 68, farmer of 206 acres with eight labourers, born in Horsell, purchased his lands 1822; Richard Rowland, aged 55, draper and farmer; James Rogers, aged 71, retired farmer; Samuel Mumford, aged 78, fundholder; his son, Samuel junior, aged 54, landed proprietor; another son of old Samuel Mumford, James, aged 51, farmer and miller; James Try, farmer; William Beauchamp, aged 56, carpenter; Nathan Searle, aged 25, shoemaker; and one name which we cannot decipher. This meeting must be described as a rather select group of relative newcomers to the village families. It comprised members of only six families among the 13 men, who averaged 54 years of age. They may be compared with the 19 men who (*see* p. 164) attended the vestry in 1737 to discuss the appointment of a workhouse-master: the latter represented 15 of the old families, averaged only 36 years old, and every one of them was either a past official or soon to be elected.

All that remains to report now are the results of the 1851 Census. The population of Chobham had again increased by less than a hundred people but the number of houses was now 419, with 14 houses uninhabited and two more in building. As in 1841, the parish was divided into five enumeration districts, the same as in 1841, but in this year the birthplace of every person and the exact age were entered as were the numbers of labourers each employer employed. Perhaps it will be of interest if we give details of these findings. Of the 2,069 inhabitants, 1,403, i.e. 68 per cent, were born in Chobham, 268 were born in the six neighbouring villages and 279 in England beyond Surrey. When comparing the birthplaces by occupation we find that of the 85 farmers, 55 were born in Chobham but of their 81 wives only 29 were born there; of the agricultural labourers the percentage born in the village was similar to the farmers but more than half of their wives were not so born. Of the professional men all 11 were born outside Surrey and only two of their wives came from the county. The most disturbing of the figures is the number of agricultural labourers and their employment: of the total of 352 men only 160 were employed in the parish on annual contracts i.e., if the statements of the farmers giving the number of labourers they employed is accurate, more than half of all resident labourers were either on daily or weekly contract, were out of work or worked outside Chobham. Besides the farming group we find nine blacksmiths, eight shoemakers, six carpenters, five each of bakers and tailors, four butchers and three wheelwrights in addition to six grocers and three victuallers. It is worth mentioning that among the craftsmen eight stated that they also farmed.

Although we set our target date of the Census of Population in 1851 we cannot really close this report of the story of Chobham without at least mentioning the great event of 1853: the great Camp at Chobham when Queen Victoria inspected her troops before their departure to the Crimean War.

We thought that a summary of the growth of population would be useful:

Date	Inhabitants	Houses
1086	100	35
1583	400	–
1664	700	143
1801	1,176	229
1811	1,329	259
1821	1,719	306
1831	1,937	349
1841	1,989	378
1851	2,069	419

The figure for 1664 is the result of applying the 'Hoskins-formula' (*see* p. 163) when the Hearth Tax records presented a chance to validate our result. Baptismal records for decennial periods after that date are, of course, available from our parish register books. Between 1583 and 1664 the population expanded by some 75 per cent, but in the following hundred years to 1770 the increase, from 700 to approximately 750, was only seven per cent. However, between 1775 and 1801 (the first Census year) population rose by around 40 per cent, giving our 1801 total of 1,176.

Queen Victoria and the Prince Consort   attending a Review of the troops at Chobham, 1853

51.   Queen Victoria reviewing the troops at Chobham, 1853.

We have found that these percentages were 'roughly' parallel with those for the whole county of Surrey as shown in Rickman's *Estimated Population of England and Wales, 1570-1800* which was planned to be part of his Abstract of the 1841 Census. His percentage increases for the county were: 1570-1670, 45 per cent; 1670-1750, seven per cent; 1750-1800, 50 per cent, proving that our calculations were reasonably accurate. Similar population figures for the 18th century are found in the decennial baptismal numbers in William Stevenson's *General View of the Agriculture of the County of Surrey*, (1809). We feel that the agreement of data relating to the growth of population after 1775 in these three sources calls for a separate and detailed investigation to establish the cause of this development.

Chapter Seven

Postscript

The different composition of the vestry between that of 1737 and 1849 confirmed a change in the relationship between the richer farmers (both yeomen and tenants) and the labouring families, but this change was only indirectly brought about by the altered ownership of farmland. We have shown that the percentage of *non-resident* owners in 1780 (45 per cent) had dropped to only 25 per cent in 1851 and was emphasised when members of the resident old families acquired such farms on the market: by 1851 the Fladgates had acquired 260 acres of farmland, while the Collyer, Chitty and Daborn families and James Lipscomb from Horsell had acted similarly. The Abdy family moved away in 1809, but their place was taken by the Le Marchants who took up residence in Chobham Place.

Another development must also be mentioned: the division of the parish when Westend became a new parish. The Census of 1871 showed that the population of the old parish had grown to 7,966, of which total 4,947 were left in the Chobham Parish and 3,019 were people in the new Westend Parish.

To this report, we must add our surprise at the choice of name for the new parish. Since the first election of overseers of the poor in Queen Elizabeth's time two men were elected by the vestry, one for the eastend and the other for the westend, the dividing line being in the High Street, so that one official was responsible for the area to the west and the other to the east of the street. In our opinion, the name 'Westend' leaves open the question 'westend of what?' so that in our view a name historically chosen would have been 'Westend Chobham' or perhaps 'West Chobham'. What in fact did happen is that the postal address 'Westend, Woking' seems to be accepted, thus establishing a completely new and not previously existing link with the giant neighbour. We admit that the people living in the westend of Chobham considered themselves different from those in the rest of the parish so that the new name sounded, for them, right, and the popular view prevailed. But it is sad that thousand-year-old links are no longer obvious in the two parishes' names.

References

List of Abbreviations

V.C.H.	*The Victoria History of the County of Surrey.*
P.R.O.	Public Record Office.
S.A.C.	*Surrey Archaeological Collections.*
S.R.O., G.	Surrey Record Office, Guildford Muniment Room.
S.R.O., K.	Surrey Record Office, Kingston.
S.R.S.	Surrey Record Society.

Chapter One: Chobham under the Abbey of Chertsey

1. *Chobham Common, a Management Plan.*
2. *V.C.H.*, III, p. 413.
3. D. Whitelock, ed., *English Historical Documents, I, c.500-1042*, 1955, p. 440.
4. N. Salmon, *Antiquities of Surrey Collected from the Most Ancient Records*, 1736.
5. G. J. Copley, ed., *Camden's* Britannia, *Surrey and Sussex*, pp. 2-3.
6. The Venerable Bede, *A History of the English Church and People*, ed. B. Rice, 1955, pp. 217-18.
7. F. M. Stenton, *Anglo-Saxon England*, 1943, p. 61.
8. Ibid., pp. 54-5.
9. Whitelock, ed., *op. cit.*, p. 440.
10. S.R.S., XII ctd., Vol. II, part I, p. vii, Introduction.
11. Whitelock, ed., *op. cit.*, p. 207.
12. J. Weever, *Ancient Funeral Monuments Within the United Monarchye of Great Britain, Ireland and the Islands Adjoining*, 1631, p. 133.
13. Whitelock, ed., *op. cit.*, p. 144.
14. G. O. Sayles, *The Medieval Foundations of England*, 1948, p. 221.
15. J. Morris, ed., *Domesday Book: Surrey*, 1975, 34a.
16. S.R.S., *op. cit.*, p. lxviii.
17. *V.C.H.*, III, pp. 418-19.
18. S.R.S., *op. cit.*, pp. xxx-xxxi.
19. Ibid., pp. xxxi-xxxii.
20. Ibid., p. 70, sec. 767.
21. P. Brandon, *A History of Surrey*, 1977, p. 39.
22. G. M. Trevelyan, *English Social History*, 1973 edn., pp. 10-11.
23. L. Wheeler, *Chertsey Abbey: An Existence of the Past*, 1905, p. 129.
24. Whitelock, ed., *op. cit.*, p. 146.
25. H. J. F. Tringham, *The Story of Long Cross*, 1934, p. 11.

Chapter Two: Chobham Park, the House of the Lords of the Manor

1. S.R.S., XII ctd., p. xxxii.
2. *V.C.H.*, III, p. 415.
3. John Aubrey, *The Natural History of the County of Surrey*, 1719, III, p. 212.
4. Ibid., p. 150.
5. Manning and Bray, *The History and Antiquities of the County of Surrey*, 1814, III, p. 212.

6. *V.C.H.*, III, p. 415.
7. J. Weever, *Ancient Funeral Monuments Within the United Monarchye of Great Britain, Ireland and the Islands Adjoining*, 1631, p. 156.
8. Aubrey, *op. cit.*, I, p. 110.
9. Ibid., III, p. 199.
10. P.R.O., Letters and Papers of Henry VIII, L, p. 873, no. 5,383.
11. *V.C.H.*, III, pp. 414-15.
12. C. S. L. Davies, *Peace, Print and Protestantism, 1450-1558*, 1975, p. 165.
13. P.R.O., Court of Requests, Req2/149/60.
14. Manning and Bray, *op. cit.*, III, p. 197.
15. *V.C.H.*, III, p. 415.
16. S.R.O., G., Loseley Mss, LM 2.
17. *Idem*, LM 20a.
18. J. Davis, *Historical Records of the Second Royal Surrey 11th Regiment*, 1877, p. 40.
19. J. D. Mackie, *The Early Tudors*, 1951, p. 441.
20. *V.C.H.*, III, p. 415.
21. J. P. Kenyon, *Stuart England*, 1978, p. 49.
22. John Strype, *The Life and Acts of Matthew Parker, the First Archbishop in the Reign of Queen Elizabeth*, 1711, Chapter XVI, p. 142.
23. Aubrey, *op. cit.*, III, p. 199.
24. Ibid.
25. Manning and Bray, *op. cit.*, III, p. 83.
26. Aubrey, *op. cit.*, III, p. 199.
27. Manning and Bray, *op. cit.*, III, p. 193.
28. S.R.O., G., PSH/BIS/6.
29. S.R.O., G., PSH/CHO/1/23.
30. Aubrey, *op. cit.*, III, p. 201.
31. C. J. Shore, *Reminiscences of Many Years*, 1878, II, p. 11.
32. A. J. Kempe, *The Loseley Manuscripts*, 1836, p. 216.
33. J. Harvey, *The Plantagenets*, 1959, p. 193.
34. *S.A.C.*, XXVIII, p. 11.
35. Mackie, *op. cit.*, pp. 410-11.
36. Kempe, *op. cit.*, pp. 217-18.
37. Manning and Bray, *op. cit.*, III, p. 197.
38. *V.C.H.*, III, p. 416.
39. Kempe, *op. cit.*, p. 187.
40. Ibid., p. 188.
41. Ibid., pp. 198-9.
42. Ibid., p. 201.
43. Ibid., p. 200.
44. Ibid., p. 187.
45. S.R.O., G., Loseley Mss, LM 2, f. 1,515/1.
46. N. Williams, *Elizabeth I*, 1975, p. 101.
47. P.R.O., E179/185/301, item 35.
48. G. M. Trevelyan, *English Social History*, 1973 edn., pp. 167-8.
49. S.R.S., II, pp. 54-5.
50. S.R.S., XI, pp. 133-4.
51. Kenyon, *op. cit.*, p. 54.
52. *S.A.C.*, XIX, p. 59.
53. Ibid., pp. 87-8.

54. Kenyon, *op. cit.*, pp. 60-1.
55. Kempe, *op. cit.*, pp. 213-20.
56. S.R.O., G., Loseley Mss, LM 2, f. 1,511/3.
57. Kenyon, *op. cit.*, p. 110.
58. P.R.O., E187/475.
59. Kenyon, *op. cit.*, p. 59.
60. M. Ashley, *England in the Seventeenth Century*, 1966, p. 51.
61. Ibid., p. 53.
62. S.R.O., G., Loseley Mss, LM 2, f. 1,519/1.
63. *Idem*, f. 1,516/4.
64. P.R.O., E179/257/28.
65. *V.C.H.*, III, p. 415.
66. C. R. B. Barrett, *Highways, Byways and Waterways*, 1895, p. 208.
67. E. W. Brayley, *A Topographical History of Surrey*, 1841, p. 87.

Chapter Three: Other Manors and Important Sites

1. R. J. Brown, *The English Country Cottage*, 1979, p. 28.
2. S.R.S., XII ctd., pp. xlvi-xlvii.
3. *V.C.H.*, III, p. 415.
4. Ibid.
5. Ibid., p. 416.
6. Manning and Bray, *The History and Antiquities of the County of Surrey*, 1814, III, p. 196.
7. Ibid., p. 197.
8. *V.C.H.*, III, p. 416.
9. Ibid., p. 415.
10. Rev J. Carter, *Bisley Bits*, 1892, p. 18.
11. Ibid.
12. Ibid., p. 25.
13. Ibid., p. 96.
14. *V.C.H.*, III, p. 414.
15. Manning and Bray, *op. cit.*, p. 218.
16. Ibid., p. 197.
17. *V.C.H.*, III, p. 416.
18. Ibid., p. 414.
19. C. R. B. Barrett, *Highways, Byways and Waterways*, 1895, p. 208.
20. Manning and Bray, *op. cit.*, p. 193.
21. S.R.S., XII ctd., p. 87/809.
22. Ibid., p. 89/814.
23. *V.C.H.*, III, p. 414.
24. An Abstract of Mr. John Attfeild's Title to a Farm in Chobham, dating from 1622-1693.
25. J. Aubrey, *The Natural History of the County of Surrey*, 1719, III, p. 202.
26. Manning and Bray, *op. cit.*, III, p. 196.
27. M. James, *Social Problems and Policy during the Puritan Revolution, 1640-1660*, 1930, p. 126.
28. S.R.O., G., 51/12/56.
29. C. MacFarlane, *Notes About Chobham from the Camp of 1853*, p. 6.
30. G. and C. Greenwood, *Surrey Described*, 1823.
31. M. de G. Eedle, *A History of Bagshot and Windlesham*, 1977, pp. 74-5.
32. S.R.S., XII ctd., p. 71/771.
33. Ibid., p. 90/816.

34. Ibid., p. 96/824.
35. Ibid., p. 73/776.
36. Ibid., p. 68/763.
37. Ibid., p. 85/804.
38. Ibid., p. 95/823.
39. *Woking Review*, 1848.
40. Manning and Bray, *op. cit.*, III, Appendix, p. cvii.
41. 'Cricket Activities in Chobham', *County Herald*, 1844-1848, 7 August 1846.
42. Ibid., 10 August 1848.
43. Ibid., 15 August 1846.
44. S.R.O., G., PSH/CHOB/7/1/6/8.

Chapter Four: Church Affairs in Chobham

1. S.R.S., XII ctd., p. xxxiv.
2. L. Wheeler, *Chertsey Abbey, an Existence of the Past*, 1905, p. 79.
3. L. O. Mitchell, *Chobham Parish Church*, 1908, pp. 6-7.
4. Ibid., p. 11.
5. S.R.O., G., PSH/CHOB/7/1/21.
6. Mitchell, *op. cit.*, p. 11.
7. *V.C.H.*, III, pp. 416-17.
8. Mitchell, *op. cit.*, p. 6.
9. Surrey Wills – Archdeaconry Court, Herringman Registry.
10. C. S. L. Davies, *Peace, Print and Protestantism, 1450-1558*, 1975, p. 154.
11. J. Aubrey, *The Natural History of the County of Surrey*, 1719, III, p. 204.
12. S.R.O., G., PSH/CHOB/7/1/1.
13. S.R.O., G., PSH/CHOB/7/1.
14. S.R.O., G., PSH/CHOB/1/1.
15. S.R.O., G., PSH/CHOB/1/1.
16. S.R.O., G., PSH/CHOB/7/1.
17. S.R.O., G., PSH/CHOB/1/1.
18. S.R.O., G., PSH/CHOB/1/1.
19. S.R.O., G., PSH/CHOB/1/1.
20. D. H. Bishop, *The Father of the Wartons*.
21. S.R.O., G., PSH/CHOB/1/2.
22. S.R.O., G., PSH/CHOB/7/2.
23. S.R.O., G., PSH/BIS/1/2.
24. S.R.O., G., PSH/CHOB/7/2.
25. Mitchell, *op. cit.*, pp. 11-12.
26. S.R.O., G., PSH/CHOB/7/3.
27. S.R.O., G., PSH/CHOB/1/2.
28. S.R.O., G., PSH/BIS/1/2.
29. S.R.O., G., PSH/CHOB/1/2.

Chapter Six: The Farmers Run the Village

1. S.R.O., G., Loseley Mss, 1,042/17.
2. Ibid., 1,036/22.
3. S.R.O., G., Calendar of Assize Records, Surrey Indictments, Elizabeth I.
4. S.R.O., G., 1/48/83 (f).
5. Manning and Bray, *History and Antiquities of the County of Surrey*, *sub* Chobham, p. 193.

6. S.R.O., K., Chobham Deposit, P34/7/2.

7. D. Marshall, *Industrial England, 1776-1851*, p. 68.

8. S.R.O., K., Chobham Deposit, P34/8/4.

9. *Memoirs of the Life and Correspondence of Lord John Teignmouth, by his son, Lord Teignmouth*, 1843, I, p. 214.

10. Sir Frederick Morton Eden, *The State of the Poor*, 1797, p. 3.

11. John Pitt, attorney and steward of Lord Hardwicke's Gloucestershire estate – 29 October 1766. British Library, Add. Mss 35,607.

12. Marshall, *op. cit.*, p. 65.

13. A. Tindal Hart, *The 18th Century Country Parson* ca *1689-1830*, 1955, p. 3.

14. S.R.O., K., Chobham Deposit, P34/17/1.

15. Rev. James Jerram of Fleet, Lincs., ed., *The Memoirs and a Selection from the Letters of the Late Rev. Charles Jerram, M.A.*, 1855, p. 251.

16. Ibid., p. 199 (at Sutton).

17. Ibid., p. 180.

18. Ibid., p. 181 ff.

19. Charles John Shore, Baron Teignmouth, *Reminiscences of Many Years*, 1878, I, p. 9 ff.

20. Ibid., p. 11.

21. Ibid., p. 10.

22. Ibid., p. 12.

23. Ibid., p. 16.

24. Ibid., p. 26.

25. Rev. James Jerram, ed., *op. cit.*, p. 299.

26. Robert Southey, *Letters from England (by Don M. A. Espriello)*, 1807, p. 206.

27. Rev. James Jerram, ed., *op. cit.*, p. 299.

28. John Blackman, *The Story of My Life*, 1886, pp. 4, 9, 10.

29. S.R.O., K., Chobham Deposit, P34/18/7.

30. Rev. James Jerram, ed., *op. cit.*, p. 311.

31. S.R.O., K., Chobham Deposit, P34/6/19.

32. Private letter from the Rev. O. R. Acworth.

33. S.R.O., K., Chobham Deposit, P34/12/5.

34. Cesar de Saussure, *A Foreign View of England in the Reigns of George I and George II*, 1725-9, p. 295.

35. 'Cricket Activities in Chobham, 1844-1846', *County Herald*, 17 May 1845.

36. Rev. James Jerram, ed., *op. cit.*, p. 251.

37. William Marshall, *Agriculture in the Southern Counties*, 1799.

38. John Blackman, *Home Scenes and Heart-memories*, 1887, p. 12.

39. Rev. Charles Jerram, *A Tribute of Parental Affection to the Memory of a Beloved and Only Daughter*, 1824, p. 36.

40. S.R.O., K., Chobham Deposit, P34/27/2/9.

41. 'Chobham: the Late Incendiary Fires', *County Chronicle*, 3 April 1849.

Indexes

This index has three parts: a General Index, an Index of Chobham Families, and an Index of Chobham Farms. The first includes persons connected with the parish but not necessarily resident in it. The second gives references to members of families known to be resident in Chobham and to the account of each family as a whole. The third provides references to farms in the parish.

General Index

Index of Chobham Families

The dates in brackets are those when individuals were first recorded.

Index of Chobham Farms